CW00557382

Properties of Blood

Volume I

The Reign of Love

Thomas Fleming

...videte itaque fratres quomodo caute ambuletis non quasi insipientes sed ut sapientes redimentes tempus quoniam dies mali sunt
— Ephesians 5:15,16

C O L O F O N

The Reign of Love

Publisher: The Fleming Foundation
fleming.foundation

© Copyright 2022: Thomas Fleming
All rights reserved
ISBN: 978-1-7337196-5-0

Date: spring 2022 – First Edition

CONTENTS

Forward On a Darkling Plain

The world, which seems
To lie before us like a land of dreams,
So various, so beautiful, so new,
Hath really neither joy, nor love, nor light,

— Matthew Arnold

MANY OTHERWISE REASONABLE MEN AND WOMEN appear to believe that their world has somehow gone wrong and is going still wronger every day. They usually do not express this belief explicitly or in general terms, but when controversial subjects are raised at a dinner table, there is often a disquieting sense that "things have gone too far" or that the powers-that-be simply do not understand the gravity of the social, moral, and spiritual crisis in which the modern world is enveloped.

Democratic processes–debates and campaigns, platforms and promises, elections and programs–are supposed to be a means of clarifying problems and putting forward solutions, but political rhetoric hardly ever gets to the nub of the most urgent problems and still less often contributes anything to clarifying questions. Whether the subject is marriage laws, immigration control, crime and punishment, moral and æsthetic standards in the arts, or even decisions of war and peace, discussions are reduced to an exchange of slogans and sound bites crafted, cobbled, and propa-

1

gated by opposing political factions. When Conservatives or liberals, if they are possessed of some common sense, are confronted with the evermore extreme projects of the revolutionary left, are so confused that they concede point after point to their opponents, and, before too long, they have surrendered another institution or tradition to its enemies. We are not even permitted to accord an honorable burial to the institutions of the dead past, but monuments must be desecrated and destroyed and the bodies of the failed champions of lost causes disinterred.

A very basic part of the conservative failure is the acceptance of leftist principles, such as equality and human progress, as basic truths with universal acceptance. They want to defend what they call "traditional marriage," but they stumble as soon as they accept the revolutionary premise that marriage is strictly a contract between two individuals for individual happiness and/or mutual satisfaction. Older conservatives may out of stubborn prejudice stick to the principles they grew up with, but their children will bend to the changing mood of the times.

The modern mind is in a hopeless muddle, and anyone who has tried to persuade friends or readers of the grave mistakes being made by people in authority will run into the same brick wall. Few people apart from intelligent leftists know what they believe, and fewer still know what they know. What passes for thought in serious publications and debate are issues of *clichés*, often contradictory, which are accepted blindly and without examination. All our discourse, from "America is a nation of immigrants" to "planet earth is being destroyed by global warming," is dominated by truths we hold to be self-evident. This is an infallible indication that the ideology that shapes public discourse is a kind of religion. There may be sects and heresies, but common dogmatic assumptions undergird every argument.

I have been working for two decades to articulate a coherent opposition to this religion. This alternative point of view is based on no new ideas or original insights but on the traditions that pre-modern men and women took for granted. This is the first volume of a work addressed to two sorts of readers. The first sort consists of Christians who wish to disentangle Christian teachings from the political ideologies that have tended to instrumentalize the faith for purposes that may be (or, more commonly may not be) blameless or even laudable in themselves but are no part of the Christian tradition. The second sort of reader is anyone, whether cynic, atheist, or agnostic, who has grown weary of hearing the Bible quoted in defense of revolutionary political measures advocated by ideologues who, by and large, seem to have little to do with Christianity as it has been historically understood. I mean, the sort of political advocate who runs around saying things like, "a real Christian would not support the death penalty," or "Christians who believe in the value of marriage would surely extend the right of marriage to homosexuals," or "democratic capitalism [or nonviolent socialism] is the fulfillment of the Christian gospel."

Although the author is an unabashed Christian, this is not a work of apologetics designed to lead gullible readers either to Christianity in general or to any church in particular. There is no political agenda, no set of policy prescriptions, no blueprint for success or roadmap to a brighter future. I leave all such dreams to political propagandists and partisans suffering from the delusion that they are pragmatic, when in fact they are powerless and disenfranchised busybodies whistling past the graveyard of the American Republic.

The principal difficulty with reformers is that they almost always want fast action before having grasped the fundamental principles at stake. Examples of their hasty reforms abound. Since, they argued, children should not be forced by their parents to do remunerative work, they passed laws making child labor illegal. They never paused to think of the superficial problems they might be creating in depriving poor families of much-needed income, much less of the probable consequences that would follow from legislation that subverts the authority of parents and erodes the autonomy of the family.

The human race, depending on how you count and who is included, has been around many thousands of years, and our social institutions have evolved as a means of securing natural necessities. Our civilization, in one form or another, has been forming our character for some three to five thousand years, which can be numbered as roughly ten to fifteen thousand generations. The idea that we can devise brilliant new answers to the ancient problems of flesh and blood is, on the face of it, preposterous. As Dr. Johnson observed, "Men more frequently require to be reminded than informed," or, to quote a leftist songwriter, "Let me be known as just the man who told you something you already knew." I have no notion of setting up any "new paradigm" or founding a new ideology. With the poet Charles Péguy I can boast that like other Christians, I am stupid once and for all.

What I do hope to accomplish is, nonetheless, ambitious enough to incur a charge of vanity. For many decades, I have been studying the pre-Christian or non-Christian foundations of a just social order and attempting to distinguish the common traditions of Christians and their predecessors from the ever-increasing tendency, for several centuries at least, to regard Christianity as a revolutionary movement that would better be termed Christianism–that is, an abstract ideology–rather than a collective noun like humanity, society, and even Romanitas ("Romanness").

Yet the founder of the religion, whom Christians regard as divine, declared He had not come to abolish the law but to fulfill it. Taken seriously, even literally, our Lord was saying that the laws and customs of the Jews, however much they might have suffered from neglect, decadence, and misconstruction, were not going to be swept aside but clarified and refined. A key passage is his teaching on divorce. In Jesus' time, a Jewish husband could dismiss his wife for any of a dozen trivial reasons and then marry a woman who pleased him better. Nonetheless, from the beginning, He assured his followers, it was not so: Adam and Eve were bound in an indissoluble mystical union, from which Moses granted divorce only as a concession to the hard hearts of his people. Christian marriage practices, then, were not to be created out of whole cloth but would be a continuation, albeit in more rigorous form, of traditional customs.

But Jewish customs, in such matters as marriage and child-rearing, revenge and self-defense, charity and war, differed only in particulars from those of neighboring nations and from the habits common to Greeks, Romans, and other peoples of the Mediterranean. With its unmistakably Jewish roots, Christianity could hardly have been accepted by large numbers of Greek and Roman gentiles, had it radically jarred with the best pagan morality. Justin Martyr, one of the earliest apologists, had enough familiarity with Greek philosophy to tell the Emperor Antoninus Pius and his philosophic heir Marcus Aurelius that Christianity is not only a rational creed but one that shares and clarifies the best ideas of Greek philosophers.

A subsequent volume will take up the household and the institutions of private property, marriage and family, as well as moral questions such as abortion and euthanasia. This first volume, which serves as a preface, takes a broad look at love and hate as the foundations of our moral and political institutions. Of necessity, it is more philosophical and theological than subsequent parts, which depend more on historical evidence.

This work can be read by anyone who can keep his mind open long enough to entertain the outrageous possibility that earlier human generations may have had a better idea of how to lead good lives than the modern subjects of Western democracies. However, it does rely on the arguments made in an earlier book, *The Morality of Everyday Life*, whose goal was to demolish the Liberal tradition of moral and political reasoning to make way for a point of view that combines objective observation with a "decent regard for the opinion of mankind," though unlike Mr. Jefferson, I do not limit that opinion to educated people of recent centuries. There will also be some reference to the sociobiological arguments of my first book, *The Politics of Human Nature*, in which I tried to show the compatibility of the traditional classical and Christian view of human nature with the evidence of anthropology and evolutionary biology.

The overall working title, *Properties of Blood*, emphasizes the importance of blood ties as the basis of the social order. The title of this volume, *The Reign of Love* takes up the positive side of love, friendship, and kinship and establishes them as the foundation not only of our ethical life but also of all social and political order. The initial chapters, which are devoted to the The Cities of Man are intended as a response to Augustine's contrast between the ideal community known as "The City of God" and the flawed and often evil institutions of the Earthly City. As an alternative to Augustine's stark contrast, I am suggesting that the City of God on this earth cannot be built on anything but the foundations built by the City of Man–or rather Cities, since there has never been and never will be one commonwealth or one type of regime that will satisfy the needs of all human societies.

It will, therefore, be necessary, to take up in some detail (I hope not tedious) the laws and customs of various societies in order to give substance to more general claims about the universality of marriage and institutionalized aggression. Inevitably, philosophers and political theorists–breeds that tend toward dry-as-dust abstractions–will find this approach unsatisfying and even amateurish. My Marxist friend, Paul Piccone, once complained, "Why do you take so long to get to the point?" In jest I sometimes reply to such criticism that, as in all adventures and travels, getting there (and getting lost) is half the fun.

In truth, I should say, that the ample use of historical, literary, and anthropological examples is offered as a casuistic alternative to the Simon-pure rationalism of the philosophers, who write as if human life, with all its fuzzy perceptions and sloppy tendencies could be plotted like points on a graph. To avoid the tedious pretense of absolute knowledge, Plato, himself the first and greatest of the great abstractors, used the give-and-take of dialogue and delighted in unresolved paradoxes; St. Thomas used, to similar effect, the scholastic method of point and counter point. Since the Renaissance, as moral and political speculation has become almost completely detached from reality, wiser writers have turned to fiction and the essay more frequently than to didactic syllogisms and universal systems. Since the word "essai" itself means attempt or trial, I think of my own efforts as so many trial balloons. Rather than attempting to draw up a broad topography of the human moral universe, I have been content to take a few soundings into some of the nether regions of our common life and its traditions.

In exploring the foundations of a Christian moral and social order, I have tended to focus on two sets of historical examples: first, those three civilizations, Greek, Roman, and Jewish, which came together to create the Christian Church, and second, those national cultures that seem most relevant to our own traditions: American, British, French (before and after the Revolution), and Italy in the Middle Ages and the Renaissance. For some subjects, I have also studied the customs and literature of the Balkan Slavs. A more comprehensive book might have been written by a scholar with a better knowledge of Orthodox traditions or even of the non-Christian civilizations of the East, but one human being can only do so much.

Wherever possible, I have tried to work with texts in their original languages rather than borrowing second-hand from textbooks, surveys, and secondary scholarship (though, as the bibliography will show, I have made a good-faith effort to grapple with the scholarship on a number of questions.) The one exception is the Old Testament, where my abysmal ignorance of Hebrew has made me dependent upon translations and on Tradition. In my defense, I should say that I am firmly convinced that Christians should study the Old Testament from their own point of view and privilege the selection and interpretations of the Greek Septuagint, which is, after all, the source of most of the Old Testament quotations in the New Testament. When differing interpretations are not a problem, I have been content to quote from well-known translations, such as the Authorized (King James) version of the Bible and various influential translators of the classics. More typically,

I have either retranslated the passages or altered familiar translations to bring out the point I am pursuing.

Since this work has not been written primarily for historians, classical philologists, or philosophers, the notes and bibliography are far from exhaustive. Where a work of scholarship has been quoted, it is generally noted, and works that have been used without specific reference are listed in the General Bibliography. Great works of literature have been cited either according to standard enumerations of book, chapter, and line, or even more generally by chapter. The object is not to assist writers of dissertations, few of whom are likely to be attracted, but to acknowledge my debt to scholars and provide suggestions for further reading. I also take this occasion to acknowledge my debt to the people who have read the manuscript and offered corrections, especially Niki Hatzilambrou Flanders, and to Michael Guravage who typeset the book.

In this work, then, I have set two tasks for myself. The first and less important task is to show Christians and non-Christians alike that the teachings of the Church are truly the fulfillment of the Law, both the Law of the Old Testament and of the best legal and moral traditions of the pre-Christian West. The second is to provide Christians with the necessary cross-cultural context of Christian teachings on marriage, family, and kinship in the hope that some of them will learn to distinguish between the Sermon on the Mount and the *Communist Manifesto*, not to confuse the parable of the talents with the capitalist theories of Adam Smith or Ludwig von Mises, and, ultimately, to see that the ties of blood, kinship, and community, so far from being obstacles to a Christian way of life are, for most of us, as indispensable to our moral life as blood and bone are to our physical existence.

Exiled Children of Eve

> I shall not cease from mental fight
> Nor shall my sword sleep in my hand
> Till we have built Jerusalem
> In England's green and pleasant land
>
> — William Blake

WILLIAM BLAKE WAS QUITE MAD, EVEN MADDER THAN MOST SWEDENBORGIANS, but many Christians (and post-Christians) less insane than Blake have dreamed of building a new Jerusalem, where the unpromising specimens of humanity they had known all their lives would live in perfect peace and uninterrupted joy. This heavenly kingdom was not located in another dimension or in an afterlife when the saints would receive new bodies, but in the here-and-now, where ordinary men and women, if they could but comprehend and follow the latest revelation, would achieve a justice that had only been hinted at in the societies of the past.

When men have tried to create Golden Age perfection out of bricks and mortar and human blood and clay, as in Savonarola's Florence, Calvin's Geneva, Robespierre's France, Hitler's Germany, or Lenin's Soviet Union; the reality is more nightmare than paradise. You cannot make an omelet without breaking a few–or, rather, more than a few million–eggs, and you cannot realize the imagined rights of man without wiping out or at least truncating some of the most basic foundations of human social life, namely, marriage and the family, the institutions of kinship and community, and the human habits of barter and exchange on which all economies depend. This is a hard lesson, and it has been learned the hard way by ideological states such as the former Soviet Union. It is also the lesson that is being taught to the residents of Western "democratic" countries whose governments are constantly increasing their size and scope at the expense of more fundamental human institutions.

The state *per se* is not the fundamental problem, and the growth of government cannot be successfully restricted by arguments about efficiency, fairness, or the natural rights of the people. The metastasizing states of the developed world are not simply misguided exercises in benevolence, nor do they result solely from the desire for money and power–though money and power certainly reward the efforts of state-builders.

The modern state is first and foremost an ideological project aimed at transforming the human race from what it has been from the beginning into some new etherial creature whose basic instincts have been repressed or channelled into socially constructive directions. Though many of the leaders of this revolutionary movement to liberate the human race have been Christian, the roots of this development lie in the anti-Christianity that has been the hallmark of progress and modernity since the Renaissance. The reality is not easy to understand, since, in a back-handed tribute to Christianity, such trans-human aspirations are often termed "Messianic," as if they were secularized fulfillments of the Christian vision.

Is Christianity Subversive?

This raises a question of fundamental importance both for believers and for secular liberals who have adopted, more or less, Christian social values: Does Christianity demand or even encourage a revolutionary overthrow of the traditional moral order and social institutions that have been taken for granted in most societies? In other words, are Christians required to pursue, both individually and collectively, utopian projects designed to eliminate distinctions between mine and thine, kinfolk and strangers, citizens and aliens?

Although Christianity has been prolific in generating utopian dreams, the utopian temptation is not specifically Christian. Plato and Plotinus had their social fantasies, as did Stoic and Epicurean philosophers and the Essene sect of Judaism, but pagans and Jews may be more easily excused for succumbing to the devices and desires of their own hearts than Christians, who are supposed to follow the teachings of their Master, who firmly declared in one of his final public utterances, "My kingdom is not of this world." That should have been a warning, at least, to those who would conflate the Christian faith with socialism or democratic capitalism or even the rule of the saints.

Jesus issued his rejection of a kingdom on earth under interrogation from the Roman administrator who would consent to his execution. When Pilate asked the suspect if he were king of the Jews, He denied the charge. Pontius Pilate's initial misunderstanding of Jesus' royal mission was, no doubt, instilled in him by critics who were eager to paint the Christ in the colors of a secular Messiah who would expel the Romans from Judaea and reinstitute a truly Jewish monarchy. (The Herods were, after all, a mixed lot descended from Idumean and Nabatæan stock, and some of them–Herod the Great in particular–appear to have scoffed at what they regarded as Jewish "superstitions.") But some of Jesus' own followers took the same line. After the feeding of the multitude narrated in John [6:15], some men were so impressed with the prophet's ability to provide necessities that they planned, as Jesus realized, to "come and take him by force, to make him king."

Despite the clear warnings of the Scriptures, some ardent believers have never ceased in their efforts to build a new Jerusalem. If we could believe an ancient story, the emperor Tiberius knew better. The emperor, according to Tertullian [*Apologeticum* 3], perhaps impressed by the example of a Jewish prophet who did not contest imperial authority, asked the senate to include the Christ in the Roman pantheon. Few historians (apart from Marta Sordi) put much stock in the tale, though it is not inconsistent with Tiberius' ironic sense of humor and just improbable enough to be true. (Sordi, 1994, pp. 17-18)

The first Christian to convert Christ's moral and spiritual message into a program for political revolution may have been Judas, who complained when Mary, the sister of Lazarus, anointed Jesus with oil, a task she and other Christian women would soon have to perform on His body. When Judas asked why the oil was not sold and the price given to the poor, Jesus' reply was an incisive rejection of the Social Gospel: "The poor you have with you always, but me you do not have always." The Christian, both as individual and as member of a corporate body (such as a family or church), will practice charity out of his love of God and of his fellows made in God's image, but he will not set up a system to redistribute other people's wealth. What then, does Christianity preach indifference to the social order or supine compliance with the powers that be and the way things are? Hardly.

Beatitudes, Not Platitudes

It is commonly believed that, as Judas went away from the disagreement over the wasted oil, he was disgruntled over Jesus' failure to lead a social revolution. It is certainly true that Jesus' answer remains a powerful rebuke to those who would confound the gospel with one or another form of state-imposed socialism. The poor, whom we always have with us, will be taken care of properly only when we freely behave as Christians and not when Cæsar, at the point of a sword, requires us to render doubly unto him so that he can purchase political power with our tribute.

Jesus, however, though he was no socialist, was also neither capitalist nor "conservative" in the Anglo-American sense, and His moral message is far more alarming than Marx or Marxist Catholic bishops seem to have realized. The melding of Christian and Marxist perspectives often goes by the name of the "Social Gospel," whose message, whether expressed by liberal Protestants or Catholic bishops, is at best a collective appeal to check-writing philanthropy and at worst a systematized hypocrisy. In essence Christian socialists tell us to go about our business as mankind has always done, lying, cheating, stealing, so long as we pay the state to redistributes some portion of our wealth to the poor–a small price to pay for a "Get Out of Hell Free" card. Christ, by contrast, turns our most highly cherished values–pride, ambition, greed, rugged individualism–upside down or, rather, inside-out.

"And seeing the multitudes, he went up into a mountain: and when he was set, his disciples came unto
him: And he opened his mouth, and taught them,
saying, Blessed are the poor in spirit: for theirs is the
kingdom of heaven. Blessed are they that mourn: for
they shall be comforted. Blessed are the meek: for
they shall inherit the earth. Blessed are they which
do hunger and thirst after righteousness: for they
shall be filled. Blessed are the merciful: for they shall
obtain mercy. Blessed are the pure in heart: for they
shall see God. Blessed are the peacemakers: for they
shall be called the children of God. Blessed are they
which are persecuted for righteousness' sake: for
theirs is the kingdom of heaven."[Mt 5:1-10]

To understand the Sermon in its context, it may help to
recall that it is delivered shortly after Jesus had been led
into the Wilderness to be tested by Satan. In an effort to find
out who this person really is, the Tempter suggests that He
perform a series of miracles that will prove his identity:
turn stone into bread to satisfy His hunger, defy gravity
by jumping off a tall building and get rescued by angels,
and accept authority and power over all the kingdoms of
the earth, for which he only has to worship Satan, a lesser
and created being. In each case, Jesus reveals Himself by
rejecting the offer: Man does not live by bread alone, but
by the word of God; We are commanded not to tempt the
Lord; and, finally, to the offer to worship Satan and rule the
world, he instructs him to be gone: "Thou shalt worship the
Lord thy God, and him only shalt thou serve."

Put in human context, Jesus has been given the opportunity
to minister to physical well being, make a display of power
over nature, and rule this world at the price of worshipping
a created being. Each offer is something that most of us,

no matter how well-intentioned, would jump at. Imagine all the good I might do if I could feed the world's poor and rule the nations with justice and charity! The price, if it is too high for Christ himself, is unquestionably too high for Christians to pay, though rulers and governments claiming to be Christian will fail these very tests repeatedly throughout history.

Properly read, Jesus' replies to Satan can be summed up by his answer to a representative of one of the world's rulers: *My kingdom is not of this world*. But neither are his own counter-proposals an expression of worldly wisdom. In this first recorded sermon of Jesus Christ, the conventional wisdom (not just of Jews but of Greeks and Romans and modern Americans who have some notion of what they believe) is turned on its head. Failure and poverty, which were regarded as unmitigated miseries in the ancient world, are celebrated. Good fortune, wealth, and power, which had been regarded as signs of divine favor, now counted for nothing.

Like most peoples everywhere, ancient Jews respected power and success. In looking back at their own history, they admired the exploits of Joshua, Gideon, and Samson, violent men who would not have been out of place in the American West. King David and his son Solomon were among their greatest heroes. David was a man of war who smote his enemies and built a powerful (albeit minuscule) kingdom; Solomon was proverbial for his wealth and women as well as for his wisdom and power.

For more recent heroes, Jews could turn for inspiration to the Maccabees, who had led a bloody insurrection that liberated their people from the Macedonian kingdom of Syria ruled by Antiochus Epiphanes. The successors to the Macedonians were the Romans, who had been ruling over the Jews, largely through proxies like the Herods, for more than 100 years. In expecting a messiah or savior, Jews commonly believed he would come as a fighting prince, another David or Judas Maccabæus, with sword in hand, to drive the Romans into the sea. Yet here is this prophet or (as some would say) the Messiah, early in his career, calmly beginning an address to the multitude proclaiming the blessedness of "the poor in spirit" or simply, as in the parallel passage in Luke, "the poor."

What do these words mean, really, "blessed" and "poor in spirit"? Blessed, for example, can mean several things in English. When we bless someone, we speak well of him. In the Vulgate translation of the Bible, this is expressed by the verb *benedicere* (to speak well of), which gives us the English word "benediction." *Benedicere* is the word used to translate the Greek *eulogein*, as in "Blessed be the Lord God of Israel." [Lk 1:68] However the completely unrelated Greek word, (*makarios*), used here in Matthew, means blessed or happy, in the sense of having good fortune. (It is translated into Latin here and elsewhere as *beatus*). The more basic word *makar*, from which it is derived, is typically used in early Greek to refer to the gods as opposed to mere mortals, and *makarios* thus retains a strong whiff of divine favor. In the plural (as Jesus uses it here), *makarios* is often applied to the rich and well-educated.

The English word "poor" is also ambiguous; it can mean either lacking in wealth or in a poor condition or quality, as in "the actor turned in a poor performance." In Greek the *ptochoi* or poor, by contrast, are at the bottom of the socioeconomic scale; they are the beggars that crouch and cringe, fearfully, in the presence of their superiors. There is really no good modern analogy for the ancient poor, since our homeless people are, for the most part, either mentally disturbed or "substance abusers" or both. The ancient beggar, by contrast, might just be unfortunate, an otherwise decent person who had fallen on hard times.

One of Jesus' listeners who had been to school might have thought of Odysseus, the noble Greek warrior who disguised himself as a beggar and had to endure insults and abuse in his own house—a story that eerily anticipates Jesus' own arrival in earthly form: the son of God who is born to a poor family, a man "despised and rejected and acquainted with grief." However, Matthew's phrase "poor in spirit" takes us well beyond Homeric myth. Odysseus may have been without resources and beggarly in appearance, but, as a proud and violent Greek aristocrat, he was anything but poor in spirit, as he would show when he put off his disguise and killed his wife's suitors. (Poor in condition though he was, Odysseus was, nonetheless, in Aristotelian terms, *megalopsychos*, that is, possessed of a proper appreciation of his own virtues.) Our Lord was telling his people that the greatest happiness one can have, the happiness usually associated with the prosperous and educated, is to possess the spirit of the cowering beggar.

What a strange statement, then, to make, that the abject and miserable, those who mourn the loss of a loved one, are the ones who have experienced divine good favor. Most of us have read or heard this sermon so many times we take it for granted as either hyperbole—He could not have meant these things literally, could He?—or as a set of Sunday school clichés that we recite without any intention of living up to them. But then they would not be the Beatitudes, but only the platitudes.

How are we to take these and other terrifying pronouncements? St. Augustine (*De sermone domini in monte,* I.1.1)
quite properly regarded the *Sermon on the Mount* as a the
loftiest compendium of Christian ethics, and, while he certainly recognized the difficulties to be encountered in living
up to such a standard, he thought it was necessary for us
to do our best. Thomas Aquinas and Martin Luther, in different ways, sought to distinguish the more practical from
the more impossible strands in the Sermon: Thomas, by
distinguishing between general commands issued to all
Christians and the counsels offered to the clergy [*S. Th* II.i.
qu. 108, art. 4], and Luther in distinguishing between what
one does as Christian and what one does as a human being
with worldly responsibilities.

In more recent centuries many commentators have been
troubled by what appears to be an impossibly high set of
ideals. John Calvin, who applied it to the everyday life of
Christians, had to soften its severity, while some more recent Protestants (for example, the so-called Dispensation-
alists) have either given it a weak interpretation or else
claimed it did not apply to our own circumstances: Jesus'
harshest prescriptions were aimed only at the unredeemed.

Some Christians (Anabaptists and the Amish, for example), ignoring the rest of the Scriptures and the traditions of the Church, have concluded that Christians are
required to be communistic pacifists. Others, particularly
Catholic socialists, convert Jesus' injunctions to practice
charity into a government-imposed program for redistrib-
uting wealth. (Cardinal Peter Turkson, as head of the Vat-
ican's Peace and Justice Department, signed a document
calling for a global economic dictatorship to control world
markets.)

A more common solution in the pews is to regard Christ's stark commands as an ideal to be celebrated in church on Sunday and safely ignored during the rest of the week. Neither of the "solutions"–Christian socialism or pew-renting conservatism–are rooted in the Master's teaching: Socialism undermines society and the law that Christ did not come to overturn, while the conventional lip-service is only an instance of the pharisaical hypocrisy He everywhere condemns. "Blessed is he who is not scandalized by [that is, does not spiritually trip and fall over] my name." [Mt 11:6]. There is that word *makarios* again! Thus it is not even enough to be meek and poor in spirit; we must accept Christ at face value, as the savior who means exactly what he says. For a Christian, then, it is imperative to rise to the challenge Christ has set us in his Sermon, but, even for non-believers, it should be a matter of some importance to understand the Christian approach to social responsibility. The Church has, after all, played a formative role in creating the civilization of the past two millennia. I am not foolish enough to claim to have some novel interpretation of the Sermon, except insofar as I can try to set it in a context that both reflects the historical circumstances and applies to our own.

In Matthew's story up to this point, nothing has prepared us for this shocking message. We know only of Jesus' miraculous conception and birth, the precocious wisdom he displayed in questioning and answering teachers in the temple, his baptism by John the Baptist, and the testing by Satan, who had promised him material comfort and power if he would only challenge his Father, as Satan himself had done, and join the ranks of the fallen angels.

Emerging victorious over the Enemy, Christ now despises the very success that Satan had promised. He has attracted a large following, not only from his home-area of Galilee but also from Jerusalem and Judea and even from the Decapolis [Mt 4:25], ten Hellenic cities that enjoyed important municipal privileges within the empire. These cities had the benefit of Greek culture, which even the Semitic inhabitants (whether Jews or Syrians) had absorbed. The mention of these Decapolitans in the audience is the first indication that Jesus is not necessarily preaching only to Jews or to men and women of exclusively Jewish cultural traditions.

What would Greeks or Hellenized Jews think of the Sermon, with its disturbing inversion of values? Those who had read some Homer–and the *Iliad* and *Odyssey* were obligatory reading in any course of education–would have contrasted Christ's ideal with the noble heroes who populate epic poems. They might first have thought of Achilles, whom some believed to have led a life of eternal happiness in the Isles of the Blessed, or of Heracles, whose career of bloody self-assertion had earned him a place among the gods. These were men of violence and wrath, who took nothing from nobody, as the saying goes. They were also members of a nobility that equated virtue with courage and defense of honor. The only lower-class character in the *Iliad*, the ugly rabble-rouser Thersites, is rebuked and beaten by Odysseus for presuming to comment on his superiors.

Early Greek poets (such s Pindar) had never tired of celebrating men of wealth and power or (like Theognis) of complaining about their own failures and poverty. Traditional Greek culture taught that shame (*aidos*) and honor (*time*) were important moral values that had to be respected. A sense of shame included having a regard for social conventions and showing respect to parents, elders, and social superiors, while honor (the Greek word *time* (pronounced roughly teé-may) literally implies price or value) was the respect to which you were entitled, by your family, social status, and personal qualities. When the great Achilles quarreled with Agamemnon and left the Trojan War, it was not so much that he missed the woman of whom he had been deprived as it was that he was losing his honor in the tangible form of a woman he had been given as a prize, a mark of the esteem in which he was held. "Agamemnon has robbed me of my honor," Achilles cries to his divine mother, "and he has robbed me of my prize." There would be little use in telling Achilles (or most Greeks) to ignore public opinion, because they would interpret such a remark to be an indication of a base character (as, indeed, it often is).

If they had dabbled in philosophy, actual Greeks or Hellenizing Syrians in Decapolis might have been less shocked and would have connected Jesus' preaching with the diatribes of Cynic philosophers who derided the pursuit of wealth and power as vanity and distraction, but in that case they might also suspect that Jesus was one more hypocritical guru, of the type satirists routinely ridiculed. Wealth is nothing, say the philosophers? Then why are they always asking for handouts and taking fees for teaching–rather than practicing–the virtues of self-restraint, chastity, and humility? Lucian made a living off this theme some hundred years later, and, five centuries before Christ's ministry, Greek comic poets like Aristophanes and Eupolis had lampooned the Sophists and even Socrates. These days, if there were actually satirists in our own world, they would be merciless in exposing the pretensions of well-heeled professors of philosophy at major universities. Fortunately for the professors, satire is a lost art.

Ancient men and women were not all self-centered hedonists who took no interest in right and wrong. If they had been amoral, they would not have been prepared to listen to anyone preaching any morality beyond the "gospel of success" proclaimed by so many self-anointed prophets of the profit-driven life. Christians in nearly every age have always been quick to condemn pagans for their sensuality and immorality, while turning a blind eye to the hypocrisy and pharisaism that is rampant in their own community. Despite the never-ending flood of sermons attacking the sins of ancient pagans, ancient peoples were not all infanticidal sodomites or movie extras in a crowd egging on Nero and Caligula to greater excesses of violence and perversity. Some of them responded, at least, to the Christian promise of salvation, because they were already accustomed to similar appeals from philosophers.

Jesus had gone up a mountain to preach his startling revelations, but, back down in the valleys and plains, ordinary people had been living, for thousands of years, lives that aimed, at least, at some level of decency. Jews, Samaritans, Syrians, Greeks, and Romans–although they disagreed on many important points of custom and morality–shared enough common assumptions that they could do business together, read each others' religious books (The Jewish Scriptures had been translated into Greek in Alexandria), live in the same towns, and even intermarry. We can get some idea of what Jesus thought of some of these customs, by looking a bit further into the Sermon.

> "Think not that I am come to destroy the law, or the prophets: I am not come to destroy, but to fulfill. For verily I say unto you, Till heaven and earth pass away, one jot or one tittle shall in no wise pass from the law, till all be fulfilled. Whosoever therefore shall break one of these least commandments, and shall teach men so, he shall be called the least in the kingdom of heaven: but whosoever shall do and teach them, the same shall be called great in the kingdom of heaven.

For I say unto you, That except your righteousness
shall exceed the righteousness of the scribes and
Pharisees, ye shall in no case enter into the kingdom
of heaven. Ye have heard that it was said by them of
old time, Thou shalt not kill; and whosoever shall
kill shall be in danger of the judgment: But I say unto
you, That whosoever is angry with his brother without a cause shall be in danger of the judgment: and
whosoever shall say to his brother, Raca, shall be in
danger of the council: but whosoever shall say, Thou
fool, shall be in danger of hell fire."[Mt 5:17-22]

Then, if our first impression of the Sermon was that this
Messiah had come to destroy all law and custom, we were
mistaken. "I am not come to destroy, but to fulfill."

What He means by this is made clear from a series of examples. The law and morality of the Jews (like the legal and
moral conventions of the Greeks, Romans, Egyptians, *et al.*)
forbade murder. The Greek *phoneuein,* used in the Sermon,
though it can be used of killing beasts, is not a generic word
for kill that would typically be used of a hunter killing a
beast; it is a strong word that may either imply the ruthless
slaughter that takes place in war or the unlawful taking of
a human life, for which the English word is "murder." That
is clearly the sense here. But Jesus is telling us that while,
of course, we should abstain from unjustified homicide, we
must also refuse to fly into the passionate anger of the sort
that might result in a killing. The traditional prohibition of
the act now includes a condemnation of the inner, moral
condition that inspires the act.

But the Fifth is not the only Commandment that Jesus is
willing to revise:

Ye have heard that it was said by them of old time, Thou shalt not commit adultery: But I say unto you, That whosoever looketh on a woman to lust after her hath committed adultery with her already in his heart. [Mt 5:27-28]

Once again, it is not enough to abstain from the sinful act–in this case adultery–but one must repress the inner desire to commit adultery. Whether this refers to the passing thought that a woman is desirable or–as I rather suppose–to an inner rational assent, which implies that I would commit adultery if I knew I could get away Scot free, is not important here. Jesus was telling his hearers that to fulfill the old law, they had to go beyond the material prohibitions while yet taking them for granted as the starting-point from which they would begin their moral race.

In improving upon the Commandments, Jesus is quite willing to go beyond the Mosaic law, which permitted divorce [Mt 19:8] and revenge.

> "Ye have heard that it hath been said, Thou shalt love thy neighbour, and hate thine enemy. But I say unto you, Love your enemies, bless them that curse you, do good to them that hate you, and pray for them which despitefully use you, and persecute you."[Mt 5:43-44]

This and other passages of Christian Scriptures are frequently cited as proof that true Christianity would dispense with all distinctions, including national boundaries.

The Rights of Nations

Viewing Christianity as the enemy, intellectuals have always felt justified in misrepresenting its teachings, either to make them contemptible (as Nietzsche and the neopagans have done) or to pervert them to what they saw as good use. So-called Christian Socialists and Social Gospelers made it appear that "true" Christianity (as opposed to the bogus faith of the previous two millennia) would dispense with all distinctions, including national boundaries.

To delegitimate the right of nations to defend their territory, leftists like to quote Paul's statement [Gal 3:28] that in baptism "There is neither Jew nor Greek," as if Paul's intent was not to repress the quarrels that broke out between gentile and Jewish Christians, but rather to obliterate ethnic and cultural boundaries. The absurdity (and dishonesty) of such an interpretation is made clear by what Paul goes on to say: "There is neither bond nor free, there is neither male nor female: for ye are all one in Christ Jesus." Surely, no candid reader would argue that Paul, who more than once instructs slaves to obey their masters and runaway slaves to return, condemned slavery per se. Paul, who has been unfairly stigmatized as a misogynist, can hardly be accused of pursuing a feminist agenda.

Some leftists have pretended that Christians cannot restrict immigration into their country, even if they believe it is harmful to their nation's security and prosperity. They cite such statements as "Thou shalt neither vex a stranger nor oppress him: for ye were strangers in the land of Egypt," [Ex 22:21, 23:9, et alibi.] but they conveniently ignore the dozens of passages in which aliens are condemned and despised.

A Jew could charge interest on money loaned to a stranger but not to a Jew. Second Esdras, among the countless curses it pronounces against Babylon and Egypt, includes the threat that those who labor will labor in vain because "strangers shall reap their fruits, and spoil their goods, overthrow their houses, and take their children captives..." [2 Esd 16:47] Like most ancient peoples, the Israelites were intensely chauvinistic and xenophobic. By their own (exaggerated) account in *Joshua* and *Judges*, they exterminated the gentile population of Canaan when they entered the Promised Land, and they were forever quarreling with their neighbors and, more perilously, with the great kingdoms of the Middle East.

The passage of time and the experience of exile did nothing to soften Jewish chauvinism. In what might be understood as an outburst of xenophobia, Nehemiah tells us that the Israelites, returning from the Babylonian Captivity, separated themselves from non-Jews and made a covenant not to intermarry with them. (Nehemiah was clearly indulging in a bit of wishful thinking.) In light of these and many other passages I might have cited, it is simply disingenuous to argue that the Jews' undoubted kindness to sojourning strangers constitutes an argument against either defensive war or restrictions on immigration.

The apparent contradiction in the Old Testament's approach to foreigners is easily resolved by a closer look at the words. The Hebrew language and the Law made a clear distinction between, on the one hand, sojourning immigrants who have been given permission to stay in the land and generously accorded the protection of the law (rendered in Greek as *prosyletos* and in Latin as *advena*), and, on the other, foreigners who have not been given this legal status (in Greek *allogenes* and in Latin by *alienigena*). While the former are treated as potential or real converts to Judaism (as the Greek word proselyte suggests), the latter are unclean. An alien could not so much as touch the bread being offered to God, and if a priest's daughter married a foreigner, she could not eat the holy food that priests and their families partook of [Lev 22:10,12]. A foreigner who approached the tabernacle was put to death, and no bread could be offered to their God from a foreigner's hand "because their corruption is in them." [Lev 22:25].

The restrictions on unlegalized foreigners were not limited to religious practice. A Jew could charge interest on money loaned to a stranger but not to a Jew, and the Jews' ethnic first cousins, the Edomites, only gained full rights after three generations of living with the children of Israel. [Deut 23:8] The wise Solomon took a census of the strangers in Israel and sent them off to do hard labor.

The writings of the New Testament, while they repeat the earlier admonitions to treat proselytes decently, have virtually nothing to say on the subject of either territorial sovereignty or immigration. The writers assume the backdrop of the Roman Empire, whose rulers and armies are authorized to defend the Greco-Roman world. When massive and unauthorized immigration did take place from the fourth to the sixth centuries, the Goths, Vandals, and Lombards destroyed the empire and put civilization on hold for several centuries.

Catholic and Orthodox rulers and their subjects have had no reluctance to defend their commonwealths against pagans and heretics, and, if they had no other piece of Scripture, the story of the tower of Babel would have informed them that their Creator had established separate peoples and warned them against any attempt to corral all the nations into a world government. Christians only began to lose their will to defend themselves during the Enlightenment, precisely the period when they began to replace their Christian faith with the unrealistic moral abstractions of John Locke and Adam Smith, Jean-Jacques Rousseau and Immanuel Kant. One-worldism is not even a Christian heresy but a post-Christian delusion. Free enterprise, tempered both by duties to family and community and by charity to others, is certainly consistent with the Christian moral order, but imperial globalism, dominated by a handful of world-controlers who make war on all distinctions of blood and affection, is the economic AntiChrist.

In saying "love your enemies," Christ was asking his followers to be "perfect even as your Father in heaven is perfect," who has given the blessings of this life to the just and unjust alike. To be as perfect as our Father in heaven is literally impossible for any man, but in the next chapter of Matthew, in teaching the multitude how to pray, Christ again tells us to do our best to imitate the Creator:

> "Our Father, who art in heaven...Forgive us our trespasses [literally debts] as we forgive those who trespass against us[debtors]."[Mt 6:9,12]

On the lowest and most literal level, Christ is asking us to forgive people who owe us money, just as the Father forgives what we owe him. However, it is also true that our debtors also include everyone we believe to have wronged us, hence the English translation, "Forgive us our trespasses, as we forgive those who trespass against us." It is a legitimate and useful broadening of the original; nonetheless, if we stick to the literal meaning of the text, the profit-seeking capitalism lauded by classical liberals and their libertarian descendants is as inconsistent with the gospels as Marxist socialism and humanitarian internationalism.

URBS AETERNA

In addressing himself to the Jews (and the stray gentiles who may have been in the crowd), Jesus was able to take for granted certain customs and traditions of moral law, whose inner and original meaning He now revealed. Although modern Christians make much of the Ten Commandments, the moral injunctions they contain, against blasphemy, theft, perjury, adultery, murder, and filial impiety were hardly unique in the Mediterranean world. Such prohibitions were the common stock of ancient moral and legal traditions. Greeks and Romans, whose moral codes were more systematic and universal than the codes of Egyptians, Sumerians, and Jews, condemned all these crimes, though (like the Jews) they had gradually relaxed their aversion to divorce. Although Greeks as much as Jews believed in the *lex talionis* (an eye for an eye), the Romans were quite severe in restricting the rights of retaliation and even of self-defense–restrictions the Church was to incorporate into its own codes.

These pre-Christian moral and legal assumptions about marriage, filial piety, and patriotism, and the prohibitions on adultery, theft, and murder make part of what St. Augustine referred to as the earthly city or commonwealth (*civitas terrena*). Augustine, as a zealous convert, naturally exempted most Jewish traditions from this category, and he was fond of contrasting the wickedness of pagan customs with the righteousness of the children of Israel. Augustine lived in a time of crisis, and his primary objective in writing his book was to defend the Church from its pagan critics.

Sixteen centuries later, it is more useful for us (and certainly fairer) to look for parallels among these three ancient cultural traditions whose convergence resulted in Christendom.

For Roman citizens of Augustine's time, whether Christian or pagan, *the* city or commonwealth was Rome. According to Roman tradition, Rome was said to have been founded by Romulus in 753 B.C., though, in fact, there had been much earlier settlements on the Palatine Hill. From their clusters of huts on the hill, the inhabitants spread across neighboring hills and down to the malarial marshlands along the Tiber, forced the proud ancient towns of Latium and Etruria to acknowledge their authority, and gradually conquered all of Italy and the Mediterranean world. In the reign of the Antonines (either side of A.D. 100), Roman authority stretched from southern Scotland to North Africa to ancient Mesopotamia and Anatolia.

Posidonius, a Greek philosopher of the early first century B.C., had taught the Romans their destiny: to rule over a stable world order, preserving and spreading the fruits of Greek civilization. This must have been a somewhat bitter pill for the more civilized Greeks to swallow. However just the Romans may have appeared to themselves, they had destroyed two of the greatest Greek cities in the world, Syracuse and Corinth, looted many others of their art treasures, and politically subjugated the entire Greek world. And yet, even at their worst, Roman generals and statesmen were more humane than most of the rulers of Hellenistic Greece had been. Alexander's successors and their descendants waged war as a business in which the primary objects were loot and slaves. To some Greeks, at least, the Roman order offered a relief from the dynastic and territorial wars that sometimes seemed more like terrorism than warfare.

Rome's ability to pacify the Greeks is partly explained by Polybius, a Greek who had gone to Rome as a hostage in 168 BC, between the Second and Third Punic Wars. He was present, when his friend Scipio Africanus the Younger captured and destroyed Carthage, and that was the year in which the ancient and beautiful city of Corinth was sacked and destroyed for its treasures. Nonetheless, Polybius, who had seen the Romans wage wars from both sides, declared that Rome's success was the result of a religious piety that made the Romans just and honorable in their dealings with foreign states [6.56.6-10].

> "For I conceive that what in other nations is looked upon as a reproach, I mean a scrupulous fear of the gods, is the very thing which keeps the Roman commonwealth together..."

Fear of divine wrath kept Roman public servants honest, Polybius argued, and that is why the punishments of Hell were still useful to keep ordinary people in check:

> "Much rather do I think that men nowadays are acting rashly and foolishly in rejecting them. This is the reason why, apart from anything else, Greek statesmen, if entrusted with a single talent, though protected by ten checking-clerks, as many seals, and twice as many witnesses, yet cannot be induced to keep faith: whereas among the Romans, in their magistracies and embassies, men have the handling of a great amount of money, and yet from pure respect to their oath keep their faith intact."[Polybius Histories 6:56:10]

In principle at least, the Roman senate did not wage aggressive or preemptive wars but always responded to an attack upon the territory of Rome or its allies. That Roman statesmen might sometimes expand the definition of foreign aggression does not detract from the novelty: In principle, Romans were only willing to wage a just war and, even when provoked, often conducted their wars with a degree of justice and mercy not often witnessed in either the ancient or modern world. The poet Vergil sums up this character in his account of the Roman historical mission [Æneid 6.853]: "To spare the fallen and subdue the proud"–a phrase that Augustine derides, in the preface to *De Civitatis Dei*, as "the inflated fancy of a proud spirit," though upon further reflection (in book V) was willing to concede the fact that the Romans had constructed and maintained the only terrestrial order that served the cause of justice.

A UGUSTINE AT THE END OF AN ERA

When Alaric the Visigoth sacked Rome in 410, therefore, it came as a terrible shock to the world. The most recent parallel is the fall of Constantinople to the Turks in 1453, but that catastrophe had been universally anticipated for decades and preceded by the Crusaders' sack of the city in the Fourth Crusade. The fall of Rome was inconceivable.

Pagans like the poet Claudian echoed the conservative arguments of Symmachus, a Roman senator of ancient stock: In abandoning the old gods Romans had invited disaster. Claudian gleefully mocked a Christian general, telling him to trust in the saints for protection. Christians were no less distraught than pagans. During the siege, St. Jerome writes (in letter 127, written in 412) that he heard

"the terrible news that Rome is besieged, that her citizens have been obliged to purchase their safety in

heavy gold and, already plundered of all their pos-
sessions, they have been besieged anew...My words
strangle in my throat. My sobs stop me from dictating these words. Behold, the city that conquered the
world has been conquered in its turn. Rome is dying
of hunger before it can die by the sword."

Earlier in his life, Augustine had lived in Rome as a teacher
of rhetoric, and, while he felt deep sympathy for the sufferings of Christian Romans, he was dismayed and angered
by pagan propaganda that blamed the disaster on the new
religion. In the days of her greatness, so the conservatives
said, Rome had invoked the protection of the gods. With
the triumph of Christianity, Rome had thrown down her
shield. When pagans said, "I told you so," Augustine asked
a young Spanish friend, Paulus Orosius, to write a Christian
apologia. Orosius explained the fall of the city in simplistic
terms. The pagan empire was insufficiently Christianized
and more or less deserved to fall. It is an appealing argument that can be used to justify any human misfortune.

Orosius' justification reminds me a bit of what a Calvinist
kindergarten teacher I had hired told one of her charges,
whose grandfather led the victorious rival faction in her
church. When the little girl came late to school, her eyes red
from crying, she gave the excuse that her pony had died that
morning. "Do you think," the teacher asked the distraught
child, "that if you had loved Jesus more, he would not have
taken away your pony?" It was, I have always thought, a
very Islamic view of God.

Orosius was not the only Christian to respond. In Gaul, Salvian wrote his *De Præsenti Judicio* (*On the Present Justice*),
in which he seemed to exult in the barbarian invasions,
arguing that while the Romans might be more civilized,

the Germanic barbarians were more virtuous and less degenerate. It is amusing to read Salvian's encomium on the virtuous Vandals in the seventh book of his work, since within a generation the Vandals in North Africa would become one of the most degenerate nations on earth. People at the court of the Western Emperor Honorius might have reached a similar conclusion if Procopius' story [Vandalic Wars III.2.25-26] is true that the Emperor, when he he was told (by his poultry-keeper) that Roma was destroyed, lamented: "And yet, it has just eaten from my hands." The poor sap thought he had lost a prize chicken named Roma–so degenerate was this son of the powerful Theodosius. Even if the tale is not true it is, as the Italians say, "ben trovato."

Augustine, in what became one of the most influential Christian books of all time, was more subtle, explaining in the *De Civitatis Dei* (*The City*–or rather *Commonwealth–of God*) that Christians, in abandoning the pagan gods, had not caused the destruction of Rome. Rome's success, he conceded, could not be denied, but what was worldly success compared with the heavenly kingdom? In the course of his argument, Augustine makes a stark contrast between God's people, both pre-Christian Jews and Christians, and the pagans whose cultural achievements were tainted by violence and moral ugliness.

Augustine's theology of pain and suffering strikes a distinctive note in the Greco-Roman culture of late antiquity, and his work is filled with theological and historical insights that justify its great reputation and influence. Nonetheless, his one-sided rejection of *Romanitas* often amounts to little more than special pleading. Greek and Roman myths are derided as violent and immoral, while parallel Jewish stories are interpreted allegorically and theologically to produce a wholesome and uplifting message. Augustine conveniently ignores the fact that Christians borrowed the technique of allegorical interpretation from the pagans–an appropriation that annoyed the most important critic of Christianity, the philosopher Porphyry, who composed an influential work against the Christians.

Romulus, Augustine declares, was evil to kill his brother Remus, while murders committed by Old Testament heroes are commanded by God, which rather begs the question Augustine has raised: If Jews and Christians are by definition virtuous, what is the point of his argument, which becomes one QED after another? Viewed by nonbelievers, which is the more horrifying story, Neoptolemus' killing of Priam, an enemy king, or Abraham's willingness to obey the divine command to sacrifice his own son?

Greek and Roman gods set immoral examples and exulted, so Augustine says with some justice, in obscene theatrical performances. Literary tragedies and comedies, he acknowledges, do not use such dirty language, but the subjects are not morally edifying. There is no mention of the classical Greek portrayal of Zeus as the god of justice who punishes sinners or of the moral wisdom taught by the Delphic Apollo and given dramatic form by Æschylus and Sophocles, whose plays constitute explorations of moral dilemmas certainly as serious as what we find in the Jewish prophets. On the other side, he writes as if he does not know of all the immoral behavior described in the Old Testament, a veritable catalogue of deadly sins–adultery, incest, fornication, robbery, murder, human sacrifice, and genocide–many of them committed, so the perpetrators claimed, under divine instigation.

When Augustine does mention the peccadilloes of Old Testament heroes, it is only to justify or palliate them, while Romans are judged not by their own but by Christian moral standards. When Romans committed suicide for moral reasons, they are derided, while Samson's action, in bringing down the Phoenician temple around him, was commanded by God. Augustine is well aware that weak-minded people might be deluded into thinking they are justified in murdering for God, but his argument could lead the unwary into just that conclusion.

On the surface, then, it might appear that Augustine was actually indifferent to the fall of Rome, but this is far from being the case. In fact, not long before he began *Civitas Dei*, he had depicted Rome in a letter [38] as a paragon of earthly virtue by which God has shown "how great is the influence of even civic virtues without true religion that it might be understood that, when this is added to such virtues, men are made citizens of another commonwealth, of which the king is truth, the law is love, and the duration is eternity."

Augustine was an educated man and (even in a purely literary sense) one of the greatest writers of late antiquity, but, like most successful orators and debaters, he tends to get carried away by the passion to win an argument, especially when the argument is over the Christian faith itself. He wrestled, over and over, with the obvious fact that much of his own success in promoting the faith derived not from the Scriptures so much as from his pagan education and rhetorical training. He cannot help thinking that his favorite philosophers—Plato, Plotinus—wrote from divine inspiration, and he cites the anti-Christian Porphyry with respect. Augustine does not even deny [18.47] that there may have been non-Jews who belonged to the heavenly kingdom.

LIGHT UNTO THE NATIONS

Christians and Jews have always believed that the Jews of the Old Testament were an instrument by which salvation came to the human race. This does not mean that gentiles and all their works were uniformly despised even in the Old Testament. Throughout the Old Testament we meet with many decent or righteous gentiles: the pharaoh who befriended Joseph, the benevolent Persian king (Cyrus) whom some rabbis regarded as the Messiah, because he returned the Jews to the Holy Land, and Job, the man of Uz. The gentile Job is the most righteous man of the Old Testament and Christians interpreted him as a symbolic forerunner of Christ.

The figure of Jonah is certainly intended as a critique of Jewish xenophobia. As a patriotic Jew, he was disturbed by the ease with which the Assyrians of Nineveh repented, but he is rebuked for becoming angry at the death of a gourd plant without considering that the Creator might be reluctant to destroy Nineveh, "that great city, wherein are more than sixscore thousand persons that cannot discern between their right hand and their left hand." Jonah's mission–and its success–make it clear that the civilization of the gentiles could instill a moral sense–that could prepare the way for repentance.

One question Augustine does not address is the comparative ease with which some pagans accepted the Christian promise of salvation. What did pagans think, when they heard Christians preaching to them about their hope of salvation? Perhaps, once again, a closer look at the text can tell us something.

There are many passages in the Gospels where a miraculous healing is followed by Jesus' pronouncement, "Thy faith has made thee whole," *e.g.*, the blind man Bartimæus [Mk 10:46-52] and the woman with an issue of blood. The Greek verb *sozein*, which is used in these passages, means primarily to save or preserve the body, to keep alive. Hence Zeus is called upon as *Soter*, savior, as later Hellenistic rulers were also addressed. Thus *soteria*, salvation, means primarily deliverance from death or illness, from danger or bondage.

When pagans heard Christians preaching salvation, then, it was not an alien thought that they could be rescued by a god or a son of a god or a favorite of god (at least temporarily) from death, and if they had heard of mystery religions or had studied philosophy, they might understand that this salvation could be a permanent condition that outlasts death. Porphyry, an anti-Christian Platonist, writes a letter of advice and consolation to his wife in which he tells her that there are "four first principles concerning God–faith, truth, love, hope," and adds the admonition that "we must have faith that our only salvation is in turning to God."

If the Christian message did not fall on deaf ears, it was partly because thoughtful pagans were yearning for a wholeness of existence, both in this life and throughout eternity, which they would spend in communion with a divinity or divinities that were entirely good and infinitely superior even to the great gods of Olympian religion. This argument, sometimes called the *Præparatio Evangelica* of the gentiles, goes back to Clement of Alexandria, Justin Martyr, and perhaps even to St. Paul who appealed to Greek traditions in his speech on the Areopagus.

Christianity did not develop in opposition to the moral and religious beliefs of pagans and unconverted Jews but in fulfillment of their highest aspirations. Christ came, as He declared, not to destroy the law but to fulfill it. The common civilization of the ancient Mediterranean world, in all its classical or extravagant varieties, was far from perfect, but Greek philosophy and literature, Roman law and political order, and the Jewish Scriptures were the foundation on which the Church could be built.

Some Christians, who object to the interweaving of Christian faith and pre-Christian cultural traditions, have gone so far as to reject traditional customs associated with Christmas and Easter, weddings and birthdays. Why they do not first reject television, computers, printing presses, and aluminum is a mystery. In recent centuries Christian Fundamentalists, Catholic as well as Protestant, have been repeating Tertullian's question, "What has Athens to do with Jerusalem?," with increasing urgency, though Tertullian, plainly, would not have been the writer he was without some grounding in rhetoric and philosophy. Attempts to create a purely Christian culture have always proved to be a dead end. Augustine himself toyed with the idea of a Christian literary curriculum–as John Henry Newman was later to attempt a Catholic reading list in English literature–but it was a futile project. No one, not even brilliant and faithful Christians, can make up a civilization out of whole cloth. It is only a little less presumptuous than the Enlightenment's attempt to reinvent the human race itself.

Doing the Lord's Work

Philosophically, Augustine was a Platonist and, like Plato and Thomas More (a Renaissance Neoplatonist), he was inclined to extremes in his speculations on human moral and social perfectibility. While it is undoubtedly true that the great philosophical tradition is that of Plato and Aristotle, there are subjects on which one or the other master may be a more useful guide. Idealists, it sometimes seems, are too often in a rush to erect the lofty and towering kingdom of God on earth, even before they have properly surveyed the ground or laid the foundations. The results of these secular attempts to build the Kingdom of God are often disastrous.

Utopian projects run aground on a fundamental principle enunciated by Cicero: The family is the foundation of the city (*principium urbis*) the seed-bed of the commonwealth (*seminarium rei publicæ*). (Dyck & Cicero, 1996, pp. 167-74) Cicero's declaration [*De Officiis* I 55 ff.]–or rather quotation from a Greek philosopher–has been repeated so often that it has suffered the fate of too many familiar truths–including the truths of the Gospels: No one takes the trouble to wonder what it means. Taken literally, Cicero's seed-bed metaphor assumes the family is the network of relationships in which citizens are reared and the source from which all civil institutions derive their legitimacy and strength. The authenticity and health of any political system, therefore, would depend directly upon the vigor of the families that comprise it: Undermine the family, and you destroy society. Unfortunately, self-described defenders of the family have used Cicero's quotation to buttress their calls for government interventions to "save" the family, when, in fact, it is governments that have been working assiduously to undermine and destroy it.

Cicero's view of the family was not an eccentric opinion. For Christians and Jews, the story of Adam and Eve has been a vivid confirmation of the family's status as a divinely established institution that stands at the beginning of human history, and political thinkers from Cicero to St. Thomas and even down to the 17th century were influenced by Aristotle's account of social evolution (in the first book of *The Politics*) as an unfolding process that begins with the married couple and culminates in the commonwealth.

Even if Cicero's statement were false, political dreamers and social revolutionaries have written and acted as if it is true, so true that they believe all their projects would run aground on the rock of the traditional family. With only a few minor exceptions, every political theory and social experiment of the past three hundred years has predicated itself on either the elimination of the family or on a drastic reduction of its traditional autonomy. Plato himself understood very well that his own utopian plans for a society based upon competitive excellence and social stability could never be realized so long as men and women forged exclusive marital bonds and parents had the authority to rear their own children.

Plato was less hard on the family in the *Laws*, and in his Seventh Letter he seems comfortable with normal Greek sentiments. He explains that the wise man will not try to compel his country to follow what he regards as the best course, using the analogy of parents: "To a father or mother I do not think that piety allows one to offer compulsion, unless they are suffering from an attack of insanity; and if they are following any regular habits of life which please them but do not please me, I would not offend them by offering useless advice, nor would I flatter them or truckle to them, providing them with the means of satisfying desires which I myself would sooner die than cherish." Still, it is the Plato of *The Republic*, hostile to the family, that has left the strongest impression.

But Plato, although his apparent aversion to the family is matched by few *ancient* philosophers (apart from Epicurus), is hardly an isolated case. The family's enemies are legion among political theorists. Many of them have attacked the historicity of the institution, offering their own substitutes for the accounts in *Genesis* and Aristotle's *Politics*. Marx and Engels, following the American anthropologist L.H. Morgan, regarded the family not as a natural institution but as the historical invention of the same patriarchal males who invented private property and the state; Freud de-legitimized the family by offering his own myth of the "Oedipus complex," according to which primal sons wrested power from a primal father in order to have sex with a primal mother; Franz Boaz and such prominent students as Margaret Mead believed they could debunk the family by trying to show that marital institutions and sexual customs, so far from being natural and universal, were very different in non-Western societies.

The accounts in Genesis, Engels, Freud, and Mead have one feature in common: They are all ætiological myths designed to explain human nature. None of them can be substantiated by scientific evidence, though one of them—the anthropological myth of Boas and Mead—has been refuted by cross-cultural anthropological studies that reveal the existence of common patterns of human social life.

Among all these mythical tales, the story in Genesis has several claims on the loyalty even of those who are neither Christians nor Jews: Almost everyone in the West knows it, and it is paralleled by similar stories in many other cultures. More significantly, the account of Adam and Eve is a serious attempt to grapple with the reality that men and women often find they cannot be as good as they think they should be. Evil exists and not just in other people whom we dislike.

Adam naturally blamed Eve for getting them kicked out of the Garden, but they left together and, until Cain killed his brother, they formed a nuclear commonwealth that sustained and defended itself. Driven out of the homestead, Cain despaired: As a fugitive he knows, "Everyone will slay me." Outside the protective circle of the family, Cain will face Hobbes's war of all against all.

Not all attacks upon the family are as bold as the frontal assaults launched by the master theorists of political and social revolution. The founders of classical liberalism also took a dim view of the family's broader responsibilities. Liberals, in emphasizing the liberated individual and his right to pursue his own destiny, have generally been less than supportive of the peculiar legal status of marriage and family and favored liberalized divorce and inheritance laws as well as the economic and political liberation of married women. They were not explicitly opposed to the family *per se* any more than they generally admitted that they were opposed to Christianity *per se*. Their object, so they claimed, was merely to liberate individuals from the shackles imposed by religious fanaticism and patriarchal authority.

I am using "liberal" in the traditional (or "classical") sense to refer to writers, parties, and movements that emphasized individual liberty and the free market at the expense of tradition, inherited privilege, and established religion. In Britain, the godfather of liberalism is John Locke, and his spiritual heirs (among whom there are, admittedly, many important differences) include Adam Smith, Tom Paine, William Godwin, and John Stuart Mill. In contemporary America, the great liberals have been the advocates of free markets and free trade who describe themselves as libertarians, when they tend toward anarchism, and as conservatives, when they speak on behalf of those who are determined to hold onto their great wealth and influence, no matter how it was acquired and no matter what the cost to others.

John Locke's entire political theory was grounded in his opposition to the patriarchal view of government advocated by Sir Robert Filmer and other advocates of monarchical rights. While Filmer traced the origin of sovereign authority back through the power held by biblical patriarchs over their extended families and ultimately to Adam, Locke set aside all such traditions and adopted the theory of the Social Contract, whose long history stretches back at least to Epicurus and his disciples. Although there are many variations on contract theory, they usually say, generally, that men originally lived in a state of nature, without either law or order. Political authority, private property, and even social institutions such as marriage came into existence as the result of an agreement or contract, made by early men who were tired of the inconveniences of uncivil society. Though Locke did not directly attack the family itself, he did advocate the right of divorce, once children were grown, and the implications of his thought, logically working their way out across the centuries, have been to regard the family as a useful, though not essential social institution.

HUMAN SOCIETY

As a Platonist, Augustine was not inclined to respect traditional human institutions and, as a Christian convert in conflict with a stubborn paganism that refused to leave the stage, he conceded few virtues (at this point in his career) to the Roman Empire, whose fall plunged the West into violence and poverty, but he was too hardheaded not to understand human reality. The City of God could not be arrived at, if the saints who were destined to live in it had not been created as social beings. Marriage and parenthood, he acknowledges, are fraught with grief, but that is not because they are bad as such but because parents and spouses suffer loss and betrayal as the consequence of sin. The home is our refuge, albeit a precarious one, just as is the city. Both are institutions that serve, if properly maintained, human happiness. [C.D.19.5.] Augustine also agrees with ancient philosophers and modern Darwinists that human beings share some of their tendencies toward sociability even with the savage beasts we too often resemble. If that is so, then, he asks, "How much more is a man in some manner borne by the laws of his own nature to enter into fellowship and peace with all men...?" [19.12] Even against the thrust of his main argument, Augustine lends some support for the idea that the terrestrial city is not utterly depraved. If the family is the seed-bed or nursery for the commonwealth, the earthly city–at its best–might then be the nursery in which one can nurture the seedlings that will some day be transplanted into the heavenly city.

But, rather than distort Augustine's language or co-opt him for purposes of which he would probably disapprove, we might extrapolate a third city, a City of Man in which men and women, seeing the truth of natural law in a mirror distorted by their passions and by imperfect knowledge, prepare the foundations for the City of God. It is better, perhaps, to use the plural, Cities of Men, since we are dealing with concrete historical manifestations of human society and not with an abstract or perfect community. In these human cities, the institutions of marriage and the family, vengeance and justice, private property and social hierarchy, while far from perfect, can offer us a dim perception of the perfected social state designed by our Creator.

Augustine himself acknowledges this possibility, in quoting St. Paul's admonition to Christians to provide for their own households: "Whosoever does not provide for his own, and especially for those of his own household, he denies the faith, and is worse than an infidel." [1 Tim 5:8]. The responsibility for taking care of one's family, as Augustine says [C.D. 19.14], belongs to "the order of nature." These duties are not, therefore, capricious commands imposed by a sovereign upon a human race that has no inclination to carry them out. Much less have they been arbitrarily or conditionally assigned to parents, whose mandate to provide for their children can be arrogated by higher powers.

What would he say, then, of a society that systematically denied the responsibilities of parents or inculcated disobedience into children? Or ridiculed marital fidelity or propagated a conception of marriage that included the casual union of members of the same sex? Or denigrated personal responsibility and promoted the notion of collective or state responsibility for material well-being? Or, or, or...This is the ideology of the modern state, and whatever Augustine might have called it, I prefer to call it by its rightful name: The City of Satan.

In recent centuries the City of Satan has all too often been proclaimed as the City of God by misguided Christians, who dressed their secular ideologies–liberalism, capitalism, socialism, democratism, nationalism, internationalism, feminism, pacifism, zionism, environmentalism–in the Church's vestments. Leaving the high road of the great tradition of Scriptures and the major Fathers, and poking their way through obscure passages and vexed interpretations, they seize upon some ambiguous phrase and, plucking it out of context, use it as a foundation for whatever moral or social or political position they are seeking to justify.

Some of the confusion arises from the honest mistakes of absolutist sects (such as the Anabaptists) whose creeds are based on a fundamentalist misconstruction of selected passages; more often, however, the error stems from the surrender to fashionable opinion. There have been Christian deists, Christian Unitarians, Christian socialists, Christian capitalists, Christian libertarians, Christian feminists, and even Christian environmentalists, none of whose creeds would bear much scrutiny from anyone who possessed the necessary context for understanding historic Christendom. In America, especially, ignorance truly is bliss for the founders and followers of the proliferating sects, though some Catholic bishops have been equally zealous in perverting the Christian understanding to justify one or another Marxist scheme of forced redistribution of wealth.

Whether intentionally or not, these ideological reinterpretations of Christianity have done a great deal of damage to the Church and to modern society. Many virile and ambitious young men have been revolted by a religion that seemed to say it is wrong to resist evil, defend borders, or compete in the marketplace. When the ranks of the clergy are filled with ill-educated sentimentalists, the church loses authority with men. It is easy to say that Christianity is incompatible with socialism and libertarianism; it is another thing for ordinary people to prove it. Many a decent person, confronted by Christian fools, has preferred to steer clear of religion. Of the spiritual leaders who, by advocating fashionable opinions, have fostered disbelief, it would be better for such a man "that a millstone were hanged about his neck and that he were drowned in the depth of the sea."

The Commonwealth of God is the Church, not the Roman Empire or the American Republic. While incompetent and wicked sovereigns have to be obeyed when they carry out the laws (so long as they do not command us to do what the Church forbids), we are not to look upon them as God's anointed delegates, carrying out a divine program of world conquest for Christ or promoting the cause of American exceptionalism. In rendering unto even a Christian Cæsar, we must not surrender to him, to a constitution, to a form of government or political theory, the things that are God's.

References

Dyck, A. R. & Cicero, M. T. (1996). *A Commentary on Cicero, De officiis*. University of Michigan Press.

Sordi, M. (1994). *The Christians and the Roman Empire*. Taylor & Francis.

LOVE AND HATE IN THE CITIES OF MAN

Shall I tell you the little story of Right-Hand-Left-Hand–the tale of Good and Evil? ...H-A-T-E...It was with this left hand that old brother Cain struck the blow that laid his brother low! L-O-V-E!...See these here fingers, dear friends! These fingers have veins that lead straight through to the soul of man! The right hand, friends! The hand of Love! Now watch and I'll show you the Story of Life. The fingers of these hands, dear hearts! –They're always a-tuggin' and a- warrin' one hand agin' t'other. (He locks his fingers and writhes them, crackling the joints) Look at 'em, dear hearts! Old Left Hand Hate's a-fightin' and it looks like Old Right Hand Love's a goner! But wait now! It's Love that won! Old Left Hand Hate's gone down for the count!

IN THIS SCENE OF *Night of the Hunter* (based closely on the novel by Davis Grubb), Preacher Harry Powell delivers what may be the best known sermon in cinematic history. His words are vividly illustrated by the words L-O-V-E and H-A-T-E tattooed on the knuckles of his right and left hands. It is a persuasive account, and one of the onlookers declares, "I never heard it better told." Some moviegoers would have been a bit more suspicious, knowing of the preacher's weakness for loose women and other people's money, and by the end of the film, if they had occasion to look back, some might have wondered if life is really a simple morality play fought out between the forces of love and hate.

Between the preacher's hysterical moralizing and the moral relativism that already dominated Hollywood in 1955, there is considerable ground, though modern Christians are often tempted into imagining human existence as an endless struggle—in language made familiar by Reinhold Niebuhr—between the children of light and the children of darkness. In staking their moral claim on the position that "love is all you need," Christians have ample justification in the Scriptures. As Paul says [Rom 13.8]:

> "Owe no man any thing, but to love one another: for he that loveth another hath fulfilled the law."

The entire thirteenth chapter of St. Paul's *Epistle to the Romans* is a summation of the Christian approach to morality and politics. Taken out of context, the statement "he that loveth another hath fulfilled the law" sounds perilously close to a John Lennon lyric, but, if we read the whole chapter as the culmination of a carefully thought out argument, we shall not make the mistake of trivializing the apostle to the gentiles.

Paul had been dwelling on the theme that under the law we cannot be saved but only condemned by divine judgment for our sins, because an infraction of any part of the law entails condemnation. Here on earth, he tells us, the sword of punishment—even unto death—has been entrusted to the rulers, and Paul cannot be imagining the responsibility of Christian rulers in the future but thinking in concrete terms of the Roman emperor and the officers and administrators who execute his will. Indeed, Paul makes it clear that he is not speaking of a utopia or calling upon his readers to overturn or reinvent the social and political order: Obedience is still owed by wives to husbands, children to parents, slaves to masters, subjects to rulers; our duty is to obey the second great commandment, to love our neighbors as ourselves. In loving our neighbor we shall not kill, steal, commit adultery, bear false witness, or covet.

Love (Greek *agape*, Latin *caritas*) worketh no ill to his neighbor: therefore love is the fulfilling of the law.

Love, then, fulfills the law, but, here in the imperfect Cities of Man, the demands of the law must also be met.

THE HEART HAS ITS REASON

The City of God, wherever and however it exists, is ruled by that kind of love that used to be referred to as "charity." "He that loveth," then, far from being in conflict with the traditional moral law taught by the Decalogue, is fulfilling it. Professional philosophers since Descartes (with a few exceptions like Hume and Nietzsche) would immediately raise the obvious objection that love–or friendship or charity–is an irrational feeling, a sub-rational reflection of our character and experience. We may "love" dogs or even a particular breed of dog because we grew up in a household where such dogs were raised, but an affection for spaniels or our siblings and schoolmates is not moral by definition. It is not rational or based on consent or a covenant (as Thomas Hobbes would demand); our affections do not involve the fulfillment of a duty nor are they dictated by a rational universal principle. Charity and justice, to simplify the philosophers, have very little in common.

For the moment, let us dodge the question, "What is justice?," and look instead at charity. Christian charity is not limited to handing out alms, though a person with charity will be generous to those in need. In carrying out the two great commandments, to love God and love our neighbor, Augustine [*C.D.* 19.14] explains, "Man finds three things he is to love: God, himself, and his neighbor...thus, he is concerned for his wife, his children, the members of his household, and other men as he is able..."

To have charity, then, is to aim at loving our neighbor as our self or, at least, treating him as we should treat a member of our family. Some, like Adam Smith, have found it convenient to ignore the First Great Commandment, which then permits Smith to reduce the Second to sentimental philanthropy.

Others have gone further, concluding that charity requires us to be "non-judgmental," and, if they are Christian, they are sure to cite, "Judge not lest ye be judged." Taken literally however, the word 'non-judgmental' could only be applied to a fool and not necessarily a pure or holy fool. Christ himself passed judgment frequently, as when he kicked the bankers out of the temple, telling them they had turned His Father's house into a den of thieves. In Matthew, He delivers an angry diatribe against the legalism of the "Scribes, Pharisees–actors," in the course of which He declared: "You pay tithes of mint and dill and cumin; but you have overlooked the weightier demands of the Law: justice, mercy, and good faith."[Matt 23:23] As His indignation against the Jewish power structure rose to its height, He declared [John 8:39-44]: "Your father was not Abraham; your father was Satan." Could He have framed a harsher condemnation?

The word "justice" used in many translations of Matthew is a translation of the Greek *krisis*, a word that is better rendered (as it is in both the Authorized Version and Douai-Rheims) as "judgment," the action of weighing evidence and coming to a verdict. In a negative context it indicates condemnation. (I wonder if more recent translators have deliberately mistranslated the text to make it less "judgmental.") In the New Testament the word is often used of the Judgment that will be passed on human beings when Christ returns. In the Sermon on the Mount, we have heard: "Whosoever is angry with his brother without a cause shall be in danger of the judgment."

The Christian is supposed to live in fear of divine condemnation, not so much of the terrifying End Times, whose arrival no one can or should predict, as of the judgment that will be passed on his conduct. This judgment or divine verdict is the first element cited as being among the weightier parts of the law, and it is followed by mercy and faith, two moral qualities that must guide his behavior if he is to escape condemnation. No Christian could be merciful or faithful if he did not pass judgment on the actions of kinsmen and friends who, if they fell short in the practice of these virtues, might be sentenced to permanent death.

Nonetheless, the charitable person will not measure the faults of others by a stricter standard than he uses for himself. In the City of God, the human lion will lie down with the human lamb, whereas the City of Satan, which professes the love of all to all equally, is actually defined by the old Latin proverb, that man is wolf to man. Thomas Hobbes was completely and utterly wrong in thinking that human life in a state of nature–if such a phrase actually can mean anything–was a *bellum omnium contra omnes* (the war of every man against every man). That condition of universal hostility was reserved for our own post-civilized and post-human era.

It is important to understand where Hobbes went wrong. If man ever lived in a state of nature, such a natural man has never been observed. The whole concept of a "state of nature" derives from the unsupported philosophical speculations of the ancient philosopher Epicurus and his intellectual descendants. Although the fable of a state of primitive anarchy from which men escaped by making a social contract has been repeated *ad nauseam* by Locke, Rousseau, and (in our own day) John Rawls, it is at best an untestable hypothesis, which cannot profitably be made the foundation for further speculation any more than we could construct a rational and scientific account of oxidation on the basis of an imaginary substance called phlogiston. In studying man, we must limit ourselves to what is known and can be known, for, if we take the lost continent of Atlantis as the starting point of our investigation, we shall end up attributing all civilization to the intervention of the Anunnaki, who arrived from the planet Nibiru.

Mankind has been around a long time, as the anthropologists remind us, and it is not safe to speak of this or that simple society–Eskimos or Pygmies–as "primitive," if by primitive we mean less subject to social evolution. Pygmies have been around at least as long as Europeans and probably much longer. At best we can say that Pygmies, Bushmen, and Eskimos represent a less socially complex and less technologically advanced–not necessarily primitive or even simpler–form of human society.

But suppose, for the sake of argument, that we can speak of a "state of nature," meaning a sort of conglomerate model or ideal pattern deduced from the simplest societies known to anthropologists–again, Eskimos, Pygmies, Bushmen, *et alii*. Far from being battlegrounds of individualistic self-assertion and anarchic violence, such societies are tightly knit by strong social and familial ties. It is only in the Satanic City of modern cosmopolitan societies where we see institutions of blood and marriage replaced by governments that rule the lives of naked individualists who, if truth be told, live more like flocks of domestic sheep (raised to be sheared and slaughtered) than like lone wolves. It is precisely philosophers like Hobbes and Locke and Rousseau, with their corrosive theories of the state of nature, individual rights, and the almighty state, who are the human architects of the Satanic City.

If the City of God requires us to regard (or at least try to regard) others as we do a brother or parent, the Satanic City tells us that we should be equally indifferent to all men and women, naturally under the pretext of being a "citizen of the world" who is devoted to the welfare of all mankind. In that city, parents will concern themselves with how to rear and educate other people's children, while neglecting their own; they will vote for healthcare and retirement benefits for other people's parents, while treating their own with no more respect than they would show to a derelict car abandoned in the backyard.

The Cities of Man are located between these two stark extremes. In them, we are told to love our own but also to treat fellow-citizens justly and, at least in more civilized cities, strangers with some decency. However, in loving our own and showing them charity, we can also find ourselves in a position where we have to defend *our* people from *their people*, that is, from strangers against whom we may even have to retaliate, meeting violence with violence. If citizens in the Cities of Man are at peace in their household, they must also be sometimes at war with other households. Then we might say there are two laws at work in the Cities of Man, the law of love and the law of hate, though, as we shall see, there are more precise words like strife or war. One does not, after all, have to hate an enemy in order to resist his aggression.

It is tempting but a bit too simple to say that in obeying the law of love we are showing our love of God and in displaying hate or anger toward aggressors or strife with those who would gain advantages at our expense we are only following the dictates of Satan. If we bracket, for the moment, the many passages in the Old Testament where we are told of what the Lord hates [Ps 11:5], we are still left with Paul's unambiguous statement that in loathing that which is wicked, we must cleave to the good. [Rom 12:9] The Authorized Version translates the Greek *apostugountes* as "abhor," a good word when its meaning was still understood as "shrink in loathing from." In Greek, the root *stugnos* indicates the feeling of hatred and repugnance aroused by that which is loathsome. In the *Acts of the Apostles*, Paul not only rebukes a sorcerer as the son of the devil and an enemy of righteousness but also proceeds to inflict him with temporary blindness.

A Christian will naturally treat with suspicion any defense of hatred and its customs, such as dueling, feuding, and belligerence. We are told to love our enemies and pray for those who do us injury. We are not even allowed to wish harm to come to our enemies. In the *Theologia Moralis* [II 28-29] St. Alphonsus de Liguori says we are obliged to display common indications of love (*dilectio*) to our enemies: what one Christian or fellow-citizen or blood-relation owes to another. On the other hand, he stipulates, we are not required to display particular indications of love by, for example, treating non-Christians as Christians or giving the privileges of citizenship and kinship to outsiders. As for acts of revenge and punishment against aggression, Alphonsus lays down the general principle that such things are best left up to the proper authorities.

If we were to love universally and without discrimination, then we could not love those whom we are bound to love but would waste our charitable energies on those who prey upon the weak and innocent. When Dr. Johnson expressed admiration for "a good hater," he was not speaking as a pagan but as a Christian who hated the Evil One, from whom we pray to be delivered, and from all his human legions. In the Cities of Man, therefore, we can expect to find the realms of love and strife (or, if you prefer, hate), neither of them in perfect condition.

> But on this side there is no end to strife,
> where violence has taken love to wife—
> a pagan tale of Venus and of Mars,
> matter of fact and heedless as the stars
> of carnage done in our too human wars.

"Love makes the world go round," as an old proverb has it. Does this mean anything more than the obvious fact, celebrated in Valentine cards and romantic novels, that sexual attraction between male and female is a necessary condition for propagating many species, the human species in particular? What is love? Philosophers since Plato and psychologists of different schools and sects have spilled much ink in a vain attempt to define it, and I am not going to enter, much less add to, the debate. If love could be strictly defined, it probably would not possess the power it does.

Whatever else can be said of it, love is a kind of passion or feeling (like pain or hunger or envy), which can be roughly described though not defined in any absolute terms. In one obvious sense erotic love implies the desire for another, even *the* other. If we limit ourselves to the desire that leads to procreation, it is the desire of opposite sexes for each other, and although men and women expect to find mates with compatible interests and habits, they are rarely looking for their twins or doubles. In this respect, Plato was quite wrong in the charming myth he puts into the mouth of Aristophanes, who (in the *Symposium*) argues that lovers are forever seeking the other half from whom they were divided.

> "The original human nature was not like the present, but different. The sexes were not two as they are now, but originally three in number; there was man, woman, and the union of the two, of which the name survives but nothing else...Terrible was their might and strength, and the thoughts of their hearts were great, and they made an attack upon the gods; of them is told the tale of Otys and Ephialtes who, as Homer says, attempted to scale heaven, and would have laid hands upon the gods."

The gods, to curb the power of the two parts of man, split them in two with the result that

> "The two parts of man, each desiring his other half, came together, and throwing their arms about one another, entwined in mutual embraces, longing to grow into one, they began to die from hunger and self-neglect, because they did not like to do anything apart; and when one of the halves died and the other survived, the survivor sought another mate, man or woman as we call them,–being the sections of entire men or women–and clung to that."

If this fable had any explanatory force, the human race would have long ago died out. The survival of the human race requires us to lust after the other and not after the same. (Even in erotic pairs of the same sex, it is conventional for one partner to take the role of the husband and the other that of the wife.) In abstract terms, then, love might be compared with the magnetic or electronic attraction of opposites, and it is not too much of a stretch to claim that such a force is responsible (if only in part) for making the world go round. On this understanding, hate (or some other negative emotion like strife or competition) would represent the repulsion of opposites, the attraction of like for like; and, if love really does make the world go round, then the opposite of love, the complex of feelings and relations we refer to as hate or competition or strife, presumably keeps the world within its orbit by preventing all things from joining together in a universal union.

These fanciful speculations may be more appropriate to poets, who have always testified to the power exercised by love and hate in human life. The first work of Western literature, the *Iliad*, seems to be about nothing but desire and hate. Paris' love for Helen sparked the Trojan War, and Achilles' hatred of his commander, Agamemnon, almost led to a Trojan victory until Hector killed Achilles' best friend and inspired an even greater hatred in the Greek hero. Like pleasure and pain, which Plato [*Phædo* 60b-c] describes as a monster with two bodies but one head, love and hate cannot easily be kept separate. Love, when thwarted, often turns to hate, and

> "Heav'n has no rage, like love to hatred turn'd, Nor hell a fury, like a woman scorn'd."

But love and hate of the same person can coexist in the same soul, as Catullus knew, though he could not explain the reason:

> "Odi et amo: quare id faciam, fortasse requiris. Nescio, sed fieri sentio et excrucior."

> "I love and I hate. Maybe you want to know why I am acting this way. I don't know, but I feel that I am, and I am on the rack."

For the most part, the poets sing of the love experienced in the here and now. "What is love?" asks Shakespeare in a song, "T'is not hereafter...Present mirth and present laughter. What's to come is still unsure." Erotic love is, proverbially, a short-lived passion, as I learned when I asked a student to distinguish between the Latin verb forms *amavi* (I loved, have loved) and *amaveram* (I had loved). The young lady, sighing in her charming Lowcountry South Carolina dialect, replied: "What's the difference? When love's gone, it's gone."

These days, most of us would agree with this young lady or the other lady who advised a poet "to take love easy, as the leaves grow on the tree," but there are tales of love and hate that go beyond the grave. The ghost of Hamlet's father walked the earth seeking revenge on the brother who had murdered him and married his wife. The Greek hero Protesilaus, the first to die at Troy, was so mourned by his wife that the gods allowed him to spend three hours with her, and when he left she died of grief. Wordsworth christened the myth, and the hero tells his wife of eternal love:

"...such love as spirits feel In worlds whose course is equable and pure; No fears to beat away–no strife to heal–The past unsighed for, and the future sure."

Orpheus, the patron saint of poets, went to Hell to fetch his bride but made the mistake of looking back to make sure she was following him. His excess of passion–and lack of trust in the gods–cost him his wife.

These tales are myths, that is to say, they contain truths too deep to be taken literally, but the Greeks were also inclined to systematic reflection, and this was a habit that grew in the centuries following the writing down of their great epic poems. Many textbook accounts of ancient philosophy give the impression that the development of Greek philosophy was a straightforward and steady advance from the religious and mythical point of view of Homer and Hesiod to the entirely rational and scientific approach of Democritus and Epicurus, who explained everything in the universe as the interaction of atoms within the void. Such an account makes philosophy, almost by definition, the enemy of religion (and of the opinions of everyday life), but it leaves out not only Aristotle, who took ordinary life and the prejudices of ordinary people very seriously, but also the important contributions of Greeks in the West, in Sicily and Magna Græcia (southern Italy), whose philosophical speculations began with religious assumptions and culminated in a mystical theology that sometimes defied common sense.

Plato's *Republic* (though not devoid of its own mysticisms) is the most familiar literary expression of the rationalist tendency in Greek philosophy, not just in physics and metaphysics but in ethics and politics. To ascertain what a just man would be, Plato's Socrates suggests an exercise in model-building: Let us construct a perfect commonwealth and then apply its features—more easily explicable for being on a larger scale—to the human individual. Thus his republic has no real geography, only an idealized setting; no history, only a set of founding principles. One might think he was talking about the United States as Lincoln imagined it, a nation without identity or history, a mere abstraction "dedicated to the proposition that all men are created equal."

All the normal traditions that shaped the lives of the Greeks and gave them joy were either to be banished from Plato's ideal state, as the poets were, or reengineered, as the family was, so as to be unrecognizable. The family, at least for the ruling class, would no longer be an autonomous institution informed by erotic attraction, parental love, filial obedience and the strong ties of blood. Male and female guardians would live in barracks, own no property, and rear their children in common. Unfit children would be adopted out to a non-guardian family. Henceforth families would be little more than departments of an all-controlling commonwealth—as they have become in totalitarian societies of the 20th and 21st centuries.

Plato's hostility to the jealous passions of the household are well-known to students of philosophy. What receives somewhat less attention is his skeptical view of Greek religion and civilization. Socrates, in the early dialogues, debunks the common morality and religion of the Greeks, and, in the less-than-candid *Apology* Plato gives him, he denies the charges of atheism and introducing false gods, defending his skeptical teaching as a blessing to Athens.

Socrates was, alas, guilty as charged. He not only did not accept the gods of his city, but, in Plato's *Apology*, he declared his moral independence of both gods and the city. This is not merely arrogance but *hybris*, as that word is understood in Greek tragedy, that is, an overweening arrogance that leads to ruin. The understanding of the divine offered in the *Apology* and the *Euthyphro* precludes the existence of the individual and passionate gods who inspired all of Greek culture, and, as Miles Burnyeat correctly observes, "With gods as moralistic as Socrates', Greek culture would have been impossible, and in consequence Western civilization would not have been what it is today." (Burnyeat, 1997, p. 10)

Greek Lessons

Socrates and Plato had fixed their eyes on another, more perfect world that might be considered a preliminary sketch of Augustine's City of God. By contrast, a typical Greek city (if such a thing ever existed outside the imagination of political theorists) was dominated by two locales: the acropolis and the agora. The acropolis (or high town) was the ancient citadel, where Bronze Age kings had ruled. In time, as the kings were replaced by aristocrats, oligarchs, and demagogues, the acropolis became the home of the gods and site of the most important temples.

The Athenian acropolis was crowned by the Parthenon, a temple to the virgin goddess Athena. The Panathenaic festival, held every four years, was highlighted by a procession in which different groups brought the fruits of the earth, especially olive oil (her gift to man) and, most important of all, the new woolen *peplos* (a type of gown) for her sacred image. The festival, which included athletic and literary contests, was a celebration of Athenian unity in which rival clans, neighborhoods, and political factions were supposed to submerge their differences.

Down in the *agora* or marketplace, however, a different kind of life went on. Men bought and sold goods, made deals, and competed for public honors. It is not that there were no temples: One of the best preserved Greek temples is set on a hill in Athens jutting up from the east end of the Agora. It is commonly called the Theseion, though it is more likely to have been dedicated to Hephæstus, the god of the forge. There were other shrines in the marketplace itself, but the greater part of this public space was devoted to two activities: commerce and politics. The very layout of Athens—and most other Greek cities—hints at a creative tension between the religious and familial side of life represented by the acropolis and the competitive, market-driven life of the agora.

It must have seemed a very messy state of affairs to autocrats and to the would-be autocrats known as political philosophers. According to Herodotus [I.153] the Persian king Cyrus, after listening to the demands of Spartan envoys to leave the Greeks alone, told his advisors that he did not fear any people who gathered together in the marketplace to cheat each other. Plato shared the Persian contempt for trade and competition. In his *Republic* the *agora* virtually disappears. The aristocratic philosopher had no use for trade, and as for the rough-and-tumble strife of politics, he wished only to eliminate the fray and establish a tyranny of love, in which the peculiar traditions of Greek cities, their superstitious attachments to the land and its gods, their hereditary friendships and blood-feuds would be merged into the common good defined by intellectually and morally superior social engineers. In one of his later books (the *Laws*), Plato recognized the impossibility of his dream and made his commonwealth somewhat more human, but in conceding to reality he did not really alter his approach: the application of pure reason to human problems.

As a means of understanding the real lives of men and women, all forms of reasoning fall short, even when they are deployed by a supreme master like Plato. In his *Politicus*, a late dialogue that is often neglected (partly because its dialectical argumentation is very tedious), he forces the reader to go through a seemingly endless process of subdividing everything on earth in an attempt to arrive at a definition of the statesman or ruler. Along the way, he (rather casually) concludes that ruling men is a rational science, which means that very few people–perhaps two or three out of 10,000–can practice it. Those who engage in market activities would never dream of possessing such a power, his student declares. [290a] The best system would be the absolute dictatorship of an enlightened godlike ruler who is not bound by laws or traditions in his pursuit of the best interests of his people. Under the benevolent guidance of the Supreme Court, 21st century America has almost realized Plato's ideal.

The *Politicus* is a brilliant piece of analysis, but there are several gaps in Plato's arguments. Some of the gaps are the result of confounding words with reality and of assuming that, if the Greeks had a word for a number of different phenomena, there must be a reality that corresponds to the word. In a rich and allusive language like English, this mistake explains many of the mistakes of any school of philosophy that begins with the analysis of words. The confusion over the word "rights" has even generated philosophical systems!

When one attempts to go from one language to another, the result can be even more comical than the writings of

Locke and Rousseau. How often has one heard the first sentence of John's Gospel invoked by preachers as proof of Scriptural inerrancy: "In the beginning was the word." Unfortunately, "word" translates a complex Greek word that is not so much used to mean a spoken or written word as to indicate rational discourse, proportion, and, philosophically, a principle of order in the universe.

Plato, who believed that words were somehow rooted in reality, was particularly prone to this mistake. For example, he takes it for granted that the "political science"–the art of governing–is a single science and that the authority held by a master of the household is the same as that exercised by the ruler of the state. He obviously begs the question of what a science is (to say nothing of the word *politikos*, which properly refers to what goes on in the life of the city and in the conduct of the city's business).

There is a similar (though not identical) confusion in English, where it is legitimate to speak of "political science" or the "science of economics," only if we are using science in the old-fashioned sense of a systematic body of knowledge, as in the "science of philology" or the "science of music theory" or even "the science of cookery." However, terms like political science or social science are not legitimate if they are intended to indicate that they are exact sciences, such as physics or physical chemistry, whose results can be quantified and whose theories can be tested. There is, for example, a medical science whose practitioners agree on the role played by microbes in a disease and can, in most cases, predict the effects of an antibiotic treatment on a specific strain of pneumonia; whereas in the case of psychology (or, rather psychologies) each school of thought has a different theory of cause, a different set of treatments, and rather disappointing track records for results.

Like Socrates, Plato viewed the passions as hostile to the rational life—and thus as irrational impulses that had to be subdued—but he did not pause to consider if they might also be natural necessities that enable us to survive and thrive. An ordinary man who did not feel hunger might starve to death. Finally, in drawing up general prescriptions for how men should be ruled, he did not ask himself what should have been the first question: What is the nature of humanity? What if his reasoning led him to conclude that the life of the hummingbird was best and thus men should feed off nectar and fly at breakneck speed by flapping their arms? This must have been the view of the comic poet Aristophanes, who in *The Clouds* portrays Socrates as an impractical meddler with his head in the clouds. Under his influence, a young man learns to despise conventional morality, including the respect that is owed to his parents.

Like many philosophers since, Plato was not content with the merely human, and he was led to design a society in which humans could not live. Some of his later admirers, such as Thomas More (if he was not being merely fanciful) fell into the same trap of designing a divine or supra-natural political order for human beings, and, since the French Revolution, the project of transcending the merely human passions of love and hate—and the institutions based on them—is no longer the exclusive province of utopian philosophers: It is the objective of most political movements of modern times.

For argument's sake, let us consider a grotesque over-generalization—something like one of the myths Plato made up; let us say this rationalist approach to the basic human passions and facts of life represents *one* but not *the only* Greek approach to human life, one that is typical of Athenian thinkers and their elder kinsmen in Ionia. Let us, again for the sake of argument, call it the Eastern Greek approach. There was, however, another approach, which I am calling Western Greek, one that took more account of human realities. Before turning to these Western Greeks, however, we have to grapple with the predecessors and heirs of Socrates.

In their search for a first principle or principles (an *arche* or *archai*) the Ionian "physicists" of Eastern Greece (Thales, Anaximander, Anaximenes, Heraclitus, and Anaxagoras) had sought to explain natural phenomena as a product of a few simple processes, such as condensation and expansion, that caused the basic material(s)–*e.g.*, earth, air, fire, water–to exhibit change and variety. (To be fair to the Ionians, one should note that these *archai* also possessed certain divine characteristics, such as immortality and immutability.)

In both metaphysics and natural science, the Ionians laid the foundation for all future serious study (as Plato can justly be regarded not only as the greatest of philosophers but also as the one who posed most of the really enduring questions); however, when rationalist criticism was applied to moral, religious, and political institutions, as it was by the free-thinkers known as Sophists, such a critique could act as a solvent on the prejudices and traditions that bind a people together into a community.

By the time of Socrates, Athens was filled with itinerant Sophists. Some of them were serious men; others, promising to teach rhetoric, were more of the type of success-hucksters of 21st century America, and all too many were like the cynical immoralists who turn up in Plato's *Gorgias* and *Republic*. They harped ceaselessly on the contrast between nature, on the one hand, and custom (or law), on the other. There was no universal morality in nature; principles of right and wrong were invented by men; and wise is the man who will see through the hypocrisies of his society and grab for the power that will make it possible for him to gratify every whim. Since traditional Greek religion could no longer satisfy the higher aspirations of the best men and women, pious people could only occasionally annoy or harass the skeptics, as they did in attacking Anaxagoras and Socrates.

Some free-thinking sophists, predictably, went in the direction of moral relativism and skepticism, much like their spiritual descendants, the *Philosophes* of the French Enlightenment. We know nothing of the gods, declared Protagoras, and man is himself the measure of all things–and not only in the judgments we make about things: For Protagoras and his more radical successors, the human perspective even determines whether things exist or not. Moral and political laws, since they are based on local and irrational customs, are of secondary importance and can be ignored. Nature is the ultimate reality and the ultimate test of any principle. Taking the final step, some Sophists (such as Thrasymachus, at least as portrayed by Plato, and perhaps Plato's kinsman Critias) argued that nature should be our only guide, because religion and morality were invented by weak people in an attempt to curb the appetites and ambitions of the strong.

To their credit, Socrates and Plato opposed this line of thought by extending the philosophic search for an absolute truth, not conditioned by mere custom or prejudice, to the moral realm. At the same time, however, they employed the methods of the Sophists and implicitly accepted one of their basic premises: that moral and political traditions should not be defended if they were irrational.

For some of his students, Socrates' significance lay in an entirely skeptical approach to Athenian, and indeed all Greek customs and beliefs, and Plato himself is hardly exempt from the charge. In fact, Plato encouraged his students and readers to subject all inherited wisdom to analysis and to reject anything that did not stand the scrutiny, and since the Renaissance Descartes and most philosophers afterwards have made the jaundiced eye an indispensable part of the philosophical approach to life, without apparently pausing to wonder if irrational traditions may not have a part to play in shaping the human character and staving off the madness to which our species is prone, whenever it relies too much on the devices and desires of its own mind. David Hume, a greater skeptic than Descartes, subjected philosophical rationalism itself to the same scrutiny that had been given to religion and tradition and concluded, as Donald Livingston has pointed out, that the philosophers had disenchanted the world.

Since Descartes, moral and political philosophers have tended to turn away from ordinary human experience, and they have drawn up moral codes and political schemes that seem more like Aristophanes' *Nephelococcygia* (Cuckoos-in-the-Clouds) than any human polity. Classical liberals wanted to eliminate or attenuate formal social classes, established religion, and irrational bonds of kinship; Marxists would abolish property and economic distinction; more recent radicals want to banish sexual differences and to subject the family to governmental control. The goal of all these projectors is a rationally designed society controlled by the state (preferably a global government) and based on principles of perfect justice without regard for personal ties or historical tradition.

This ambitious objective, however, has remained largely unrealized. Men, good and bad, still pursue wealth and power. Even incompetent and negligent parents may love their children more than their governmental caretakers do, and, though fewer and fewer men and women in the West are getting married, the institution is far from extinct.

The persistence of our primitive passions even in postmodern conditions should come as no surprise. The human race is old, not, perhaps, when measured either *sub specie æternitatis* or by cosmic time or geological ages, but rather old nonetheless. If we can believe the palaeo-anthropologists, some creature like *Homo sapiens* has been around for about 120,000 years. If there are roughly 3 generations per century and something like 3000 per hundred thousand years, then the 15 generations since the Renaissance represent 0.4% of the generations of the past 120,000 years or, in terms of total years, modern culture represents less than half of one percent of human history.

These utterly bogus statistics are introduced to add scientific verisimilitude to a bald and otherwise unconvincing narrative. They are also rigged to favor my argument, because the human population has been increasing exponentially in recent centuries. However, it is also true that the experience of *Homo sapiens*, however long it may be, constitutes only a small part of the story. Man has been a work in progress for some time: *Homo erectus*, a species with a brain developed highly enough to be capable of speech, emerged about 1.8 million years ago. As a percentage of 1.8 million, 500 ends up as 0.000 on the primitive calculator I started with, and we have not even considered the careers of more ape-like predecessors. From this perspective, our little experiment in rational living in no particular time and place with with only weak ties to kith and kin almost disappears from sight, and the facts of love and hate appear as inescapable as the doom that overtakes the heroes of Thomas Hardy's novels.

Studies of primate behavior have yielded a rich harvest of insights into human problems. Our nearest kinfolks among the primates are the chimpanzees, whose social interactions are complex but dominated by a rule that sounds remarkably like a basic principle common to ancient Greeks and Jews: Help friends and punish enemies.

Many Christians reject evolutionary theory as an atheistic reduction of Creation and its mysteries to mechanical processes. They have a point: A great many evolutionists have been anti-Christian or atheist. But, the same generalization might be made of legal scholars and literary critics. While a literalist reading of Genesis would seem to exclude millions of years of evolutionary processes culminating in man, a similarly literalist reading of the entire Old Testament would not be compatible with many key teachings of Christian morality on such questions as monogamy, divorce, and charity. Christians who begin with a literalist reading of the Pentateuch, which they then apply to the Scriptures, are starting at the wrong end. It is the Old Testament that is to be read in light of the New, and not *vice versa*.

The Church has always taught that the Holy Ghost works through history, enlightening the darkened mind of the human race. About to leave this world, Jesus himself did not tell his followers that he was leaving behind the Old Testament as a once-and-for-all textbook on everything they needed to know. On the contrary, he told them: "The Comforter, which is the Holy Ghost, whom the Father will send in my name, he shall teach you all things, and bring all things to your remembrance, whatsoever I have said unto you." [John 14:26] Obviously, the Holy Ghost, unlike the Supreme Court of the United States, will not and cannot reverse His position or contradict himself. But, we are assured that we shall find the knowledge and wisdom we need if we are to understand the constantly changing challenges.

Before plunging headlong into fundamentalism and obscurity, let us see if the Greeks have anything more to teach us than the skeptical methods of dialectic and logic. This requires us to shift our focus from Eastern Greece–from Ionia and Athens–to the West, to Sicily and the parts of Southern Italy known as Magna Græcia.

Stepping Westward: Empedocles' Universe of Love and Hate

An evolutionary understanding of human nature can liberate us from our rationalist disposition to ignore our human and pre-human traditions as we speed toward Utopia along the fast track of theoretical abstractions. However, the application of evolutionary theory to human social and political questions is usually filtered by different and often conflicting political ideologies, each with its own peculiar predilections and particular agenda. In a "democracy" every man is free to pick his favorite heresy, though most people will fall somewhere within the Liberal tradition, whether on the conservative-libertarian side or on the Marxian side.

Before deciding to swallow the Liberal tradition whole, however, one might consider some alternatives, ancient as well as modern, which seem to accord with the facts of nature rather better than either rugged individualism or compassionate collectivism. There have been political thinkers who took into account such observable facts of human nature as the differences between the sexes, the significance of kinship, the role played by the passions in human life, and our basic human needs to feed and shelter ourselves, to mate and rear children, and to defend lives–our own and those of our friends and relations. I have already mentioned Aristotle, Cicero, and Thomas Aquinas, but I might just as well have named the representatives of the Scottish Enlightenment–Francis Hutcheson, David Hume, and Thomas Reid–or even the American pragmatist Josaiah Royce, whose highest principle was not pure reason but loyalty to the principle of loyalty.

In seeking insights, let us not be afraid to follow paths that, while they were once celebrated highways, have long since been abandoned, like neglected country roads crumbling into impassable pathways. Sometimes the earliest thinkers to make a serious effort at tackling a subject were capable of gaining insights not easily observed by later philosophical systems. Aristotle may have been the first philosopher to attempt a systematic study of kinship and friendship, but he is far from being the first Greek thinker to take the passions of love and hate seriously. Greek poets seem to write about nothing else, and the philosopher Heraclitus made strife or war a cosmic force. It was a mystical Sicilian from Acragas (Agrigento), Empedocles, who tried to explain the universe in terms of the contest between love and strife.

Empedocles is best known for his theory of the four elements: earth, air, fire, and water. What an absurdly useless theory, you may be tempted to say: Every schoolboy today is taught that there are over 100 elements. If we could reincarnate Empedocles with the same mind he had in the 5th century, he would no doubt be impressed with the marvels of modern science, but he might well inform us that the elements he was proposing were not of the type to be found on the periodic table. His purpose was to understand the dynamics of the universe, the human as well as the cosmological. He might ruefully concede that as physical science his theory is useless, but as a creative response to a serious problem, he might argue that he still has something to tell us.

Empedocles put forward his four elements in response to the problem posed by Parmenides of Elea (another Western Greek). Parmenides may deserve to be called the first true philosopher, because he was the first to achieve a logical breakthrough, which he stated in the puzzling terms that, "What is, is; and what is not is not and cannot be." What he meant, apparently, is that when we say that something exists, really exists, then its existence excludes its opposite, namely non-existence. Paradoxical as it may seem, this break-through enabled later philosophers to develop both a strict logical system and the concept of absolute being that theologians know as "God."

Parmenides, descended from a nation of Phocæan freebooters, was a bold thinker, and, in his poem *The Way of Truth*, he drew what seemed to him the only possible conclusion, namely, that diversity and change were impossible (at least in absolute terms), since the ultimate reality had to be eternal, unchanging, and one.

When critics tried to poke holes in his theory, Parmenides' disciple Zeno (also of Elea) reduced their arguments to rubble, using his famous paradoxes of the arrow, the stadium, and Achilles and the tortoise–paradoxes that have yet to be successfully refuted. The common sense of ancient Greeks (and of us moderns) persuades us to view reality as an infinite series of points. Zeno proved that such a theory leads to the absurd conclusion that to run a hundred yards, one must first run half the distance, but to complete that half, one must first run half of the half, and so on *ad infinitum*. It is not that Parmenides and his followers were unaware of change and diversity: Parmenides even composed a work on *The Way of Seeming*, trying to account for the world as it appears. Nonetheless, so far as we know, he could not reconcile these two quite different approaches to the universe, our sensory perception of the world and the reasoning from accepted postulates to inevitable conclusions.

Empedocles thought he was up to the task of reconciling the two approaches. To account for change and diversity, Empedocles proposed four unchanging elements that he named earth, air, fire, and water. These elements were joined and separated in an unending cosmic rhythm of creation and dissolution. The four elements were not the material entities and forces indicated by names like air and fire, but first principles (like those of the Ionians), and, also like the Ionians' first principles, they were divine beings with names. Fire can be called Hephæstus and Water *Nestis*–the name, apparently, of a Sicilian water goddess. (Bignone, 1916, p. 542, n. 3) The cosmic rhythm was the result of the actions of two forces, Love (*philotes*, which means, more strictly speaking, friendship or affection) and Strife (*eris*).

A double tale I'll tell, of how the one
From many grew...

It is a complex theory of evolution, which includes an account of the development of complex organic life out of simpler and less complete forms, but I shall try to sum it up in crude terms relevant to this discussion. When Love, or, to speak more abstractly, the power to attract opposites, is dominant, the four elements associate together to produce complex substances like flesh and blood, but when Strife, which brings like to like but repels opposites, is on the increase, the elements begin to break apart.

Empedocles appears to denigrate Strife, preferring blameless love that is forever flowing into our strife-dominated and guilty world. In fact, Aristotle thought that Empedocles regarded Strife as a principle of evil, but this may reflect Aristotle's point of view as much as Empedocles', though Aristotle himself recognized that the elimination of strife would lead to problems. (Inwood, 1992, pp. 46-47)

The Greeks were a quarrelsome people, and it would not have taken much to convince any serious-minded Greek that love is, in principle, better than strife. In Empedocles' lifetime, the Greek world was wracked by incessant warfare: Athens and Sparta against the Persians, Sicilian Greeks against the Carthaginians, Athens against Sparta and her allies. In the closing years of Empedocles' life, Athens made up its mind to invade Sicily–a fateful decision that led directly to the Athenian defeat in the Peloponnesian War, which sunk forever Athens' aspiration to be a world power. After his death, the merciless Carthaginians would invade Sicily, destroying Himera (scene of the great Greek victory in 480 B.C.) and Selinus and devastating Empedocles' own city of Acragas, which would be occupied by Carthaginian squatters.

Even people of a less troubled age might understandably detest strife in all its forms. However, Empedocles' reign of love, when it is complete, turns the universe into something resembling the unified and unchanging sphere that Parmenides described as "Being." This would seem to preclude organic, thus human life. Since the works of Empedocles have survived only in substantial fragments, it is impossible to know if he ever resolved this paradox or was even aware of it.

As much as they detested war, the Greeks excelled in it and celebrated courage as the ultimate virtue. Just as Latin *virtus* in origin means "manliness" and thus "power," Greek *arête* may possibly be derived from *aner*, "man," though other etymologies are equally possible. Greeks were too hard-headed not to realize that in any functioning society some level of strife was necessary or at least inevitable.

Hesiod, the first philosophical poet, had already distinguished between the good form of strife, which leads to healthy competition, and the evil form that is rooted in envy. In his *Theogony* Hesiod had decried Eris, strife, as evil [225 ff.], but in his later poem, the more down-to-earth *Works and Days*, which is devoted to the life of the farmer, he corrects himself [11 ff.], saying there are two kinds of Eris: the one that leads to war and violence causes man great unhappiness, but the other (which we could call emulation or the spirit of competition) makes a poor farmer envy his richer neighbor and resolve to work harder. "In this way potter competes with potter, carpenter with carpenter." One difference between bad and good strife is that the former is imposed capriciously by supernatural forces–the gods–while the latter is "a permanent force inhabiting earth, of which we may make use according to our desire." (Fränkel, 1975, p. 116)

Heraclitus, an Ionian philosopher a little older than Empedocles, had also treated strife or war as a necessary component of the universe. Viewing life as a tension of opposites, he declared war to be "father of all, king of all," because without hostility or repulsion, there would be no change. "War is common," he wrote, "strife customary, and all things happen because of strife and necessity."

Some degree of strife and conflict is essential to organic life, and while "survival of the fittest" is probably an over-optimistic summation of the evolutionary process, genetic competition within and between species filters out the less fit and encourages the propagation of the fitter. The alternatives–domestic breeding for specific characteristics or genetic isolation on an island–may produce adorable kittens and puppies or (in the case of the Galapagos that inspired Darwin) a situation in which finches fill the evolutionary niches ordinarily occupied by all bird species, but, judged in terms of fitness, neither pets nor the finches of the Galapagos may be described as entirely successful experiments.

The political equivalent of pet-breeders and isolated islands is an all-powerful state, which represses competition and imposes peace at the price of liberty. The reign of love can only be imposed on human societies by absolutism in its various forms. Empedocles, by contrast, was described as anti-tyrannical and *demotikos*, that is, a supporter of the people's rights and of the principle of *isotes* (*equalness*). This does not necessarily imply anything like the radical Athenian democracy of the late Fifth Century, but it would probably make him an opponent of tyranny, which was the most common form of government in Greek Sicily, and a supporter of a system in which power was shared among the property-owning taxpayers.

In human life, strife, whether it takes the form of competition or of a preference for me and mine that may create hostility to you and yours, is essential to the health and functioning of a well-ordered society. In his *Discourses on*

Livy, Machiavelli observed that the strife between the plebs and patricians at Rome was universally condemned, but it was their experience of conflict that enabled the Romans to resist aggression. In Herodotus, when Cyrus the Persian overthrew the Lydian kingdom, Croesus, the Lydian ruler, advised him to forbid the Lydian youth to take part in strenuous or military exercises and to cultivate a love of luxury that would keep them docile subjects. Empedocles, detecting the fondness for easy living which Plato later denounced in the Sicilian Greek character, is supposed to have said that the people of Acragas ate as if they would die tomorrow and built as if they would live forever.

Empedocles was a multi-dimensional thinker. While his most enduring legacy is probably the theory of the four elements, mixing and separating as they are moved by the cosmic principles of love and strife, he was also a mystical moral philosopher. However, his two philosophies–cosmological and moral–are not separate. Just as the universe evolved from an ideal condition of love and unity, there was once a *human* Golden Age, the reign of Kypris/Aphrodite, in which men lived without strife even with animals. Such myths can be useful, affording us insights into the nature of man that go deeper than any merely rational analysis. Taken literally, however, as too many myths are, they can encourage utopian delusions and, ultimately, totalitarian government.

ACRAGAS — A CITY OF MAN

The landscape and layout of Empedocles' city of Acragas, as at Athens, was the result of a dynamic tension between religious shrines that express the unity of the people and the marketplace where economic and political competition is carried on. Arching over all the other tensions in a city–between male and female, rational and irrational, the gods of earth and the gods of sky–is the polarity between acropolis and agora that can be seen in Athens and other Greek cities. In Agrigento today, the most impressive ruins are of fifth-century temples built on a ridge between the acropolis and the sea, but in earlier times the acropolis of the city was home to the most important religious construc-tion(Zuntz, et al., 1971). In Greek we might say, following Empedocles, that the Acropolis and the Agora of ancient cities are the realms of *philotes* and *eris,* and their respective institutions are characterized by community and society or, to use the German of Ferdinand Toennies, *Gemeinschaft* and *Gesellschaft.*

In any form of reality known to us, there can be no realm of love or hate that is uncontaminated by its opposite tendency. In Empedocles' vision, even when such a stasis is achieved, say, in a perfected reign of love, strife begins flowing in. A healthy community will keep these two tendencies distinct without making a rigid separation–there were usually tem-ples, after all, in the Agora, while the Acropolis celebrated the military defense of Athens in the form of the Temple of Athena Nike. There were also, no doubt, the Greek equiva-lents of the sellers of sacrificial animals and the changers of money that Jesus chased out of the temple in Jerusalem.

Still, it is important, at least in principle, to keep these as-pects of life distinct, no matter how intertwined they may be in everyday life. The rule of love dominates in the fam-ily and in religion; it is accepting and non-discriminatory within the group. We love our children and siblings not so much because we can honestly say that they are bet-ter than other people but because they belong to our little community. The rule of strife, on the other hand, is the law of the marketplace, of athletics, and of politics, where competition for success is based more on merit than on friendship–though this is more often an ideal than a reality.

In our personal lives, we make a mistake in applying the laws of love to the realm of strife, and vice versa. No one should marry a spouse to get even with a faithless lover or claim to make war for philanthropic motives. In the former case, we are deceiving and betraying the person with whom we have promised to share our life and have deprived him or her of the possibility of a happy marriage. In the latter we are deceiving not only the victims of our "tough love" but ourselves–or at least the people whose votes and moral support give the ruling classes the power to kill strangers. When Americans declared war on Japan at the end of 1941, it was for the normal and healthy purpose of avenging the deaths of so many Americans who died in the sneak attack on Pearl Harbor, whereas the terrible destruction visited upon the peoples of Iraq and Afghanistan was justified–with almost unparalleled hypocrisy–as a defense of international human rights.

Tyranny arrives either when the forces of market and politics invade religion and family, as happens in capitalist societies, or when religious principles of sharing and equality are imposed on competitive enterprises–as under communism and socialism. Both destructive forces are at work in the City of Satan, but in the Cities of Man a perpetual tension is maintained between the bonds of love, manifested in family and clan, and the divisions caused by strife.

If a family is united by love, it is also divided against the rest of the world by the laws of revenge. Though Christ has taught us to love our neighbor, his disciples did not entirely eliminate the weapons of revenge. "Vengeance is mine, saith the Lord," and vengeance was too engrained in the human soul to be eliminated, but, as a divine force, it could be taken away from feuding families and clan leaders and entrusted to a commonwealth whose rulers owed their authority to their Creator. That, as we shall see, was the solution offered by St. Paul, though it has yet to be thoroughly implemented in the world.

In the almost infinite variety of human social and political fabrics, we can almost always trace the ancient threads of love and strife. The institutions of marriage and parenthood, the customs of blood revenge and profit-seeking exchanges, and the aspirations toward aristocracy or equality–in all of them we can glimpse the cosmic rhythms poetically depicted by Empedocles. Many an ambitious ruler, seeking to extend his power, has stubbed his big toe on the brute facts of kinship, and many an ideological revolution that failed to reckon with the blind forces of greed and competition has been brought down by the primitive passions and instincts they had hoped to eliminate or at least suppress. To understand why this is so will require a patient look at the resilient institutions of marriage and kinship that have resisted the French and Russian revolutions and have even managed, for the time being, to survive the more devastating revolution known as "democratic capitalism."

Before moving onto the wider circles in which human persons are formed, we need to take a brief look at those chimerical creatures, individuals, and the duties imposed on them by love and hate.

REFERENCES

Bignone, E. (1916). *Empedocle: Studio Critico; Traduzione e Commento Delle Testimonianze e Dei Frammenti*. Fratelli Bocca.

Burnyeat, M. F. (1997). The Impiety of Socrates. *Ancient Philosophy*, 17(1), 1–12.

Fränkel, H. (1975). *Early Greek Poetry and Philosophy*. Harcourt Brace Jovanovich.

Inwood, B. (1992). *The Poem of Empedocles*. University of Toronto Press.

Zuntz, G., ... (1971). *Persephone: three essays on religion and thought in Magna Graecia*. Clarendon Press.

The Disappearing Individual

I am not like anyone I have ever met.
I may not be better, but I am different.

— Anonymous

J FIRST ENCOUNTERED THIS BIT OF INSPIRATIONAL OPTIMISM emblazoned on the wall of a college dormitory room. The student who had put up the poster was a nice young man and not at all the sort to be quoting Rousseau, even in the simplified version marketed to aspiring egotists. But, when individualism is the fashion, even the most obsequious members of human herds will have to regard themselves as trail-blazing individualists forging ahead on the road less traveled by.

The incongruity of a sensible fraternity boy (and perhaps future Rotarian) solemnly proclaiming his individuality with a mass-produced poster was not entirely lost on friends who listened to the same pop tunes, watched the same TV shows, and dated the same girls. This budding individualist, who enjoyed the tepid thrills of East Coast surfing, gloried in the nickname "Murph the Surf," which had been borrowed from the surfer who in 1964 organized what was known for a few months as the "jewel heist of the century." Four years later the jewel thief, Jack Roland Murphy, was convicted of murder, but the real Murph the Surf's saga did not end on death row or even in a life sentence. While in

87

prison, Murph the Murderer met several visiting celebrity athletes, doing mission-work to the prisoners, and, like Chuck Colson and many another upwardly mobile miscreant, he discovered a new career as a preacher to the prisoners. As a latter-day Elmer Gantry, Murphy finally found the fame and wealth he had previously sought in vain from sport and larceny.

No one appears to have questioned Jack Murphy's *bona fides* as a born-again Christian, much less to have wondered why a sincerely repentant murderer would not demand the death penalty for himself. It is as if we all knew, even then, that American celebrities live, much like Jean-Jacques Rousseau himself, by a different code from the rest of suffering humanity. That, as O.J. Simpson and Bill Clinton seem to have believed, was the point of acquiring celebrity status. It is not love but fame that means you never have to say you're sorry.

Like his name-sake, the student individualist was a walking dictionary of clichés and, in most respects, exactly like the rest of us sex-obsessed college boys who drank our Budweiser, smoked our Marlboros (or in my case unfiltered Lucky Strikes), and never missed an episode of the *Beverly Hillbillies*. By far the greatest cliché in Murph's mental outfit (as it was in mine) was the conceit that he was a unique individual. Rousseau did not invent this affectation, but he was instrumental in making romantic individualism the height of fashion in the late 18th and early 19th centuries.

A more literal rendering of this, the second paragraph of *Rousseau's Confessions*, is perhaps even more disturbing than the poster's more simplified text:

I know my heart and have studied mankind; I am not made like anyone I have been acquainted with, perhaps like no one in existence. If not better, I at least claim originality, and whether Nature did wisely in breaking the mold with which she formed me, can only be determined after reading this work.

Following obediently in the footsteps of Jean-Jacques Rousseau, William Godwin, and an entire army of non-conformists marching in lock-step toward a brighter day, we modern men and women love to proclaim the unique-ness of our individuality, but the identities we create are largely bric-a-brac cobbled together from style section arti-cles clipped from newspapers, pop song lyrics, and favorite movie scenes whose dialogue we have learned by heart. We are all, like the Woody Allen character in *Play it Again Sam*, waiting for the chance to say the lines that have given us a code to live by. In Hollywood, the masses' eagerness to conform themselves to movie scenarios is so well known that action films have to contain signature lines like, "Go ahead, make my day," and political scenarios have to in-clude tag lines like "There you go again" and "Tear down that wall!," "Hope and Change" and "Make America Great Again!" Ronald Reagan was the first professional actor to become President, but after him every President has been an actor, the Greek for which is *hypokrites*.

Our tastes are molded by the brand name gimcracks made by Apple and Sony and, if we are connoisseurs of food or wine, of some set of product lines recommended by *The Wine Spectator, Bon Appétit,* Tripadvisor, or Yelp. We adopt signature hats or imitate the fashions made popular by the film stars we have chosen to adore; we devote ourselves to unique hobbies that just happen to be all the rage in the circles we run in; we develop our distinctive perspec-

tives on politics and morality from reigning academic gu-
rus, trendy political pundits, and the website flavors of our
choice. If we are patriotic conservatives, we listen to ranting
talkshow hosts on the radio, and if we are more highbrow
liberals, we fall in line with *The New Republic* or *The Nation*
or even (would it were not so!) *The Huffington Post*. After all
this borrowing, collecting, imitating, and *bricolage*, we claim
for ourselves an independence that is directly proportional
to our servile dependence upon mass culture.

Classical Liberal individualism is obviously the antithesis
of the Christianity that Liberal propagandists set out to destroy so many centuries ago, but this has not prevented
Christian thinkers from attempting to reformulate Christian moral theology in individualistic terms. (The obvious
analogy is with Christian Marxists who pervert the Gospels
into "the social gospel.") Kierkegaard's emphasis on personal self-reliance and contempt for "the crowd," Pope John
Paul II's philosophy of "personalism," and Lord Acton's
Catholic version of classical liberalism (now reformulated
as Christian libertarianism) all exemplify—as much as atheist existentialists and libertarians—this modern tendency to
isolate the individual from the context of friends, family,
and community and treat this imagined abstraction as the
irreducible moral atom of human life. But, as I hope to show,
the individual is as hypothetical a construct as atoms, which
are really constellations of subatomic particles that for the
most part do not exist except in molecular combinations.

I could try to drag my readers on a forced march through
the Scriptures and the Fathers, pointing out along the way
the absence of any term that can honestly be translated as
'the individual,' but some would object that they put no
stock in religion or that Christianity has, as it were, moved
on. Perhaps a better place to start is the beginning of the

cultural tradition that is supposed to have discovered the freedom of the individual. If the Greeks were never individualists in our sense, at least we may reasonably conclude that individualism is not universal even in Western cultures. But, before plunging into the violent world of Homeric heroes, we might ask ourselves if the consequences of individualism, which we can see all around us, really do fulfill the promises that have been made by individualists since at least the 18th century.

ATOMIZED MAN

Rousseau's delusion (which is also the delusion of the entire liberal tradition and its antecedents in the Renaissance) has had many implications for modern life. Most obviously, it encourages us to belittle the significance of friends and and kinfolks. Rousseau himself abandoned his wife and children and repaid the kindness of David Hume by taking out a newspaper advertisement claiming he was the victim of Hume's persecution. The archetypal English liberal, William Godwin, wrote an extraordinary novel *Caleb Williams*, in which he portrays himself as a self-conscious young man, more intelligent and more highly principled than any one he meets, and yet this moral champion lived without benefit of marriage with his feminist mate, and, when their daughter, acting on Godwin's philosophy, ran off with the poet Shelley, the philosopher periodically squeezed the wealthy genius for money. Similar stories can be told about many liberal and leftist ideologues, and Paul Johnson devoted an entire book (*Intellectuals*) to make this point. Unfortunately, as Johnson's own personal scandals testify, so-called conservative individualists are no more immune to moral irresponsibility and hypocrisy than leftist collectivists.

Few Americans are so bold as Rousseau and Godwin, but we move ourselves and our families at the drop of a hat or the offer of a little more money. If we work for a large company, we may have little choice when told we must move from Huntsville, Alabama to Seattle, Washington, and the ruthless self-denial once demanded of professional military officers and missionaries is now expected of computer technicians and corporate executives. As we move, we lose not only our connection with a particular place but also with friends. Since it is proverbially difficult to make new friends as we grow older, the whole concept of friendship, in an increasingly mobile society, gradually becomes foreign.

If I am pointing a finger, it is at myself, a typical footloose American. At the age of 14 I was moved from northern Wisconsin to the low country of South Carolina, where I attended both high school and college. At 21 I shifted to Chapel Hill, North Carolina for graduate school. Five years later I took a teaching job in southwestern Ohio and after three years returned to South Carolina but, at the age of 39, moved my entire family of six to northern Illinois. By that time, like most people, I was capable of forming alliances and enjoying amicable relations with colleagues, but friendship was and is an increasingly doubtful proposition.

Many people respond to this crisis of mobility by pretending to find friends everywhere. I have noticed this particularly among the wives and children of military officers who are attempting to make the best of a bad situation. Every two to three years they have to construct intimate shallow relationships, which they know will be abandoned, though at least in the military there is some chance of crossing paths again with old fellow-officers and their families. To all appearances they are hares with many friends. Others–and they may be worse off–accept the facts and harden themselves against other people. I fear I belong more to the latter than the former type.

The difficulty goes far deeper than the modern inability to take part in the pleasures of sincere friendship. As I shall be attempting to show in the following chapter, friendship in its various forms is one of the formative experiences that make us moral human beings, and the failure to make friends and fulfill the duties imposed by friendship can come perilously close to the cold-hearted wickedness we ordinarily associate with individualists and sociopaths like the real Murph the Surf. Since isolation, detachment, and alienation are among the dominant themes of late modern and postmodern social analysis among such disparate schools of thought as the Southern Agrarians, Frankfurt School Marxists, and Existentialists, the point hardly needs to be belabored: Our obsession with being individuals is one of the great curses of modernity. It would not, however, be entirely fair to condemn individualism out of hand. It is only a theory, admittedly, but so is Pasteur's theory that microbes cause diseases or, more to the point, the atomic and subatomic theories that enabled American researchers to construct nuclear weapons from which no sane person would not pray to be delivered. Atomic theories are, nonetheless, rooted in physical reality, and moral individualism expresses a part–though by no means the whole–of human moral reality.

Theoretical individualism rests on the assumption that each of us has or is an irreducible self, a Democritean atom that cannot be broken down into constituents and enters into combinations only by an act of will. Josiah Royce, grappling with the question of what we mean by 'the self,' discovered that in ordinary English usage the term is employed not only loosely but in several contradictory manners. This should be a serious problem, especially for individualists, who–if you attempt to speak with them on this subject–appear have no very clear idea of what the individual self is. They merely take it for granted, much as Freudians take for granted the existence of the fantastical id, ego, and superego.

Royce concluded that our consciousness of self derives largely from contrasting ourselves with others and on a variety of scales. Each of us is a smorgasbord of attitudes and tastes–in music, manners, clothing, politics, morals–that we define in opposition to others. The psychological unity of the self is itself socially constructed as we respond, even as children, to 'an endless series of contrasts' with the attitudes and opinions of others.

THE INDIVIDUAL DISAPPEARING IN THE REARVIEW MIRROR

To understand the apparent failure of moderns to attain to full humanity, we have to acquire a context for comparison. Here, we are fortunate in being able to turn to our highest literary and intellectual traditions. Friendship is an important element in Shakespeare and Dante; indeed, in Dante's *Commedia* the poet is assisted through Hell and Purgatory by a series of friends, Vergil in particular, who have been sent by another friend–his beloved Beatrice, who is in Heaven. When challenged by Cato at the entrance to Purgatory, Vergil (Dante's guide through Hell and Purgatory) explains that he took on this mission at the behest of a lady in heaven, whose friend, lost in his suicidal follies of ambition and lust, stands on the verge of death and damnation. Beatrice describes Dante, significantly as *L'amico mio–e non de la ventura*– 'my friend though no friend of fortune!'

Thus it is Beatrice's friendship–and not any rational exercise or fulfillment of duty–that will lead Dante to divine love. Friendship, more than philosophy and theology, is the driving force that urges Dante toward his salvation.

Friendship was also the basis of Roman political life and the subject of one of Cicero's most popular essays, the *De Amicitia,* which partly formed Dante's views on the importance of friendship. But the worlds of Homer, Dante, and Shakespeare are alien to us moderns who think we can make friends at every new company where we work for a year or two or even on a weeklong cruise. We are so used to trivializing the word, that we do not even notice it when cynical television commentators and politicians routinely use the expression "my friend" in reference to strangers and even enemies.

If friendship is the moral foundation of Dante's and Cicero's universe, it is the individual that occupies center stage in ours. Before going on to consider what friendship used to mean to morally serious people, we must first lay the ghost that goes by the name of 'the individual.' When we speak of the individual and his rights, we may mean only that the individual is an ethical ideal that was anticipated by the ancient Greeks and has come to be realized in our civilization. This is, for the most part, a harmless and even wholesome point of view: Much of what has been best in our civilization derives from the Greek and Christian emphasis on the dignity of the human person, and it would be a grave mistake to throw out the baby of human dignity with the bathwater of individualism.

On the other hand, even the most significant cultural developments may not be uniquely or supremely important. The development of symphonic music in the 18th century resulted in the masterpieces of Haydn and Mozart, Beethoven and Brahms, but European man might not have been musically destitute if he had to be content with the techniques of Scarlatti, father and son, Handel, and J.S. Bach.

To take an example closer to the American heart, the Constitution of the United States was a valuable tool in checking the development of arbitrary power, but a document or system designed to foster liberty is not, after all, liberty itself. Augustine observes (in *De Doctrina Christiana*) that the Scriptures are extremely valuable in helping to guide us on the way, but they are not in themselves the truth and the life, and, once a believer has become mature in faith and love, he only needs the Scriptures as an instrument for teaching others. [I. 39] Human dignity is something to be prized, but not necessarily at the expense of marriage or a stable social order. We may and should respect the decencies of Victorian life, but we may not necessarily be willing to sacrifice all our other interests on the altar of "freedom and dignity." Life, as well as liberty, makes its demands.

The pursuit of individualism does not usually stop at the point of acknowledging freedom and dignity as worthy ethical ideals. Using the word "individual," we can also, especially when we speak of individual rights, be referring to what we imagine to be some universal given of human nature. This assumption, often hidden, leads to much mischief, and we should do well to ask ourselves: Is individual dignity something like good table manners or the rule of law–that is, a valuable cultural artifact worth preserving and cultivating–or is it an essential part of the human condition, like having two legs, two eyes, or the natural desires that enable (or rather force) human beings to survive and reproduce? At this point, let us postpone the question of whether individualism is an adequate basis for ethics and look only at its status as a universal human given.

One way of approaching this question—one I adopted for *The Politics of Human Nature* (Fleming, 1988)—was to examine the vast ethnographic literature on 'primitive societies.' Readers have informed me they found the endless discussion of primitive tribes more than a little tedious. Thomas Molnar, who was kind enough to read drafts of the first few chapters, asked with some exasperation if it was really necessary to prove that men and women were different or that marriage and family were universal institutions. Even Molnar, wise man that he was, had not quite grasped the fact that Marxism was only a stage in a revolution that, after destroying monarchy and private capitalism, was moving on to more essential matters.

To avoid the tedium of anthropology, we can turn instead to the portrayal of 'the individual' in the West's first major work of imaginative literature, one that has been providing literary, historical, and moral context for civilized men and women for nearly three millennia. I am referring, it hardly needs to be said, to Homer's *Iliad,* in which we confront a world in which friendship and kinship are predominant and the alienated individualist a sort of monster. The *Iliad* is not and was not for everyone, of course, but as Chesterton observed: "There was never one moment, in the long history from Herodotus to Herr Spengler, when all the men who counted in any age did not talk of the Fall of Troy." The Western man who does not or cannot talk of the Fall of Troy is a savage who counts for nothing in this or in any age, no matter if he be President or Prime Minister, yea even if he be a Chief Executive Officer.

THE "PRIMITIVE" MORALITY OF THE GREEKS

In the ninth year of the Trojan War, Agamemnon, the High King of Mycenæ, has been asked by a Greek prophet, Calchas, to restore his concubine to her father, a priest of Apollo who has inflicted a plague on the Greek army. The king is outraged:

> Having said his piece, the prophet sat down, and stood up among them the hero son of Atreus wide-ruling Agamemnon, enraged. His *phrenes* (diaphragm?) were filled up black all around with rage, and his eyes shone like fire.

Disgruntled, the King threatens to take one of his commanders' concubines, and he does not exempt the greatest hero, Achilles, who has egged on Calchas to speak out boldly. When Achilles boasts he will return to his ships and leave, if he is interfered with, Agamemnon demands the hero's concubine. Achilles now enters into the rage that is the subject of the epic poem:

> Anger broke out in the son of Peleus, and the *hetor* in his chest brooded in two directions, that he should either draw the sharp sword from his thigh, shove the others away, and slaughter the son of Atreus, or that he should suppress his bile and control his *thymos* (an unlocated organ of passion). And while he was urging these matters in his *phren* and in his *thumos*, and was beginning to draw his great sword from the sheath, Athena came from the sky. For white-armed Hera had sent her, loving and caring for both men alike in her thymos. She stood at his back and took the son of Peleus by his tawny hair,

appearing to him alone, but none of the rest saw. Achilles was stunned and turned around, and immediately he knew Pallas Athena.

The goddess forbids Achilles to kill the King but urges him to upbraid him to his heart's content.

This little episode, if read carefully, can tell us a great deal about how early Greeks conceived of the human person in relation to his world. It cannot be simply an artifact of the pre-rational mind, much less a break-through-in-progress of the "bicameral mind" (the title of a book that is perhaps the most preposterous piece of ignorance that has ever been palmed off on modern readers). The scene has rung true with readers ever since, and it has resonated with later Greeks and Romans, Renaissance scholars and poets as well as with casual readers, who have not shared the early Greeks' faith in the gods or their acceptance of Homeric psychology. If it is "primitive," then it is the sort of primitivism that still resonates in the soul of modern and postmodern men and women.

When modern scholars try to understand the Greek mind, they almost inevitably begin with the standard liberal conception of the human individual and his duties to the decision-making collectivity we call, rather imprecisely and misleadingly, the state, which either protects or invades the individual's rights. When they cannot find either conception in Homer, they conclude first, that they are dealing with a mind so primitive that it cannot grasp such elementary facts as the individual, much less his duties, and second, that the Homeric mind cannot conceive of moral decision-making.

Like most traditional peoples, Greeks were embedded in a network of family, friends, and community, and they were also subject both to divine influence and to their inner passions that functioned as biological urges. If we look again at the opening scene of the *Iliad*, we can also observe that the passions instilled by gods, as well as those that are merely human, are located in various physiological organs or processes. Agamemnon's *phrenes* swell and blacken, putting him into a rage. These *phrenes* are clearly a biological organ, probably the diaphragm, and Homer describes them as the seat of strong passions and sense-perceptions like hearing, but they are also the site of the *noos* (mind) in which they see pictures of their earlier life or meditate plans.

The *phrenes* can appear to be either an actual physical organ or a more abstract faculty of sense-perception and feeling or both. A sharp distinction between physical and mental is not always or necessarily observed by ancient Greeks or modern Americans. In Greek, the *phrenes* are only one example. There is an entire spectrum of such organic functions, ranging from the *hetor/kardie*–the physical heart–and the *thymos*–probably the spirit or soul, originally imagined as a vapor (*cf.* Latin *fumus*, "smoke") but sometimes treated as if it were organic. The *psyche,* on the other hand, is the animating force that leaves the body upon death. The *noos,* while generally a non-organic function–the mind that perceives–it can also be seen to have a physical location–much as we imagine today that our mind is in our heads for no better reason than our brain and principal sense organs are there.

It is almost as if these various organs and psychological functions operate independently, helping the hero in his bravery or driving him in his follies. Achilles, humiliated by Agamemnon, is enraged, and, it is said, the *hetor* (heart) in his chest is divided in two, whether to pull his sword and kill Agamemnon, or to stifle his *cholos* (bile). While he is debating, the goddess Athena comes and pulls him by the hair, telling him to sheathe his sword and be content with insulting Agamemnon. This conflict would be presented as an internal debate in an English novel, but here the passion of rage is an organic fluid, while the voice of reason is represented as a divine external force actually laying hands on the person. Whatever the individual person is would seem to be the border area between the superhuman divine and subconscious organic processes.

Bruno Snell, in his revolutionary book *Die Entdeckung des Geistes*, Translated as *The Discovery of the Mind* (Snell, 1953), took the straightforward position that since the Homeric Greeks had no word for the separate persons we call individuals, they must also have lacked the concept. As an analogy, Snell points out the childish and primitive depiction of the human person as a simple stick figure, which is then developed, with triangles and other figures, into the human representations found on Geometric vases. I hope it will not be too great a travesty of a great scholar's argument if we reduce it to two propositions: First, since Homer had no word for the individual person, he could not conceive of such a thing, and, second, when he did try to deal with his actors, he could only imagine them as fragmented beings strung together with wires pulled by supernatural powers.

Although Snell's thesis has been justly criticized repeatedly, (Schmitt, 1990) the analysis of Homeric terminology does in fact afford valuable insights into the Greek mind at the dawn of our civilization. There are, however, other aspects of the question to consider. In English we still attribute psychological and moral qualities to such organs as the heart, the liver, and the spleen, and we can still speak (albeit in an archaic and literary tone) of cowards as lily-livered or refer to the bowels of compassion. There was a time in our history when the theory of the humors–bodily fluids that influence character–was taken seriously by serious men (Ben Jonson, for example). Homer's biological language is not so strange, perhaps, as it has been made out to be. Nonetheless, no matter how far we are prepared to take such an argument, it can only partially shorten the distance between us and Homeric man. As E.L Harrison observed, Homeric man felt more "exposed to external influences than is the case with ourselves." (Harrison, 1960, pp. 63-80) while expressions in English, are with us a mere *"façon de parler; whereas with Homer something more positively felt, more pervasive is involved."* Even in 16th century English, there were other ways of talking about human emotions more precise than the largely metaphorical language of organs and humors.

From the other direction, we can narrow the gap a bit by agreeing that, even in the most 'backward' or 'primitive' cultures, people must make practical decisions that require some intuitive understanding of routine distinctions between subject and object, animate and inanimate, human and non-human. No matter how firmly they may believe in fate or destiny, most people in most cultures seem to hold each other accountable for their actions. What seems a paradox to philosophers was common sense to a Greek–and probably to most modern men and women.

This paradox is particularly striking in Greek tragedy, where bad choices and bad ends are routinely attributed to destiny without in the least diminishing the culpability of the moral actors. Sophocles' Oedipus was fated to kill his father and marry his mother; however, it was not fate but his arrogant nature that drove him to kill the old man at the crossroads. We may say that Sophocles was a "fatalist," but he writes as if his characters had free will–an important point well made by the very unscholarly G.K. Chesterton.

Obviously, Homer's heroes are capable of attributing praise and blame to the comrades they distinguish, the one from the other. The Greek word for 'head' (*kephale*) is sometimes used in the sense of person, (Fränkel, 1975, p. 77, n.3) and his heroes do have names, after all, which implies that they could tell each other apart–some of them seem self-willed to the point of egomania. But in addition to a regular name, like Achilles, each hero also has a sort of surname, a patronymic: Peleides, son of Peleus or Atreides, son of Atreus. Indeed, the heroes are as often called the son of their father as by their own names. This would seem to indicate that while the individual persons are clearly discerned by others, they are also identified as members of a descent group.

Homer's heroes perform acts of individual bravery and speak of winning renown, and Achilles became for later Greeks the supreme example of a man who chose his own destiny without regard for social pressures. On the other hand, as Jan Bremer has written:

> "In Homer's time the individual did not yet know of the will as an ethical factor, nor did he distinguish between what was inside and outside himself as we do. When referring to themselves, the early Greeks, like other Indo-European peoples, did not primarily consider themselves to be independent individuals but rather members of a group."(Bremmer, 1987, p. 67)

Bremer's second point, that early Greeks–and perhaps most Greeks of classical times–conceived of themselves primarily not as individuals but as kinsmen or neighbors or fellow-soldiers, is certainly right, but if his first point is equally valid, that the "individual did not yet know of the will as an ethical factor," we might quickly lose all interest in these epic poems except as light entertainment(Fleming, 1985). Before rushing to condemn the savagery of early Greeks, let us consider the scholar's loaded language. What is this all-important "individual," if not a social construction of later times, and what is this will except a reflection of Enlightenment philosophers, Kant in particular? It is a strange fact that the very scholars and intellectuals who are eager to delineate the social constraints on thinkers from earlier societies cannot, apparently, grasp the fact that they too are operating under the ironclad constraints of popular notions like "progress" and "equality."

'To know the will as an ethical factor' is a gift reserved for few mortal men in any era, but ordinary people, even when they do not possess these abstract concepts, are capable of sitting on juries and pronouncing on questions of guilt and innocence. Ajax is the most dull-witted of Homer's heroes, but he has no trouble condemning Achilles for his selfish and willful conduct. I quote from the novelist Samuel Butler's Victorian translation:

> "Achilles is savage and remorseless. He is cruel and cares nothing for the love of his comrades lavished upon him more than on all the others. He is implacable–and yet if a man's brother or son has been slain he will accept a fine by way of amends from him that killed him, and the wrong-doer having paid in full remains in peace among his own people; but as for you Achilles, the gods have put a

wicked unforgiving spirit in your heart, and this all about one single girl ..."[IX 628-36]

Ajax is quite reasonably contrasting the Greek's kin-based social and legal system, in which homicide is treated as a crime against the family, with Achilles' obsessive sense of personal self-worth that is offended to death even by the loss of a concubine. A baseball or football coach today might make a similar argument in order to persuade an unfairly treated star player to play his heart out for the sake of the team. It is quite true that Achilles is a godlike hero, impervious to all base temptations, but it is equally true that, in contrast with Ajax, Odysseus, and the other heroes, he is a spoiled brat.

It is precisely because Ajax sees himself and Achilles as members of a community (in this case the army and its leaders) that he can so confidently pass judgment against the arrogance of any man, however noble, who elevates himself above the necessities of the group. It is not at all clear to me that Ajax or his counterparts on the American frontier were morally inferior to acutely reasoning moral philosophers at major universities.

In the end, Achilles turns out to be just the monster that Ajax has denounced. He explains to his friend Patroclus that his real hope is that both Greeks and Trojans will kill each other off, leaving Achilles and Patroclus to monopolize all the loot and all the glory. When Patroclus is killed by Hector, the rage of Achilles is so great that even the golden Apollo is reluctant to approach him. In killing Patroclus, Hector had only done his duty as a Trojan leader, but Achilles is without reason or mercy. It is only when Hector's aged father is brought, under divine protection, to the Greek camp that Achilles can be moved by thinking of what his own father would suffer: Even the individualist monster can be humanized by thinking of a close member of his family. If Priam, instead of appealing to the image of old Peleus, had lectured Achilles with a Kantian admonition to "do his duty," the result would have been quite different.

RATIONAL INDIVIDUALS — REALITY OR SOCIAL CONSTRUCT?

Homeric heroes do not hesitate to assert their rights and privileges, but their individual self-assertion is limited, in the first place, by their social context and, in the second, by their belief in physiological processes that affect (or determine) character, mood, and decisions. Community solidarity and organic forces are not, however, the only powers that can inhibit their individual will: They are also checked, not only by physiological passions below the surface, but also by supernatural powers that are above them.

Athena's intervention in the quarrel between Achilles and Agamemnon reminds us how powerful and terrifying the Greek gods can be, and yet, while the goddess certainly influences Achilles' decision not to kill Agamemnon, it is quite clear that the decision is his to make: As the hero prudently observes, it is better to obey the gods. Some scholars, rightly objecting to the reduction of the gods to mere æsthetic contrivances, have drawn the conclusion that freedom of the will was unknown in Homer's time, but as helpful as this conclusion would be to the argument I have been making, such scholars seem to me to have drawn their line in the sand a good deal too sharp and too deep. Homer's characters not only appear to have a will of their own but treat each other as independent moral actors.It is at least probable that human is not entirely under the gods' control: "Der Mensch is nicht einfach und völlig von den Göttern bestimmt," (Schwabl, 1954, p. 50)

The same can be said of the gods, who in many ways serve as nobler models of humanity. Although there may be traces of a belief in animal or part-animal divinities in such expressions as owl-eyed Athena and cow-faced Hera, these gods are idealized human beings, perfectly beautiful (except for the lame Hephæstus whose disability excites laughter), intelligent, and immortal. They are not, however, all-powerful or all-knowing, and, in the *Iliad* at least, they do not always seem to conform to any general rule of justice but are as much dominated by their passions as by any reasons of right and wrong.

The gods are more powerful than human beings, but they do not have an unlimited capacity for doing as they please. Not even Zeus can have his way in everything: He too is subject to *Moira* (destiny or law of nature) and to the combined efforts of his wife and her allies. Gods are subject to the usual passions–love, hatred, envy, and revenge–and when they are not making war on human beings, they are fighting with each other. Zeus is undoubtedly wise and powerful, a god of justice, but it is all he can do to keep his wife, brother, and children in line. The gods can bully, cajole, threaten, and extort, but they cannot entirely command the wills of their human inferiors.

Even if the argument for Greek primitivism has been pushed too far, it is, nonetheless, quite clear that Greeks in Homer's time–and in much later times–did not sharply distinguish the rational and free-willed individual from his community, his gods, and his physiological organs that generated feelings and thoughts, functioning as the "subconscious" and other similar concepts in modern psychology. If the human person can be conceived of as merely the frontier where gods and organic processes converge with family and social context, we might even be tempted to subscribe wholeheartedly to Bremer's declaration that Homeric Greeks could not have "known the will as an ethical factor" and to conclude that Homeric morality is a contradiction in terms.

If the greatest literary masterpieces of ancient Greek are so primitive as to lack even a rudimentary moral sense, why should not Christians or post-Christians dismiss the works of Greek literature as the charming fairy tales of moral infants? That certainly has been a line of thought that has gained currency among some classical scholars, and it is certainly a comforting conclusion for literary intellectuals who would rather study postmodern theory than spend so much time and energy learning dead languages.

The answer to this question depends, of course, on what we mean by "morality." If we regard moral decisions as being made purely rationally and objectively for the sake of what we regard as right and influenced by neither emotion nor any other non-rational factors (such as the duties of kinship or patriotism)–if, in other words, we truly are all Kantians now, as one scholar imprudently declared–then it hardly makes sense to speak of "Greek morality" before Socrates. (Adkins, 1960, p. 2) It makes even less sense to waste one's time and energies on culture so primitive that it has nothing to say to anyone in the modern age.

Before rushing headlong to agree with the Kantians, we might pause and ask ourselves a few elementary questions. Are people in the modern age in fact morally superior in their actions to the ancient Greeks? Yes, we have a code of international law and theories of human rights and human dignity, but none of this hindered Stalin and Hitler from starting unjustified wars and killing millions of people they had never met. These theories did not prevent Harry Truman from dropping atomic bombs on two Japanese cities filled with civilians or other American Presidents from permitting the use of napalm against the people of Vietnam, nor did even the most elementary considerations of truth get in the way of President George W. Bush and his advisors when they made unjustified war against the people of Iraq. By any measure we choose to apply–rates of homicide and rape, genocidal wars, the sexual exploitation of children–modern and postmodern men and women, whatever else they might wish to claim for themselves, have no case to make for their moral superiority. If our superior Kantian moral sense does not serve to check our baser and more violent passions, we might wonder how useful or significant it is.

ATHENS AND JERUSALEM

The argument over the primitivism of ancient Greek morality has been distorted by either/or dichotomies: Enlightened Kantianism has been contrasted with pre-rational moral codes, Christian are opposed to pre-Christian world views, and there is a conflict between those who find anthropological evidence relevant and those who, like Sir Hugh Lloyd-Jones, reject it. A few moments spent on these controversies should help to lead us out of the wilderness of academic quibbling.

One of the great merits of Lloyd-Jones's approach derives from the respect with which he treated classical texts. He possessed the great virtue of finding ancient literature meaningful and relevant, and he refused to be taken in by the claptrap of literary theory and the cliches of ill-digested anthropology. I would be much remiss, even ungrateful, if I failed to acknowledge the debt I owe to his irascible skepticism, though even he seemed at times to accept the premise that "civilized" morality should be defined in terms of the past 500 years, in the sense that he accepted the conventional cleavage between modern and pre-modern ways of thought.

Christianity, for Sir Hugh, was a temporary distortion of the higher morality that had evolved among the Greeks and Romans but began to be restored, along with a better understanding of classical languages, during the Renaissance. He had small use for Christian piety and even less for the postChristian pieties of leftists who adopted the language of the gospels in order to preach only Marx and him apotheosized in Communist states. I share his distaste for the "sinistroid" reinventions of Christian morality as much as I appreciate his tenacious defense of the ancients, but, in opposing the Marxist version of Christianity, Lloyd-Jones mistakenly accepted their interpretation of the Christian tradition.

Athens and Jerusalem, though in some limited sense antagonists, converge in the creation of Christendom, which incorporates the best elements of both traditions. The denizens of both are enemies of the Capitalist/Marxist states of the modern world, where proletarianized consumers, torn out of every meaning-giving context–social and divine–pretend to be morally independent individuals even as they are being engineered into moral clones that hardly resemble human persons. This process of turning human persons, embedded in community and religion, into robotic "individuals," far from being retarded by theories of liberal individualism, has actually been facilitated by the philosophers.

What if it turned out, after all, that modern civilization had gone mad on a false and unscientific theory of rationalist ethics that is no more relevant to the human experience than phrenology or mesmerism? What if the Homeric view is closer to the mark (that is, more relevant to the human condition) than the speculations of Kant and Descartes? What if human moral decisions are rarely made by rational and autonomous individuals but take place on a frontier where blind physiological processes meet the inexplicable supranatural? In the absence of any positive proof of rational individualism–and I have yet to find one scrap of solid evidence–perhaps it would be wiser if we were to confess our ignorance and admit that we can learn something, not just from the "primitive" peoples studied by anthropologists but from the literary masterpieces that have shaped our civilization. It is not much of a stretch to say that the gods of the Greeks are realer and more moral than the hollow painted idols constructed by philosophers and social scientists.

"I often think now how strange it would be," remarks Arthur Machen's mystical Welshman in "A Secret Glory"

> "...if it turned out that we have all been in the wrong about everything; that we live in a world of the most wonderful treasures which we see all about us, but we don't understand, and kick the jewels into the dirt, and use the chalices for slop-pails and make the holy vestments into dish-cloths, while we worship a great beast–a monster, with the head of a monkey, the body of a pig and the hind legs of a goat, with swarming lice crawling all over it. Suppose that the

people that they speak of now as 'superstitious' and 'half- savages' should turn out to be in the right, and very wise, while we are all wrong and great fools!"

SOCRATES AND CHRIST

Lloyd-Jones quite correctly traced the development of Greek critical thought on morality back to its origins in Homer and Hesiod, though Greek ethical conceptions underwent a transformation, it goes without saying, between the time of Homer and the writings of Plato and Aristotle. One important development that affected this evolution was the rise of the *polis*, very roughly translated as city-state, which challenged the ethical primacy of kinship and friendship. As Gabriel Herman summarized this development:

> "...the ancient world was criss-crossed with an extensive network of personal alliances linking together all sorts of apolitical bodies (households, tribes, bands, etc.). The city's framework superposed itself upon this existing network–superimposed itself upon it, yet did not dissolve it." (Herman, 2002, p. 6)

Tensions between one's loyalty to family and friends and the demands of the *polis* are a frequent subject of Greek tragedy, as seen most dramatically in Sophocles' *Antigone*, where a young woman's loyalty to the demands of religion and family are viewed as a challenge to the claims of the city and its rulers.

Socrates and Plato, as has been argued earlier, did a great deal to undermine pre-rational loyalties, but they did not deny the significance of family and friendship, much less reject the claims of the commonwealth: Socrates worked out his ideas in a community of friends and students and preferred death to exile from Athens. As we shall see, when we take up the subjects of kinship and friendship, neither pagan Greeks nor pagan Romans ever liberated themselves from these ties, and Livy, writing in the enlightened age of Augustus, portrays Coriolanus as a nobleman whose willful pride makes him a traitor to his people and his family. Then, if there is any case to be made for ethical individualism before the Renaissance, it must be found in the Christian Scriptures and Tradition, and if not there, then nowhere.

In reading the Gospels, we are struck over and over by Jesus' radical demand that his followers pursue a course of perfection, which seem to include a blanket rejection of family ties:

> "For I am come to set a man at variance with his father, and the daughter against her mother, and the daughter-in-law against her mother-in-law. And a man's foes shall be they of his own household. He that loveth father or mother more than me is not worthy of me: and he that loveth son or daughter more than me is not worthy of me."[Mat 10:35-37]

The radical language–and this is no isolated passage– accords rather poorly with "conservative family values." But, like so many of Christ's most radical pronouncements, it must be balanced against other and more numerous passages, which are taken up elsewhere in this book, where the institutions of marriage and family are taken for granted or praised–His first miracle at the wedding in Cana, the habit of calling his disciples "brothers," the depiction of the Holy Family, *etc. etc.*

There is also the question of context. Christ is sending his disciples into the world to preach and declaring to them that love of God and his Son and preaching the Gospel take precedence over even the most important of human relationships. This is a well-worn rhetorical formula, sometimes designated by the German word "Priamel." Sappho offers a simple example:

> "Some say an army of cavalry, others foot soldiers and still others a fleet of ships is the fairest thing on the dark earth, but I say it is whoever one loves..."

Sappho, who lived in a society that loved weaponry and war, is far from denigrating the beauty of Greek warfare; in fact, she is taking it for granted but putting it second to the beloved. When Pindar wrote, at the beginning of his First Olympian Ode, that "water is a very fine thing, and gold, like a fire blazing in the night, overtops all noble wealth, but if ...you wish to sing of athletic contests ...let us not proclaim any contest greater than the Olympic Games," water and gold, so far from being deprecated, are at the pinnacle of the natural and social worlds, excelled only by the joy that a man has in gaining an Olympic victory.

Christians are required to put their love of God and hope of salvation above all lesser goods, but such an aspiration in no way diminishes the positive value of kinship and friendship, much less elevates the Christian "individual" above his social obligations. I shall take up each of the New Testament's apparent renunciations of everyday obligations in the appropriate places, but the notion that Christianity is a religion of separate individuals, each "bound for glory" on his own private pilgrimage, is easily dismissed. From the beginning, the Christian faith had a corporate existence, whether known as "the brothers" or the Ecclesia (Church).

In standard Greek, an *ekklesia* is the assembly of citizens who are corporate members of a commonwealth. Only acknowledged members can participate fully in the meetings and exercise the privileges of citizenship. The church, then, from the beginning, was a corporate commonwealth whose citizens were believing Christians.

INDIVIDUALISM AS NAIVETÉ

To speak in very rough terms, we are exploring two moral worlds so different as to seem opposed. One is the world of corporate responsibilities to kinfolks, friends, neighbors, and fellow-citizens who owe each other certain duties; the other is a world of detached individuals, either competing ruthlessly for success or living quietly under the control of a vast governmental system that speaks in the name of their rights. The first world is that of those pre-modern societies from which our modern world developed; the second is the declared ideal–though hardly the reality–of our own world. While modern Christians have tried to import individualist and Marxist theories into the Church, the very language of Christianity–whose members are "brothers" living in "communion" within the "assembly" known as the church–gives the lie to these distortions.

If men have never or only exceptionally been individualists, that is not because they have not been selfish and competitive. Mankind from the beginning–long before the self-assertions of Achilles, back in the prehistoric days of Adam and Eve, Gilgamesh and Enkidu, Cain and Able, Eteocles and Polyneices, Romulus and Remus–has been a contentious species, whose members are often unable to get along with each other, even within the little community of the household, but, even in their striving with each other for supremacy and in their compulsive greed and ambition, they have hardly ever succeeded in liberating themselves from the ties of blood and love. The pure individualism taught by some classical Liberals and libertarians is somewhere between an illusion and a pious fraud. This does not mean, however, that there is nothing good to be salvaged from liberal theories of human individualism.

In an age dominated by theories of collectivism and statism, a sense of individual dignity, reinforced by skepticism of political ideology, can be an indispensable weapon in resisting tyranny. Even the modern distortions of Antigone's resistance to tyranny can have a wholesome effect. For someone who has not thought through these questions, a simple refusal to accept the state's justifications for its destructive policies may be the beginning of wisdom; however, skeptical individualism canalso damage one's sense of connection with friends and family and be used to justify immoral and illegal behavior. I once told a leading libertarian that a journalist we both knew was describing himself as a 'libertarian.'

"What is he," he asked me, "a tax-evader or a child-molester?," explaining that no one becomes a libertarian except to justify some crime or vice. The generalization was much too broad, but there was a germ of truth large enough to cast some doubt on any philosophy of individual rights.

The moral failure of so many individualists is not simply one more example of the danger of running to extremes or of getting too much of a good thing. The real flaw in theories of individualism is that they are not descriptions of reality but unrealistic aspirations. It is not that men and women should not strive for some degree of moral autonomy–that is, after all, part of what it means to be human–but that they should not imagine that they came into this world as individuals free to pursue any dream, fulfill any destiny.

"The individual," in the extreme sense used by self-described "individualists," is not a human universal (such as the *libido dominandi* or division of society into age-groups) nor even a stock character in the repertory of Western man (such as the religious hypocrite or the *nouveau riche*). It is more like an ideal that is hardly ever to be realized this side of Paradise.

It is true that since the 18th Century, the individual–or something like it–has been an ideal human condition to which the philosophically minded can aspire, as people once aspired to holiness or virtue. Setting aside the question of whether it is possible for anyone, much less everyone, to be truly an individual, we have to go back to the question that was raised earlier, whether such an ideal is an ultimate good, one among many goods, or a mixed blessing that may sometimes seem more like a curse.

In grappling with this question, let us try not to be seduced by mere words like "freedom" and "rights," "slavery" and "liberation." Most of the changes rung on these themes are not only mere cant. All too often they serve as trumpet calls for war, devastation, and tyranny. Suppose some political idealist promised to set you free from your oppressors, but, after emerging victorious from many hard-fought battles, you discovered that you had only exchanged the devil you knew for the one you did not know and, in the bargain, had lost everything you had formerly possessed. Such is all too often the fate not only of those who take part in armed revolutions but also of those who believe the promises of social reformers.

The seduction of minds begins with the abuse of words, and no one, not even philosophers, is immune. In fact, philosophers and their students are too easily seduced by the glittering surface of words, and if they find their inherited vocabulary of technical jargon insufficiently bewildering, they coin some new term, such as "categorical imperative," or "dialectical materialism," or "neocolonialism," or even "objectivism," which they then treat as a scientific discovery or a fundamental law of human society or universal human right. This tendency to confuse the invention of terms with the discovery of truth is no recent development. The founders of Stoicism, perhaps because they came from the fringes of the Hellenic world, coined all too many novel terms, provoking Cicero's complaints against philosophers who do not make the effort to write clearly and persuasively. Modern theologians are among the worst offenders, and the fancier the lingo in which they cloak their platitudes, the greater is their imposture.

Political and ethical theorists, under the delusion that they are investigating human reality, seem to do little but quibble over traditional terms and invent new ones to impose on the unwary. Even good old words, when they are given an academic varnish, can be just as misleading as the latest invention of a newly minted Ph.D. on the make. In political arguments, both sides usually take for granted a basic set of concepts, such as the "individual" and the "state" and act as if these Latinate English words described a universal aspect of the human condition.

Both terms are, however, highly elusive. If by "state," we mean any form of political organization, then Adam and Eve lived in a state, but if we have in mind a permanent government that can act independently of the people it commands, the state is an historical invention that began to take rudimentary shape in the ancient world but was not truly formed, even in outline, until the Renaissance. To describe the attributes of the ancient Athenian "state" is much like ticking off the color of eyes and hair qualities of the unicorn.

Similarly, the individual, conceived of as an independent and self-determined person who rationally makes decisions in his own interest, is an artifact (or illusion) of the 18th century. Whatever the merits of individualism in modern political philosophy, it has scant relevance to ancient Greeks, who lacked (as I have been arguing) even the words to express such an idea. The extent to which thoroughly modern and postmodern men and women can be regarded as individuals is not entirely obvious. Most (all?) of what most of us believe about most (all?) things has been injected into us by some person or institution that influenced our development: a parent or teacher, a church or television show or pop song. E.E. Cummings, an individualist himself, once made a skeptical guess about the percentage of individuals in human history:

> "there are possibly 2½ or impossibly 3 individuals every several fat thousand years. Expecting more would be neither fantastic nor pathological but dumb."

We moderns, who regard ourselves as liberated individuals, name our children after mass-marketed pop stars, identify with name brands and commercial sports franchises, and spend most of our lives under the control of institutions, from daycare to dying hospices, from Rotary to NOW to Alcoholics Anonymous to the mega-churches to which we have been attracted by their TV commercials.

Pre-modern men and women were—and are still—more real-
istic. Far from seeing themselves as individuals, much less
individualists, they were conscious of their position in an
enveloping network of friends and relations. To the extent
they could conceive of individualists or even solitary men,
they were horrified. For the Greeks, the *polis* defined the
proper social life. Homer's Cyclopes, who lived as patriarchal shepherds, were bestial creatures, and his Achilles,
although a very great hero, is also a monster who appears
to despise the ordinary bonds of friendship.

Then, if there are occasions and contexts where we simply
must use words like "individual" and "individualism," let
us agree that they stand for an ideal of moral seriousness,
of taking responsibility for one's own actions, no matter
what excuse might be offered by our background or circumstances. If rich men and poor men alike have become
criminals, it does no good to excuse their crimes on the
grounds of poverty or affluence. Individualism can thus
be useful as an ethical-political posture that emphasizes
personal responsibility but not a universal or inclusive principle that trumps all other considerations.

We are, to some extent, trapped in a paradox: On the one
hand, we are saying that all human beings are to a great
extent the products of the communities that have formed
them, while, on the other, claiming that each of us has to
accept responsibility for his own decisions and actions. It
is a bit like arguments over the role of fate and free-will in
Greek tragedy that were referred to earlier. Was Oedipus
destined, by a curse on his family, to kill his father? Or did
he, in a fit of temper all too typical of his character, kill the
men he met at the crossroads? Which is true? The answer is
that both are true, that it would have been blasphemous to
suggest, as Oedipus and his wife Jocasta do, that the gods

plays no role in human affairs, but equally blasphemous to blame them for our own mistakes.

THE PERNICIOUS MYTH OF THE INDIVIDUAL

The term individual is derived from *individuum*, a Medieval Latin word, meaning "undivided being." In applying it to human beings, we run into two difficulties. The first and easiest to grasp is that "undivided" implies a single nature, whether material or spiritual. A materialist would have no trouble in agreeing that man is a purely material being, that soul and consciousness are epiphenomenal, that is, accidental byproducts of biological processes that give us illusions like free will and the human mind. Most non-materialists will hesitate to go down this road, though mystics or even some Platonists might be willing to say that the only true human reality is mind or spirit and that the entire material world is illusion. Christians, who believe that even the Savior took on a material body, are hardly likely to abandon 2000 years of tradition. The term "individual," which is both so ambivalent and and encumbered by such philosophical baggage, should then be used with extreme caution and never as a substitute for "person" or "human being."

The second difficulty with the term "individual" is a great deal more technical. In Medieval philosophy the term *individuum* was used in several senses. It could be used to refer to the particular species or member of a genus, as in the statement "Bugs is a rabbit." *Individuum* could also be applied to angels, which were more or less purely spiritual beings and thus not divided. I am being deliberately sloppy here in order to avoid discussing the rather serious question of how many angels can dance on the head of a pin.

There was a division of opinion on whether angels were immaterial, as St. Thomas taught, or material but without extension. Fortunately, for the purpose of this discussion, it hardly matters which side we take in so important a debate.

Unlike human beings, who are divided into body and soul–and the body into arms, legs, *etc.*–an angel is an essence undivided in itself: There are no parts. Up to this point, so far as I can understand the argument, Medieval Christian philosophers were in agreement. One point of contention, however, was Thomas Aquinas' argument that if angels were, as he insisted, pure forms and non-material, then, each angel was its own genus.

I'll make the argument as simple as I can. Thomas argued that forms could be multiplied into separate instances only through being expressed in material chunks. For example, the form whiteness was undifferentiated and only produced separate instances by being incorporated into material things like snow or chalk. It followed that each angel, being a pure form, was a species comprising a single genus that contained no other species. [Sum. Th. Ia, The First Part, Questions: 50-64 and Questions: 106-114]

Humans are quite different. We can say that Socrates is divided into body and soul, but we can also say that he is human, which means that, while he shares humanity with other men and women, he is distinct from them. In logical and rhetorical (not biological) terms, the members of a group are, each of them, a species within a genus. Thus Socrates was a species within the genus man. Thomas held that each angel, by contrast, constituted his own undivided genus.

In conceiving of men and women as individuals, we may be misled into viewing them as angelic beings, and we seem to be implicitly denying the significance of our material existence–the impulses and appetites that Homer, like modern scientists, attributed to non-rational organic processes. We are also blinding ourselves to the reality that in being members of the same genus, we human beings are not radically separated from each other. Between a dull-witted and diminutive pygmy and a tall Scottish scientist, there is a common human element that is more significant in some ways than all the distinctions of height, color, and brain-power.

This is all rather abstract and speculative, and people who do not value the judgment of either Thomas Aquinas or his Medieval critics will be getting understandably impatient. There is, however, a broader point: Words are often a trap for the unwary. You don't have to be a Scholastic philosopher or even a Latinist to understand that to speak of "the individual" might imply that a human person is both unique in itself but cut off from his fellows. As Metternich famously observed, "Speak of the social contract, and the revolution is made." The same might be said of terms like equality, human rights, social justice, and rugged individualism. When we give up traditional language in favor of philosophical or scientific jargon, we may be making a pact with the devil.

Before the Enlightenment, the English word "individual" was used in a technical sense to refer either to the Trinity, as an indissoluble and undivided entity, or to the separate members of a species or group. It was not until the 18th century that it began to be used as a colloquial substitute for person. I do not know why. Perhaps it just seemed more-high-toned. The intrusion of technical words into everyday discourse, however, can make trouble, if only by making the connection between language and reality just a little bit vaguer. When the phrase "civil unions" began to be used as a substitute for "civil marriage"–though the two are precisely the same thing, both in fact and in law–it was a significant step toward the legal recognition of marriage between members of the same sex.

Words are slippery, and while it is true that the term "individual" can have a precise meaning for moral and political philosophers, we ordinary people, when we use it, may mean no more than "person" or (in America) "guy," as in: "I went into the bar and I met this individual with an interesting background ..." The OED dryly notes this usage as "vulgar." In this sense, individual is only hyper-urban jargon for person in the same way that "perpetrator" is police jargon for criminal. The decay of precise usage, however, may be less innocent than is immediately apparent. In this case, the misuse and overuse of "individual" is used to perpetuate one of the favorite American myths, that ours is an exceptional nation, founded by "rugged individualists" who left settled communities in Britain and Europe to come to a New World, where they never stopped moving from place to place in search of opportunity and adventure. However, a closer look at our colonization and migration patterns reveals a different story: In many cases, towns along the Atlantic seaboard and later in the Middle West were settled by family groups and something like whole villages.Going West, American frontiersmen were less often lone individualists like the mythical Daniel Boone than they were men of family and community, like the real Daniel Boone. The subject of American exceptionalism is taken up in a later volume.

The proper word for a human being, considered in his own right, is "person," a neutral term that does not specify the human being's connection to or disconnection from his society. Wives and children are human persons and possessed of human dignity, but there are legal and social circumstances when it would be misleading to speak of them as individuals. Is a newborn or pre-born infant an individual? It hardly seems likely, but, if not an individual, then in what sense is the infant to be protected? Pro-life advocates will leap in to say that he is a "legal person with rights," but that is transparently absurd. Even a five year old child cannot vote, sit on a jury, make a contract, or sue in court. The confusing misuse of terms encourages a fatal misuse of human persons.

Marxists and libertarians would like us to accept their myth-historical accounts of social and political life, in which collectivism and individualism are the only two choices. But, before liberals invented the individual and leftists invented the collective hive, ordinary people and philosophers understood very well that, while human persons were distinct, they inevitably existed in a familial and social context. Inevitably the liberation of the individual has meant the dismantling of fundamental social institutions from the family to the Church and the construction of vastly larger political mechanisms with coercive powers that an Alexander or a Nero never dreamed of possessing.

Despite their theoretical differences, liberals and leftists by and large agree on the supreme importance of the individual. It is true that Marxists place great emphasis on the state as the mechanism by which the needs of the individual are satisfied, but both see traditional institutions (marriage, parenthood, the church) as obstacles to the individual's fulfillment. The goal is more or less the same. When the

Marxist state gradually withers away, all that will be left are human individuals pursuing their dreams of individual happiness, while the main result of classical liberalism has been to enfeeble all the intermediate institutions that once nurtured personal autonomy. The way of Marx and the way of John S. Mill, while they appear to lead in opposite directions, curve steadily to the point where they converge.

It would lead to less confusion it we began to speak of persons, rather than of individuals. The word "person" does not imply radical independence or complete self-sufficiency. If such creatures as liberal individuals ever existed, they would be entirely powerless, incapable of banding together to resist the growing power of the despotic state. Statists and collectivists understand this reality, which is one of the reasons they make war on the family and the Church, which are independent sources of authority capable of protecting the interests of the members.

Man is by nature a corporate being who belongs to a family, a tribe, or a religious brotherhood. It is only within a society, especially in a civilized society, that family members, kinsmen, neighbors, and co-religionists can cooperate in protecting each other from the depredations of thugs, gang-leaders and the bureaucratic tyrants who administer the organs of the modern state. It is only as members of a certain kind of society that human beings can aspire to the moral dignity classical liberals have in mind when they use the term "individual."

Why does any of this matter, someone might ask? Is this all not just one more debate over the language of political theory? Let us look at a familiar conflict among moral perspectives. Suppose an art dealer has installed an exhibition of homoerotic photographs involving minors. When local authorities close the display, the immediate leftist response is to sue in the Federal courts for the protection of the gallery-owner's individual rights on the grounds of the First Amendment. Of course, the real objective is the destruction of conventional morality, but the language of rights is more convenient. Many classical Liberals, Libertarians, and self-styled conservatives, while they might disapprove of the photographs and probably do not wish to destroy moral norms, would grit their teeth, hold their nose, and defend the owner's individual right to self-expression, typically citing Voltaire's famous statement, "I may disagree with what you say but I will defend to the death your right to say it."

Is anyone so stupid as to believe such nonsense? Let's put a little meat on the bare bones of Voltaire's rhetoric.

> "I am a Jew and while I disagree with the Nazi Party's plan to exterminate my people, I will defend to the death their right to argue for genocide."

Or ...

> "I am a parent who wants to protect my child from evil, but while I disagree with child-pornographers, I will defend to the death their right to create and advocate kiddy porn, so long as no real children are exploited."

Someone with a pre-modern or pre-liberal point of view, whether ancient Greek or Medieval Christian, would look at the issue from two quite different perspectives, the one moral and the other political. Understanding the natural law, he will have little sympathy with "Gay" Rights or their propagandists. What is wrong in nature cannot be given authentic rights by passing a law. A government that institutionalizes wrong is tyrannical. Turning to the American Constitution, the pre-liberal will note, first, that the First Amendment was written to limit or deny the power of the Federal Government in matters of religion and political speech. He would also note that this government is called "federal," because it is a league of sovereign or semi-sovereign states in which each state is supposed to be able to manage its own affairs. The 10th amendment was drafted, specifically, to prevent the federal government from dictating policy either to the state of Ohio or to a city chartered by that state.

If he is of a philosophical bent, the pre-liberal will recognize that the federal principles of the American Constitution and Bill of Rights go back to an understanding of local government and the principle of subsidiarity rooted both in the Old Testament and in the writings of Aristotle, Thomas Aquinas, and Althusius, which provide a philosophical and religious foundation for the preservation of the "little platoons" in which daily life is transacted.

Arguments over freedom of expression are good illustrations of Georges Sorel's famous observation that every assertion of the rights of man ends up increasing the power of the central state. Naturally, radical individualists deny any intention of expanding the power of government, and they will almost inevitably cite one of Ayn Rand's empty platitudes from *The Virtue of Selfishness*, such as

> "Individualism regards man–every man–as an independent sovereign entity who possesses an inalienable right to his own life, a right derived from his nature as a rational being."

It is a considerable accomplishment to have packed so many unprovable (and improbable) assumptions into one sentence! If each human being is a sovereign entity, then he is a law unto himself: That is the very meaning and nature of sovereignty. If his right to his own life is inalienable, then it cannot be taken away from him, even if he attempts to take away the life of some other sovereign entity. Randians would deny this, citing their principle of non-aggression, but how can such a principle be defended without committing aggression? Is human nature entirely rational? If it were, and Rand were right in her philosophy, then we should all be "objectivists," but most of us are not. That should mean either that Rand's philosophy is false or that we are not rational–in which case Rand is also wrong or at least irrelevant to the human condition. If we concede that most human beings have some capacity for reason, that does not exclude the possibility that men are also naturally driven by non-rational passions: greed, lust, the desire for power, of course, but also maternal affection, friendship, and benevolence. Why is reason alone to be the defining element in human nature?

Perhaps the fatal flaw in the language of individualism is an ineradicable fact of human nature: A human person is not a self-sufficient creature. Under most circumstances, he simply cannot fend for himself, even if he is possessed of the resourcefulness of Robinson Crusoe, and, even if he can eke out a living by herding goats or scratching the ground, he cannot acquire enough skills to lead a complete human life. It is unlikely to find a man who is an excellent hunter, herdsman, and farmer, and still more unlikely to find such a man who can make comfortable clothes, carve statues, craft religious rituals, play music, and tell stories. And, even if he were a combination of Da Vinci and Daniel Boone, he could not marry himself nor reproduce–except by artificial means requiring an army of scientists and technologists.

Self-sufficiency–or, to use Aristotle's term, *autarky*–need not be the ultimate goal of human social life, but it is certainly a condition that is commonly regarded as propitious to human happiness. The dream of self-sufficiency is not restricted to Southern agrarians or Aristotelians. Here is the principle reduced to a popular level by "Captain America," the archetypal film hero of the 1960's, who is paying a compliment to a man who lives off the land with his family.

> "No, I mean it, you've got a nice place. It's not every man that can live off the land, you know. You do your own thing in your own time. You should be proud."

The Classical Liberal "individual" is anything but autarkic, and the couple and household, while one and two steps above the individual, cannot hope to master all the skills or provide all the necessities and benefits that a broader or complex community offers. In the individualist myth, however, separate human persons are imagined to find fulfillment by exchanging products and services with other separate human persons. If you view yourself as an individual, you can be a producer and consumer but not truly a partner except in the narrow sense of members in a limited liability partnership set up for a specific purpose. If our humanity only finds complete expression through its relationship to the humanity of spouses, children, kinfolks, and fellow-citizens, the individualist is stunted and weak, and he remains–whatever his wealth or power–a case of arrested development.

Individualism–like every other "ism"–is a dead end, precisely because it elevates one aspect of human nature over all others and feeds parasitically upon the bodies of its subjugated rivals; it is suicidal parasite that destroys its host. To dream of man as he might be, if perfected, is a worthy exercise, but only if that dream is rooted in the reality of man as he is. Part-angel we may be, or as ancient Stoics believed, a mortal organic being with a divine spark, but that divine spark is trapped in the body of a big-brained ape that not so long ago learned to talk and to restrain his passions at least some of the time. The City of God, if it is to be built on earth, must occupy the land and heritage of the cities of men.

References

Adkins, A. W. (1960). *Merit and Responsibility: a Study in Greek Values*. Clarendon Press Oxford.

Bremmer, J. (1987). *The Early Greek Concept of the Soul*. Princeton University Press.

Fleming, T. (1985). Review of Jan Bremer's The Early Greek Concept of the Soul and David Claus' Toward the Soul. *The Classical Journal, 80*(2), 165-168.

———— (1988). *The Politics of Human Nature*. Transaction Publishers.

Harrison, E. (1960). Notes on Homeric Psychology. *Phoenix, 14*(2), 63–80.

Herman, G. (2002). *Ritualised Friendship and the Greek City*. Cambridge University Press.

Schmitt, A. (1990). *Selbständigkeit und Abhängigkeit Menschlichen Handelns bei Homer*. (No. 5). Franz Steiner.

Schwabl, H. (1954). Zur Selbständigkeit des Menschen bei Homer. *Wiener Studien*, 67, 46–64.

Snell, B. (1953). *The Discovery of the Mind, trans. TG Rosenmeyer*. Author.

FRIENDS, COMRADES, AND NEIGHBORS

Greater love hath no man than this,
that a man lay down his life for his friends.

— John 15:13

THAT'S WHAT FRIENDS ARE FOR is something we say after doing a small favor or performing a minor service for someone we may barely know. Like most platitudes we repeat without thinking, this expression, which might have once referred to some concrete duty required by a particular relationship or stipulated by two parties to an agreement, has been so worn away by thoughtless repetition that, if it retains any significance whatsoever, it is to equate "friendship" with doing things that cost us nothing or even imply chicanery. "Be a pal," we sometimes say when we want someone to do something slightly shady, and, in the mouth of a politician or journalist, the term "my friends" is almost always preface to a lie.

Even in private life, the ancient power of friendship can be invoked as a means of persuasion, not always for a noble purpose. In graduate school one of my fellow students was studying for a standardized French examination, but he could rarely tear himself away from the television set long enough to attend the evening class that prepared students to pass the required test. As the exam drew near, he asked me "to be a pal" and take the exam for him. The idea was preposterous and offensive but, just to see what he would say, I asked him what was in it for me. On a practical level, I suggested, perhaps a college professor's annual salary for 20 years to compensate me for the risk I should be taking. His counter-offer was his "friendship," which, as I pointed out, was worth very little if the "friend" would require a favor, as dangerous as it was dishonest, as the price.

Years ago I was discussing the question of friendship with an historian whom years in the academy had made wise to the point of cynicism. Both of us had been been disappointed to discover the unreliability of supposed friends, and we were seeking a practical definition that would not set the bar of friendship impossibly high. I proposed this rather limited definition of friendship: *A friend is someone who is willing to save your life or rescue you from grave difficulty if the effort costs him comparatively little.* If I were drowning in a raging torrent, I should not demand that a friend risk his own life to save mine, but I should expect him to throw me a rope or call for help.

My jaded friend, with his vast knowledge of the American political experience, proposed a more modest definition: *A friend is someone who will not stab you in the back unless he would reap some tangible benefit from his betrayal.* Such a man might seduce your wife if he desired her but not for the sole purpose of making you miserable or making a display of his own superiority. I sometimes wonder, now, with the benefit of more experience of "friends"–or rather colleagues–if he too had not set the bar too high.

This conversation would probably not have been possible a hundred years ago, but modern life is not conducive to forming, much less sustaining friendships. Friendship and its duties are not much discussed by advice columnists, much less by moral philosophers who in principle would be inclined to deny the division of the moral universe into friends, to whom some duty is owed, and non-friends, who can only demand that we do not violate their civil rights. Friendship has disappeared and not just from academic discourse. It is not even a common theme in modern fiction or popular entertainment, unless we count television shows about people who abuse each other and songs in which "my friend stole my sweetheart from me."

If old-fashioned friendships have become rare, popular novels and movies have, nonetheless, rung the changes ten thousand times on the theme of ill-assorted "buddies," who are taught by hardship and crisis to "bond"; with each other. The mere fact that the white cop and black criminal, American and Russian intelligence agents, rich banker and poor laborer, or even man and woman, Christian and Muslim, gay and straight, or human and alien have little or nothing in common is the heart of the story. The moral of these tales is that diversity is a blessing, strangers and people different from us are closer than relatives and people like us, and that opposites attract. While readers and movie-goers go away from the tale feeling good about their own generous attitudes, they cannot fail to be aware that in real life such differences are most often fatal to any enduring personal connection, let alone friendship. It is no secret that in the murky world of internet courtship, professing "liberals," who oppose all forms of racism and bigotry, tend to seek people of their own color and background. I suppose even "liberals" need a religion that will enable them to be hypocrites.

FRIENDSHIP AS AN
IMPOSSIBLE IDEAL

The modern obsession with befriending "the other" goes back at least as far as Montaigne's famous "Essay on the Cannibals," in which Latin American savages are depicted as superior to French Catholics. The wise and benevolent alien–whether Turk or Persian or Chinese–became a common theme in the Enlightenment, a generation or more before Rousseau infected the European imagination with his fantasy of the noble savage. But if we are taught to seek our highest friendships among exotic strangers, then we might think everyday friendships with relatives and neighbors to be humdrum affairs. On the other hand, perhaps only a culture that has rejected the local and provincial in favor of the universal and the bizarre could be taken in by tales of wise Turks and noble savages.

Friendship–as distinguished from the befriending of opposites and aliens–counts for little in modern thought. The great class of exceptions are writers who have set their minds against the iron laws of progressive modernity. C.S. Lewis in *The Four Loves* pays an old-fashioned tribute to its power and nobility: "Friendship is unnecessary, like philosophy, like art....It has no survival value; rather it is one of those things which give value to survival."

Lewis's declaration is inspiring, but is it entirely true to say that friendship has no survival value? A man's desire for food and women, after all, has a good deal of survival value, and rational thought and the capacity for making sense of the world may not be entirely without material benefits. E.O. Wilson, at best an agnostic, regards the idea of God as conferring fitness (in the Darwinian sense) on religious people who, even in the 21st century, have more children than atheists. I wonder if the very loftiness of Lewis's profession might be discouraging to ordinary men and women leading workaday lives. Certainly, friendship, if it is to play a significant role in our lives, cannot be so lofty an ideal as to be enjoyed only by angels or humanitarians.

With this one caveat, we find reassurance in Lewis's defense of friendship as essential to human happiness. Lewis was no philosopher, but a literary scholar and novelist, and it is precisely novelists and poets, more deeply in touch with human realities than philosophers, who have preserved some appreciation of friendship. Lewis's friend J.R.R. Tolkien portrays several enduring friendships in *The Lord of the Rings*, none perhaps so movingly as that between Frodo and his servant Sam Gamgee. The "fellowship of the ring" is nothing if it is not a band of friends, no matter how disparate in race and temperament.

The novelists who valued friendship make up a very mixed company, almost as mixed as Tolkien's union of elves, dwarves, hobbits, and humans. It includes the Catholics Chesterton and Belloc, but also E.M Forster, and Dashiel Hammet, whose novel *The Glass Key* was described by Raymond Chandler as "the record of a man's devotion to a friend." Chandler's own fictional hero, Philip Marlowe is something of a loner, but he is capable of friendship and loyalty to men of all sorts who deserve respect.

These novelists, in valuing friendship and loyalty, were out of step with the times in which they lived. As alien as friendship is to the modern and postmodern way of looking at the world, ancient and Medieval literature is filled with stories of faithful friends: Orestes and Pylades, Damon and Pythias, Roland and Oliver, Dante and Vergil, and (to go a bit later) Hamlet, who tells his friend Horatio,

"Since my dear soul was mistress of her choice, And could of men distinguish her election Sh' hath sealed thee for herself."

For Shakespeare's Hamlet, friendship is an act of the soul that stamps the friend with an indelible mark of owner-ship. This high standard for friendship—not lived up to by Hamlet's other friends—is a common feature of ancient and Renaissance treatments of the subject.

Perhaps the most familiar and proverbial pair of friends is found in the Old Testament: David and Jonathan. Jonathan, the son of King Saul, was so struck by the courage David displayed in killing Goliath, that he conceived for the young hero an unwavering devotion. When David, hold-ing the head of Goliath, was presented to Saul, "the soul of Jonathan was knit with the soul of David, and Jonathan loved him as his own soul." [1 Samuel 18:1] The friends swore a covenant, and Jonathan, in a concrete gesture sym-bolizing their merged identities, exchanged clothes and arms with David with his own garments and weapons. Readers of Homer will immediately think of Patroclus, who is killed wearing Achilles' borrowed armor. The lending and exchange of armor and clothes is a concrete illustration of Aristotle's observation that a friend is "another self."

Jonathan's friendship was so intense that he refused to carry out his father's command to kill David but, instead, warned his friend and did his best to dissuade his father from carry-ing out his threat. Saul is eventually reconciled to David, but when his three sons (including Jonathan) are killed in bat-tle with the Philistines, the king kills himself, conveniently making David's accession uncontested. David's inevitable accession, which had been foretold, was known to Jonathan, who might have reasonably expected to succeed his father, but it did not chill his loyalty.

In the Jewish tradition, the friendship of David and Jonathan is exemplary because it is not based on material gain or physical pleasure. During the Renaissance their friendship was subjected to a Platonist interpretation, which, in our own time, has inspired gender-obsessed literary theorists with homoerotic fantasies. It requires only a moment of rational analysis to reveal the silliness of such an approach. Setting aside all questions of revelation or religious faith, one has to decide whether or not the writers of the Old Testament were themselves favorably disposed toward homosexuality or lived in a society that encouraged such relations. If the answer is yes, then why did they not let David and Jonathan come out of the closet? If the answer is no, then why would they tell a story that even hinted at homoerotic themes? Ironically–if that is the right word for it–the "Gay" interpreters of 1 Samuel seem to assume the historicity of the account almost to the same degree as the Fundamentalists, with only the *caveat* that homosexualists believe that the text has been censored by so-called homophobes. Such speculations, in addition to being a waste of time, serve only to obscure the plain meaning of a text.

Few of us have ever experienced, at least after reaching the age of 21, so intense a friendship as that of Jonathan for David or of Damon for Phintias (or, in a mistake hallowed by time, Pythias). Cicero, who is the extant source for the story, tells us these friends were Pythagoreans who had merged their households, and when Phintias was sentenced to death for plotting against Dionysius, the tyrant of Syracuse, Damon agreed to act as hostage while his friend went off to settle the business of their common household. [*De off.*III.x.] The tale goes back to Aristoxenus of Tarentum, who apparently wanted to vindicate the Pythagorean tradition by showing what true friendship they were capable of.

Normal people rightly take inspiration from these heroic models of friendship, but there is a danger in expecting too much out of any human attachment. Too many writers who have celebrated friendship (Montaigne, especially, but also Plato and his disciple Ficino) hold up an ideal of self-sacrificing loyalty that seems closer to the example of Christ than is practical in everyday life, where friendship has to compete with other social attachments, such as marital love, parental duty, professional responsibilities, and civic virtue, all of which impose particular duties. The otherwise cynical Montaigne says that in a friendship (such as he experienced only with his friend La Boétie), "Our souls mingle and lend with each other so completely that they efface the seam that joined them." (De Montaigne, 1958, p. 139) It may be fortunate for Montaigne that his friend died after only a few years of mutual acquaintance.

Emerson, who thought of Montaigne as an alter ego, offers even more idealistic account of friendship, which he declares to be both "a paradox in nature," because it runs counter to our selfishness, and–better–"the masterpiece in nature." However much Emerson honored friendship, some of his closest associates thought he was more interested in attracting disciples. Both Margaret Fuller and Nathaniel Hawthorne thought Emerson's idealism was too elevated for everyday intercourse. Hawthorne thought Emerson was too interested in being the Great Man around Concord, while Emerson, who always professed to admire Hawthorne as a man, could not read his books–a fact that astounded Henry James.

Montaigne approves of Menander's cautious evaluation that a man would be happy to have even the shadow of a friend. Menander's skepticism, however qualified it might have been in the dramatic context in which it was given, is all too justified, especially if we restrict friendship to the impossible ideal of Montaigne and La Boétie or David and Jonathan or Damon and Phintias. I wonder if such impossible ideals may not sometimes get in the way of the practical requirements of more mundane attachments. If Damon or Jonathan had been married men with children, their wives might have had a few caustic observations to make on the limits of friendship and its demands.

To such complaints, the philosophers might give the traditional reply, that women are incapable of friendship and that nothing could be more impossible than for a man to be friends with his wife. Montaigne loved women (if not necessarily his wife), but for him neither erotic passion nor marital affection was to be compared with the deeper affection of friendship. Such a low opinion of married love is generally ascribed to the ancient Greeks, but there are numerous examples of Greek husbands who were fond of their wives, and Euripides, in his play *Alcestis*, not only presents a wife who sacrifices her life to save her husband but repeatedly uses the language of friendship to describe their relationship.

Montaigne might have quoted other passages of Menander that offered a more practical view of a friend as someone who, if you shared your grief with him, would not smile. In fact, now that we have much more of his work than was available in 16th century France, we can see that friendship and kindness were among the practical virtues that the Greek comic playwright most admired. The plot of the *Dyskolus*–the most nearly complete text to have been recovered–turns on friendship. The old grouch, who has tried to live independent of other men, realizes he depends on the kindness of a good man; his daughter's suitor Sostratus is aided first by a meretricious hanger-on willing to pander to a friend's illicit desires but then by a true friend Gorgias (his beloved's half-brother), who will only help in an honorable cause. As Gorgias says to his honorable friend, "I have been your friend since before I saw you." [615-16] As the brother of the girl he intends to marry, Sostratus is in his essence a friend.

Moral friendships can only exist among morally responsible men and women, but, if friendship were only possible among rarified spirits willing to sacrifice all other interests for the sake of their friends, this quasi-sacred bond, which would have limited relevance for the rough-and-tumble of everyday life, would be on par with the celibacy and communism required of monks. In a world of beer and hotdogs, friendship would be caviar and champagne–precious products to be enjoyed only on special occasions. In truth, however, friendship in its various forms is the attractive force that binds human persons into the corporate structures of society and commonwealth.

Greek Lessons in Friendships

Friendship is not a simple phenomenon. On the contrary, in every society there are varieties of attachments we should probably acknowledge as some form or another of friendship, and, if we go from culture to culture, we shall find as many variations on the theme of "friends" as on "spouses," "priests," and "rulers." Nonetheless, just as in the case of marriage, religion, and politics, there are fundamental similarities that override distinctions in language and social structure. Nations and individuals are certainly not any more identical in their moral traditions than in their physical appearance, and yet it requires no stretch of the imagination to see that a Pygmy and an Icelander are both human and have many more common characteristics, when compared with even the species closest to mankind on the *scala naturæ*, than they have differences. If we confine our attention to the three ancient cultural traditions that converged to create our so-called western civilization–Greek, Judaic, and Roman–we are struck, first, by differences in terminology and attitude and then by their convergence to a common human norm from which, perhaps, only post-modern westerners diverge.

Friendship is, however, a more complicated matter than other universal institutions that can be defined, to one degree or another, by their purpose or as a set of primary functions. A textbook in social thought might tell us that the purpose of politics is governance or the exercise of power to maintain order and that religion, depending on one's point of view, is either a set of practices and beliefs aimed at propitiating powers greater than the merely human or an entirely human system for subjugating the ignorant masses. The purpose of marriage can be seen in the hard core of physical reality underlying its many forms: the begetting and rearing of children. Friendship, by comparison, is difficult even to describe, much less define, partly because in any society it takes as many forms as there are presumed purposes.

Ancient writers (Aristotle in particular) spoke of different types of friendship that served different needs. I might make a friend on the basis of utility, that is, his ability to confer on me some benefit. I might also choose a friend because I found pleasure in his company, either because we had much in common or even because we did not. We may more easily take pleasure in the company of someone who shares our affection for American football and the music of Fauré, but we might also enjoy the conversation of someone who has studied Chinese philosophy and prefers drinking wine to any sport ever played. A certain diversity in friends can be the means by which we broaden our appreciation for the varieties of human life. But, as Greek philosophers would instruct us, these considerations of pleasure and utility should come second to the highest types of friendship, namely those that lead us to a better life.

In taking up the varieties of friendship among the ancient Greeks and Romans, I am not intending to offer an exercise in classical scholarship, much less to produce any new ideas. On the contrary, I shall be scratching the surface only deeply enough to point to some common attitudes that may force us to reconsider what friendship was and is.

Ancient Greeks took relations between friends very seriously. It is probably impossible to understand Greek literature and philosophy without first having some idea of the meaning and importance of friendship. Plato devotes an early dialogue [Lysis] to exploring the meaning of friendship, forcing his young followers to confess that they do not have a clue as to what it really is. He took up, one by one, various possible motives for making a friend–utility, like being attracted to like or unlike, etc., and found them all wanting. What he intended his students to learn from such a dialogue is a matter of debate, though it has been argued that the Lysis set the stage for the more conclusive analysis made by Aristotle. (Price, 1989, p. 9)

If a definition of friendship eluded Plato (or if Plato preferred to dodge the question), most Athenians took its importance for granted and had some rough and ready notion of what it was. While Greek philosophers extolled friendship as an ethical ideal, ordinary Greeks were, if anything, even more used to speaking of friendship as the moral basis of human society. There were, as we shall see, different types of friendship among the Greeks, and sometimes the duties owed by one comrade to another might conflict with the duties of a child toward his parents or of a citizen toward his city, but, while the terms for the different varieties might vary, it is not too difficult to see some underlying themes in these personal and social affections. Because of the high esteem in which Greeks held friendship–and because of their clarity of mind in talking about the subject–there is no better place to begin grappling with friendship than with the Greeks. As one classical scholar has observed:

> "Friendship called forth the deepest feelings of the Greeks. In its highest form it was more honored than the love between opposite sexes; it was felt to be more profound, and, so far as the Greeks conceived romance, more romantic. Moreover the obligations of friendship were very real and binding, and were normally honored even by those whose friendship fell far short of romantic devotion. A man in danger could look to his friends for defense, a man in need could look to them for help in money; and in both cases he seemed usually to have received what he asked. The refusal conferred a stigma." (Earp, 1929, p. 31)

In Homer, the very word for friend or friendly (*philos*) means something like "one's own" and thus dear. The people who most belong to us are members of the immediate family, and it is tempting, if somewhat irresponsible, to imagine some relationship with the Latin *filius, filia*, "son" and "daughter." Such an etymology might have pleased Aristotle, whose first illustration of friendship is the natural friendship a parent feels for his children. The primacy of kinship in the category of friendship explains the puzzling statement made by Menander's young man.

While modern Americans may be tempted to read into the Greek concept of friendship their own emphasis on friendly feelings and diminished sense of kinship, (Konstan, 1996; 2006, pp. 169-84) this mistake can be dismissed by looking at Aristotle's observation [*Poetics* 14.4] that in a play we are not much afflicted when someone is killed by an enemy or by someone indifferent to him, while if the sufferings take place within friendships, as when a brother kills a brother or a father a son... (Belfiore, 2000, pp. 19-20) In Homer, as C.S. Lewis has quite neatly explained, *philia* is "that inalterable relationship, far deeper than fondness and compatible with all changes of mood, which unites a normal man to his wife, his home, or his own body–the tie of mutual 'belonging' which is there even when he dislikes them." (Lewis, 1991, p. 24)

Kinship is a key element in Greek social life, from the time of Homer down to the present, and ancient Greeks, far from distinguishing kinship from other types of friendship, seem to have regarded people united by close blood-ties as the preeminent exemplars of friendship. Since English-speakers do *not* make this equation of friend and relative–though we do speak of kith and kin, friends and family–I have postponed discussion of kinship to a later chapter and will concentrate on friendship in the English sense of people bound together by affection and/or loyalty rather than by ties of blood and marriage.

Perhaps no aspect of ancient Greek life is so alien to us as the value they placed on friendship. Poets celebrated it, philosophers, while taking friendship as one of the major givens of human nature, subjected it to analysis, and ordinary people in court routinely make appeals to the fundamental importance of both kinship and friendship. While the Greeks never shrank from repeating popular commonplaces, their ordinary view of friendship is so strikingly different from our own that we shall miss a great deal if we do not appreciate the depth and richness in their approach to friendship, "a complex web of personal, political, business and family relationships." (Blundell, 1991, p. 39)

The *Iliad* is rich in examples of friendship in varying degrees and kinds. Achilles and Patroclus are closer than brothers, so close that later Greeks thought their passion might be homoerotic–an erotic relationship that does not occur in Homer's epic world. These two are so close that it is altogether fitting that Patroclus dies wearing Achilles' armor, which he has borrowed, making his death a sacrifice for his friend, who is for Aristotle "the other self": *Amicus alter ipse,* as the Romans had it.

What does friendship among Homeric heroes require? In the political context, friends are supposed to stick up for each other in the council of chiefs and praise each other's virtues. When Achilles and Agamemnon exchange insults at the beginning of the *Iliad*, they are treating each other as open enemies. In a war, friends are obviously supposed to help each other, and, if one falls, the other is supposed to rescue him or at least retrieve his body. In a typical sequence of events in the *Iliad* [Book as in XIII], Greek A may attack Trojan Z, who is then helped by X and Y, while B comes to assist A, who kills Z, only to be killed by Z's friends. A tussle breaks out as each side tries to drag away both bodies and call for more general assistance from friends, some of whom are connected by ties of blood or friendship between families. In the intricate ballet of slaughter, one theme stands out: the duties owed by friends and kinsmen to each other, in death as much as in life.

In a real sense, all the Greeks in the host before Troy are supposed to be *philoi,* friends, or at least comrades. When Achilles refuses to return to the battle, even though his friends Odysseus and Ajax have pleaded with him, Ajax rounds on him with scorn and anger, telling Odysseus "this man keeps the brave heart in his chest savage, the wretch, nor does he attend to the friendship of his comrades." [Il IX 629-30] The army is a body of friends, but Achilles selfishly clings to his anger and only returns to the battle when his loyalty to the dead Patroclus takes precedence over his hatred of Agamemnon.

In Attic tragedy, friendship plays no less important a role, and many plots turn on the diverse and often conflicting duties owed to *philoi:* Familiar examples include Æschylus' *Choephoroe,* Sophocles' *Ajax* and *Philoctetes,* and Euripides' *Iphigenia in Tauris* and *Iphigenia at Aulis* (where the question is whether Agamemnon should be loyal to his brother or to his daughter), and *Orestes.* In the *Orestes,* one of Euripides' most often cited works in antiquity, the contrast is not only between the duties Menelaus owes to his nephew Orestes and those he owes to his father-in-law, but also between the constancy of Orestes' friend Pylades (actually, a cousin, though the point is not brought out in the play) and the unreliability of his weak-kneed uncle.

Since friendship is neither pure altruism nor selfish exploitation, reciprocity is the norm. Be friendly to friends, Hesiod advises in his *Works and Days,* composed early on in the archaic age, and give to those who give. [352-69] Do not be the first to offend a friend, but if he gives offense, repay him with interest. [706-14] Among the Greeks–and not only in the age of Homer and Hesiod–the basic moral rule is: Help friends, harm enemies. This was, as Plato saw, what the ordinary Greek viewed as justice. In reviewing (only to reject) earlier views of justice, Socrates [*Rep.* 331 E], cites a Greek poet's definition as "rendering to each man what is due," which one of his interlocutors interprets as owing good to friends and ill to enemies. (Dover, 1994, p. 180) It sounds harsh to us, partly because we attach so little value to friendship, but in the Greek world "respect for friends could be ranked alongside reverence for gods, parents, and laws." (Blundell, 1991, p. 31) The practical implementation of this rule is the *lex talionis*, which requires us to reward our friends for their favors to us and to punish enemies for the harm they inflict–"life for life, eye for eye, tooth for tooth, hand for hand, foot for foot, burning for burning, wound for wound, stripe for stripe." [Ex 21:23-25]

A friend who causes harm or fails to provide help is auto-matically converted to an enemy. This was a truism among the high-strung Greeks, who were quick to take offense. Pru-dence dictated caution both in the selection of friends and in the development of trust. Aristotle [*Rhet.* 1389b23-25] endorsed the proverbial saying of the sage Bias of Priene, who tells us to love [that is, make friends] as if one is about to hate and to hate as if one is going to love.

Since, as St. Paul tells us, friends should "rejoice with them that do rejoice and weep with them that weep," [Rom 12:15] envy should have no place in a genuine friendship. Greeks certainly recognized the reality of fair-weather friends, who are loyal only so long as we are able to reward their loyalty. More troublesome, perhaps, are those who cannot endure the thought of our good fortune. Æschylus' Agamemnon, at the height of his success, acknowledged the danger of foul-weather friends who could not endure a friend's prosperity. [*Ag.* 832 ff.] but allowed another's good fortune to magnify their own sense of failure.

Dante, a Christian who embraced classical virtues, celebrates friendship and condemns envy. For example, in the *Convivio,* he argues that it is natural to be a friend to others, that praise is better than blame, though one should admonish a friend for his faults as one would one's self, and that envy, which exists only when men have the common ground which might be the basis of friendship. In *Purgatorio* XIII, as he sojourns among the envious, Dante hears the cry, "I am Orestes," recalling the story he had read in Cicero, that when a ruler was seeking to kill his nephew, both Orestes and his friend claimed the privilege of dying for the other. The episode comes from the Roman playwright Pacuvius, who gave a Roman twist to a Greek story, perhaps that of Euripides' *Iphigenia among the Taurians,* in which Orestes insists on dying with his friend. Cicero, who cites the story, wonders how many of us would be willing to go to such lengths to demonstrate our loyalty. [*de Amicitia* VII]

Then, if we can learn nothing else from this brief survey, it can teach us that for them, friendship was not a sentimental luxury but the basis of the moral and social order. It was based not on feelings only but on the carrying out of the practical duties that one friend owed another, within the household and in the public forum, in war as much as in peace.

ARISTOTLE — THE
PHILOSOPHER OF FRIENDSHIP

The burdens of friendship are still perceived by men and women who have not been influenced by philosophers (from Plato to Sartre) who have rejected the opinions of ordinary people. By contrast, Aristotle based his ethical and political analysis on the popular traditions and everyday life of the people he knew and observed. A keen naturalist and a physician's son, Aristotle, even in his works on ethical subjects–moral, political, and æsthetic questions–began his studies, in the spirit of a proper naturalist, with observation of how people lived and what had been said by earlier generations of respected men.

I should at this point state the obvious: I am not claiming to offer any new interpretation of Aristotle or to enter into such vexed questions as how he related his model of ideal friendship, in which two virtuous men are drawn into friendship by their very virtues, with lesser friendships based on utility or pleasure. My only point is to use Aristotle as a convenient point of reference for making sense of the Greek understandings of friendship.

To gain a little appreciation of what ancient peoples thought friendship was, we can turn to Aristotle's handbook on oratory [*Rhetorica*], in which the philosopher tries to summarize what most people think about friendship. This is no bold speculation: The orator, if he is to succeed in persuading a jury or public assembly, cannot engage in flights of fancy or bold speculations, because it is to conventional opinions that he must appeal.

Friends, says Aristotle, are those who want good things for their friends not for any reason but for the friends' sake.

When someone feels this way about you and you about him, then you are friends. What sort of people make good friends? People who share our interests, who are morally good, who appreciate our good qualities. Friendship is not an abstract quality or a mere thought: It is the product of action, of doing and receiving kindnesses.

Aristotle goes on to explain that friends, unlike people afflicted with sexual desire, are expected to resemble each other, if not physically then at least in habits and taste. Theognis, an early Greek poet often quoted as proverbial wisdom, advises us to adjust ourselves to our friends' differing dispositions, much as an octopus takes on the shape and character of the rock it is clinging to. [213-18]

In acknowledging the central facts of friendship and kinship in human life, Aristotle did not part company from the Greek consensus that can be observed in popular poetry, though he did provide a deeper level of understanding. At times, he writes as if he has been studying sociobiology. One cannot be just to one's children, for example, because they are so much a part of oneself. Parents, he says, love children as their very selves, and brothers love each other as being born from the same parents: Their identity with the parents makes them identical with each other [*Eth. Nic.* 1161b]. It is the reality of friendship, not the abstractions of liberty and equality that are at the heart of his understanding of the social and political order.

In the *Nicomachean Ethics*, Aristotle outlines the overlapping of justice and friendship, but in the *Eudemian Ethics* he makes the point more explicitly. [EE VII.10] "Justice and injustice"

"...are chiefly a question of friends....Therefore justice and friendship are the same thing, or close to it....We spend our days with family, relations, and pals, children, parents, or wife, and our personal acts of justice directed toward friends are up to us, while just behavior directed toward others is established by law and not up to us."

A just act, therefore, is not moral if it is coerced by a government that compels us, to take an obvious example, to pay taxes to help strangers.

Aristotle observed that friendship (*philia*), in popular usage, meant something like affection, concern, or love, and the most natural (as well as the most powerful) form is the love between parents and children. More broadly spread throughout the community, it is friendship, rather than justice, that holds the city together. Although most people would rather receive than give love, the hallmark of friendship is loving, and the strongest example is the unselfish love of a mother who may even be willing to give her child up, if that is in its best interest.

Friendship is the basis of all human associations that require sharing and mutual responsibilities. To the extent we have a "relationship," there is friendship to the same extent–and justice. In this sense, justice and friendship (or love) are concerned with the same things. Aristotle's arguments seem to lead to a conclusion that most Greeks would have readily accepted: It is only by loving others and by treating them as part of ourselves that we can behave justly toward them. To moderns suckled on Descartes and Kant, this is a shocking and immoral proposition.

In sharp contrast with his teacher Plato, Aristotle [Pol. III 3-4] virtually defines the commonwealth as a partnership of friends and family and not in terms of territoriality or mutual defense pacts or even laws guaranteeing free trade and intermarriage (though such rights are included in a commonwealth).

It is clear that a *polis* (commonwealth) is not [merely] a territorial partnership for the purpose of not wronging the partners and for economic exchange. For there to be a *polis*, these things are necessarily present, but where they are present they do not necessarily make a *polis*, which is, actually, a partnership of households and kindreds in living well, for the purpose of a life that is complete and independent.

The citizens of a commonwealth are interrelated, as Aristotle notes, by blood and marriage, which is why clubs and clan associations with common cults are so important. These associations arise from the feeling of friendship, which is the motive for living together. Thus the good life is the end or purpose of society, to which family and associations of friends serve as the means.

Languages are never entirely precise, especially when words are being used to describe some vitally important part of human experience. *Philia*, after all, covers relationships both of blood and affection. Greek can, however, distinguish between the affectionate and general bonds of kinship and friendship, on the one hand, and alliances based on particular interest or shared objectives. The latter term in Greek is derived from the word Hesiod used to distinguish a certain kind of friendship from family relations: *hetaireia*, from *hetairos*, which means comrade or ally. This is the routine term for members of a political faction or conspiracy, and it is frequently applied to comrades-in-arms.

In his dialogue the *Lysis,* Plato used military friendships, forged in combat, to illustrate friendships based on considerations of utility. Naturally, many comrades become friends in a broader sense, and it is not always easy to make a precise distinction–either in English or in Greek–between the friend we like for his own sake or for shared experiences and the political ally with whom we eat and drink, as we are plotting a revolution or office coup.

A PHILOLOGICAL DIGRESSION

Languages shape–and are shaped by–the culture of the people, and, when we learn a new language, we are also learning to view reality from a different perspective. Modern European languages, though they have influenced each other and have developed as parts of a common culture, still have many things to teach the learner. In American English, we frequently see misleading advertisements saying, "You have already won" or "You are guaranteed a loan of $2500." Both of these offers are, of course, contingent upon certain conditions, such as having the winning number or a steady job.

In languages with a lively use of the subjunctive mood, it is more difficult to mislead people by such claims. The subjunctive, in case you have forgotten your Latin or French, is typically used in constructions where there is some uncertainty about the statement being made, because, for example, the speaker is only guessing at probabilities or responding emotionally (in fear, doubt, or desire) or expressing some contingency indicated by "if." To use the indicative in such cases seems a palpable lie in Italian or German. Slavic languages lack the subjunctive and, like Modern English, have to fall back on circumlocutions that get the point across but are not a necessary part of the language. A Russian friend of mine, irritated by Italian subjunctives, once tried to argue that Slavic languages are more "honest" in rejecting such nuances. I replied to him that the reverse is probably true, that Slavic languages (like postmodern American English) encourage a wishful confusion between what is and what might be, between reality and hope.

On the other hand, Slavic languages are consistently precise in distinguishing verbal aspect, which determines whether an action is viewed as complete or incomplete. In Serbo-Croatian, for example, when you say that so-and-so drank wine and use the simple verb "piti," you are describing a continuous or repeated action that would have to be translated as "was drinking" or "used to drink." To express the idea that someone drank a glass or bottle of wine to completion, you would have to use a perfective compound verb. In English we can make the distinction between "was drinking" and "drank up," but, since it is not built into the language, we often have to rely on context. As an English speaker learning Serbo-Croatian, I found myself having to think more acutely about the verbal aspect of what I was intending to say when I used a verb.

I have introduced this little bit of superficial philology to make a simple point: By comparing the various words used for "friend" in different languages, we can begin to think more critically about what we mean by the word in English. The root notion of many words for friend is affection. Setting aside the complex case of Greek *philos*, it is apparent that Latin amicus (from *amare*, to love), English/ German *friend*/*Freund*, (and the Serbian cognate *prijatelj*) all derive from verbal roots meaning to love or like. At the most primitive level, then, a friend is someone we like or love. In French, "ami(e)" from Latin (*amicus*)–a male or female friend–can also be a boyfriend/girlfriend or lover. It is an association that does not come quite so naturally to an English-speaker.

There are other root notions. Slavic *drug* appears to be related to the other Slavic word *drug*, which means "other," which generated a constellation of uses in Slavic and Baltic languages, including "co-heir" and military comrade. From this point of view, the friend is "the other" with whom you share fellowship or a responsibility. Some hint of its meaning can be gleaned from the use of *drug* to mean *Kamerad* in the Communist sense. I am told that the character used in Mandarin Chinese to designate what is translated as friend has associations with exchange of gifts. A Chinese scholar has explained to me that this is only one of several possible explanations, but, supposing for the moment it is true, it would not only tell us something about the Chinese understanding of friendship but it might also give us an insight into one of the duties of friendship. The giving of a gift in pre-modern societies, as Marcel Mauss has explained, was not a simple act that might or might not arouse a sense of gratitude: Gift-giving established a bond of mutual obligation, as anyone who has read either Homer or the Beowulf understands.

From these observations, it should be obvious that friendship has many facets and emphases that are indicated by different words and expressions. A friend is someone we like, but it can also be someone whom, in distinguishing from ourselves, we regard as a partner in our interests, or an associate in some activity.

ROMANS AND CHRISTIANS

No previous culture has so influenced the Modern world as Rome, and the Latin language of friendship offers clarity in some areas but ambiguity in others. *Amicitia* (friendship, from *amicus*, friend) denotes a more precise and formal relationship than *philia*, one that does not ordinarily include kin. In his *Pro Quinctio* [26], Cicero, a writer who is often an excellent source for ancient common sense, distinguishes between family ties, which are characterized by *pietas* (reverent loyalty), and friendship which is strengthened by truthfulness. Who can be entirely truthful about his parents and children? In politics, however, *amicitia* (like *hetaireia* in Greek) might refer to a political alliance, though it is never easy to distinguish between allies who are actually friends and those who are content to use each other's influence. (Brunt, 1988, pp. 351-81; Konstan, 1996; Taylor, 1949) Plutarch informs us that Themistocles the Athenian is supposed to have said that he hoped he would never sit on a tribunal where his friends would not get more from him then strangers would. [*Aristides* 2.4] This was a thought that many Roman politicians would have found congenial. Cicero, at least in his writings, was more circumspect, but he acknowledged that a judge might honorably extend a sort of affirmative action to his friends.

Christians, however selfish or corrupt they may be in everyday reality, are shocked in principle by the ancients' easygoing acceptance of nepotism and favoritism, which they regard as civic counterparts of simony (the sale of offices in the Church). Cicero was a strict moralist in his writings, but as a practical politician, he was well aware of the dangers of political idealism. He once said that his friend Cato acted as if he lived in Plato's *Republic* rather than among the dregs of Romulus. As a moralist, he preached incorruptible virtue, but he knew how impractical this would have been in Rome. In his first big case, the prosecution of Verres, a very corrupt provincial governor, he appealed to Rome's highest traditions of civic virtue, all of which Verres had violated in his administration of Sicily and was now violating in Rome where he sought to corrupt the court. If Verres were to get off, argues the zealous young prosecutor, it would not be for any good or normal reason, such as "the mutual favors done by friends, the bonds of kinship, a record of deeds well done, not even moderation in one or another vice that might palliate his other vices–so great in number and scope." [Ad Verrem I.15.47] Cicero takes for granted the significance of friends and relations and does not moralize too much about their potentially corrupting influence. Verres, by contrast, offended the Roman sense of decency by buying votes from men who probably despised him.

For ancient Greeks and Romans, then, "friendship" was a complex notion that might include kinship, an affectionate bond between men who respect each other, and a practical alliance for some agreed upon purpose. However complicated the idea(s), these connections–and not some rational abstraction like rights or justice–were the foundation of social and political life. Good men tried to be just, but it was not always entirely possible then (nor is it now) to keep personal loyalties from interfering in the discharge of public responsibility.

Greek and Roman writers celebrate friendship with idealistic enthusiasm and praise the relationship as the source of benefits and pleasure, but they are also keenly and cynically aware of the celerity and frequency with which friends betrayed each other. If faithful friends are a joy, faithless friends are a curse. The archaic poet Theognis is forever

condemning the friends who had failed him and warning
his young friend Cyrnus to beware of friends and comrades
who say one thing and think another. In the Fourth Century a speech of Lysias [VI.7] condemns an opponent for
reversing the moral code by harming only his friends and
not his enemies.

The Old Testament offers a similar variety of judgments. "A
friend loveth at all times, and a brother is born for adver-
sity." [Prov. 17:17] David and Jonathan, as has already been
noted, were exemplary friends. The Lord speaks to Moses
face to face as one friend speaks to another. [Ex 33:11] On
the other hand, David complained that a friend had proved
faithless and "lifted up his heel against me." [Psalm 41:9]
Still worse, a wife, close relative, or friend might seduce you
into worshipping strange gods. [Deut 13:6] Micah sums up
the perils of life succinctly: "Trust ye not a friend, put ye
not confidence in a guide: keep the doors of thy mouth
from her that lieth in thy bosom." [7:5] These dire warnings might be misconstrued as condemnations of friendship
(and marriage); in fact, however, they are the opposite: The
examples of wives, kinsmen, and friends are cited precisely
because they are the strongest and most significant human
attachments.

In everyday matters the Gospels paint a conventional
picture of friends. The friend makes merry with
friends [Luke 15:29] and rejoices over the happiness of
the bridegroom. [John 3:29] After Jesus taught his disciples the Lord's Prayer, he explains part of the significance
by referring to the obligation of friends to help each other:

"Which of you shall have a friend, and shall go unto
him at midnight, and say unto him, 'Friend, lend me

three loaves; For a friend of mine in his journey is
come to me, and I have nothing to set before him?'"

The friend appealed to is at first reluctant to get out of bed,
but being importuned, he complies with the request. Thus
we must not be reluctant to beseech the Father. [Luke 11:5-8]

The relation of friend to friend, like that of close relatives
and kinsmen, is taken for granted both in the positive
sense–as when Jesus brings his friend Lazarus back to
life–and in a negative, when it is said that friends and
relatives may be a obstacle to faith and will even betray
the followers of Christ [Luke 21:16]. Nonetheless Jesus
refers to his disciples and hearers as his friends [Luke 12:4]
and goes so far as to define his faithful disciples as his
friends: "You are my friends if ye do whatsoever I command you." [John 15:14]

VARIATIONS ON THE
THEME OF FRIENDSHIP

In everyday language, then, we apply the term "friendship" to many different sorts of personal connections. If
we loosely define friendship not by what it is supposed
to be in essence but by the duties it imposes, we might
describe it as a relationship in which one or both of the
parties have or are supposed to have a moral obligation
to do each other favors, we can see at once that there is
a variety and scale of intensity in such relations. We owe
a variety of particular debts to kinfolks, workmates and
teammates, neighbors, lovers, and–for want of a less sentimental word–"soul-mates." Inevitably, some friends belong
to several categories: We might live next door to someone
with whom we fall in love or play on the same team or

even share the deeply felt mutual respect and affection demanded by philosophers. Despite the inevitable fuzziness and complexity that result from caring about other people, we should, nonetheless, distinguish the nature of these separate types of relationship before going on to look for common elements.

We can begin by distinguishing those who are friends by nature from other types. By nature, I mean the ties of blood, kinship, and marriage, which, although they will be taken up separately, cannot really be kept entirely distinct from other guises of friendship, such as neighbors, comrades, and lovers. (Marriage is also a tie of blood in the sense that in the children the parents are genetically united.) At this point, it will have to be enough to say only that the English phrase "friends and family," while it makes a distinction between ties of blood and ties of affection, couples kinship and friendship in a way that suggests that we have friendly feelings toward members of our family and that in making friends we are coming to treat outsiders as members of the family. Since the topic of blood-ties is reserved for the following chapters, no more needs to be said at this point.

COMRADES, LOVERS, AND SPOUSES

Enough has been said already both about the passions of love and strife and of the Greek distinction between friends and comrades, of relations rooted in love and those based on competition in the pursuit of victory or success. Comrades, team-mates, business colleagues, and political conspirators cooperate and can even act as friends–indeed, they often are friends in other senses–but the initial attraction of the relationship is the utilitarian goal of achieving a common purpose, whether the goal is winning a game, seizing power, or making money.

Although some virtues–courage and honesty–are part of the make-up of the ideal team captain, we do not chose a captain on the strength of his general virtues but because of his abilities to lead us to success. Everyone outside of the academy is aware that human life is too complicated and to be shoe-horned into Cartesian or Kantian (much less Marxian or Misesian) categories.

If sports teams provide a clear example of *camaraderie*, business and professional life gives us the parallel example of collegiality, the relationships typical of colleagues who work together for a common purpose. On a football or baseball team, each player has an assigned position, and, while two pitchers or offensive linemen might be in competition, they are not routinely competing for rewards with players in other positions. Winning games is a shared objective that can be achieved only by cooperation. In the corporate world, there is much talk of teamwork and team leadership, but the reality is often more like the cut-throat competition between gladiators who, to survive, must defeat and even kill their team-mates.

In universities, church hierarchies, think tanks, and other organizations devoted to objectives less clearly defined than victory on the field, colleagues are engaged in a never-ending struggle for increases in salaries and perquisites, power and prestige. Sometimes it appears that the intensity and ferocity of the struggles are inversely proportional to the advantages that can be gained. Though it must be admitted that the bitter infighting that accompanies papal elections is over real and tangible wealth and power, small communities can be torn apart by rivalries just as intense

within a small congregation of Presbyterians or Congrega-
tionalists. For one reason or another, friendships among aca-
demics and clergymen are often more fragile than among
athletes or among people who work on fishing boats or in
construction.

If one of the characteristics of friendship is the concern felt
and demonstrated by one friend for another, then, surely,
the passionate attachment of lovers and spouses who swear
they cannot live without each other deserves the name of
friendship. The tragic marital affection of Alcestis and Ad-
metus and the guilty passion of Lancelot and Guinevere
inspired the even more improbable love of Dante for his
beloved Beatrice and Petrarch for his Laura. Such idealized
passions, within or outside of marriage, seem out of place
in the postmodern world, where they have been replaced
by hookups and short-term enthusiasms. Nonetheless, romantic love in or out of marriage is often something more
than erotic obsession, and, when it is cemented in a no-exit
marriage, such love is not easy to distinguish from various
forms of friendship.

Marriage can be an opportunity for a kind of friendly camaraderie whose object is the rearing of children and the
maintenance of the household economy as a little commonwealth. This subject is reserved to a later volume, taking
up the household, marriage, and children, and it is enough
here to point out that marriage is most conducive to friendship, when it is viewed as permanent or at least not transitory, and when the two parties are not in competition,
whether as work-mates or as rivals, and when a traditional
division of labor allows a sphere of freedom to both men
and women.

Comrades-in-arms, lovers, and spouses can all in different ways display the different facets of friendship. Though many would agree with Montaigne and Aristotle that erotic passion and friendship are mutually exclusive, it seems a waste of time to deny what so many people believe, namely, that spouses and lovers can become quite good friends.

Friends and Neighbors

If lovers and spouses are drawn together by the mysterious forces of passion in which a man and woman become of one flesh, this passionate attachment might be placed at one end of a spectrum whose other end could be defined by the mere chance of propinquity or neighborhood. It may be hard to imagine the significance of neighborliness in the postmodern world, where people change houses every few years, but in days of old–roughly from the time when men first put down roots until perhaps the 1950s–most ordinary people had to rely on their neighbors almost as much as they relied on kinfolks. For Americans today, the neighborhood is a vague concept, defined either by a sense of familiarity or by real estate developers who laid out the streets and named them after trees or spices or their children. However, in many traditional societies–and not all of them "primitive"–neighborhood has a deep social and moral significance.

In Dante's time, neighborhood was an indispensable reference point for the familial, social, economic, and political lives. In the *Convivio*, he puts a slight twist on Aristotle's definition of man as political animal. Man must live in a society whose sole purpose is:

> "a life of happiness, which no one is able to attain
> by himself without the aid of someone else, since
> one has need of many things which no single indi-
> vidual is able to provide. Therefore the Philosopher
> says that man is by nature a social animal. And just
> as for his well-being an individual requires the do-
> mestic companionship provided by family, so for
> its well-being a household requires a neighborhood
> (*vicinanza*) for otherwise it would suffer many de-
> fects that would hinder happiness."

Readers of Dante, who are not familiar with ancient
thought, may be tempted to regard the introduction of
neighborhood as an innovation, though Dante is simply
following St. Thomas in identifying neighborhood (*vicus*)
with Aristotle's *kome* (village), the next highest level of organization above the family.

The English word neighbor (like Latin *vicinus* and Greek
geiton) refers to someone who lives nigh, that is, nearby,
perhaps on adjoining land. The Greek and Latin terms are
perhaps more evocative: The Greek is derived from the
word for land, while the Latin is derived from vicus (related
to Greek *oikos*, house), which can refer either to the quarter
of a city or to a homestead.

Neighbors share our joys as well as our miseries. In the
Old Testament, the woman in debt who feared her sons
would be sold into slavery is told by the prophet to go to
her neighbors to borrow pots, which will miraculously be
filled with oil to sell. In the Gospels there are several para-
bles involving neighbors. The man with lost sheep calls his
friends and neighbors together [Luke 15.6.] for help, while
the woman who found her lost penny wants her neighbors
to rejoice with her. [Luke 15.9]

Greek literature–particularly comedy and oratory–is even richer in instances of cooperation and friendship among neighbors. One of Aristophanes' characters goes to neighbors to get water [Thesm. 241], and Lysias tells of someone asking a neighbor for a light for his lamp. ["Murder of Eratosthenes" 14] If robbers or enemies attack, Athenians call on neighbors and "demesmen" for help. Neighbors are important for the help they can provide, but it is also pleasant, recalls a character in Aristophanes, during the rain to sit chatting with a neighbor. [*Pax* 1041]

Hesiod warns that in a crisis neighbors may be more valuable than kinsmen (who often live too far away to help in an emergency); nonetheless, one should not make a mere comrade (*hetairos*) equal to a brother. [*Erga* 706] The choice of the word *comrade* (often misleadingly translated as *friend*) is significant, because it implies a distinction from kinfolk. Greek does not have a common expression like friends and family, because there is no sharp distinction. All close members of a family are friends, and to the extent we regard someone as a *friend*, we are treating him as a kinsman, while a comrade is a mere collaborator.

In Athens, the stereotype of the prying neighbor was invoked by Lysias [7.28] as part of a legal defense strategy, since the neighbors would certainly know if you had done something criminal or disreputable.

In a stable society, getting along with a neighbor is less a question of choice or taste than of practical necessity. To have good neighbors, one must be a good neighbor. The practical advantages are obvious, but there is a moral basis to the relationship even in a very "backward" society. Neighborliness–like kinship–implies some degree of friendliness (if not exactly friendship), but it is not simply a feeling but a set of reciprocal obligations. In Alcala, a community in the South of Spain that Julian Pitt-Rivers studied not long after WW II,

> "Neighbors are thought to have particular rights and obligations towards one another. Borrowing and lending, passing embers, help in situations of emergency, discretion regarding what they may have chanced to discover, compose the obligations in which neighbors are forced by their proximity..."

Neighbors everywhere are expected to do favors for each other. The English "favor," like Latin *gratia* (and derivatives in Italian, French, and Spanish), implies both a feeling of gratitude and the actions that inspire such a feeling. It is not insignificant that both the Greek *charis* and Latin *gratia* are used in the New Testament to refer to Grace, the divine (and undeserved) favor that makes salvation possible. This Grace creates an obligation, but it is one that we can never fully discharge.

The need for cooperation in the future dictates a spirit of cooperation in the present: I help you today because I know that you will help me in the future. (That is the burden of Robert Axelrod's *Theory of Cooperation.*) In English we say, "I'll scratch your back, if you'll scratch mine," while Greeks and Romans used to say, "One hand washes the other." The need for delicacy in human relations, however, tends to soften the edges of the crass rule of tit for tat. Jesus instructs us not to invite friends, brethren, or rich neighbors to a dinner in expectation of a reciprocal offer. [Luke 14:12] This is not a counsel of perfection but quite practical advice. In Alcala, it was bad form to be too obvious about doing tit in expectation of tat.

The moral understanding of neighborliness is not limited to Greeks, Jews, and Christians. Confucius ranked the moral duties of neighborliness and filial piety just after self-possession and a sense of shame and ahead of sincerity of speech. I do not know if this is the best order of moral duties, but no one who is not a good son or good neighbor is likely to be a man of good moral character. This, then, raises the obvious question: Who really is this neighbor to whom I owe proper treatment? Does proximity in residence really entail a particular moral obligation or do we owe the duty of neighbors to everyone in the world?

Who Is My Neighbor?

For more than 100 years, some Christians have argued that Marxist socialism is the secular fulfillment of Our Lord's repeated warnings against the temptations of great wealth and His injunctions to practice charity. Inevitably, the preachers of the "Social Gospel" or "Liberation Theology" will trot out the parable of the Good Samaritan as proof of their equation of Marxist principle with Christian (particularly Catholic) teaching. Non-Marxist Catholics, perhaps uncomfortable with the apparently revolutionary tendencies in the Gospels, tend to dwell on the practical drawbacks of socialist experiments, and, while these critiques are certainly correct, they fail to address the main question posed by "Christian" socialism: Is Marxism compatible with–or even demanded by Christian moral teaching? A careful (though brief) examination of the parable, both within its immediate context and within the broader context of the Gospels, can make it quite plain that the socialist explanation not only leads to unfortunate consequences but–and this is really more important–is entirely false as an interpretation of Scripture and contrary to Christian moral theology.

The context alone should give honest Marxists pause. The parable is told in the tenth chapter of Luke's Gospel. Christ has commissioned the 70 and told them how to act on their missions. The 70 return in joy to report of their miraculous powers, and Our Lord thanks the Father for the blessings his disciples have received and witnessed, adding rather ominously that prophets and kings had desired but failed to see and hear those things that his followers have experienced. The implication is clear: Even the greatest events in the Jewish tradition are being exceeded by the plain and ordinary people who have become Christ's disciples. The question being raised is not our obligation to share the wealth but the break-through represented by the mission of Christ's followers.

At this point a "nomikos"—not a lawyer, as some translators make out, but a man learned in the Jewish Law of the Torah—asks him: "Master, what shall I do to inherit eternal life?" When Jesus replies by spelling out the two Great Commandments—to love God and love your neighbor—the finical expert, wanting to prove himself right, asks Him: "And who is my neighbor?" Jesus' answer is the parable of the Good Samaritan, the story of a man, beaten and robbed, who had been ignored by a priest and a levite, who passed him by, but cared for by a Samaritan, a member of a group despised as heretical mongrels by the Jewish religious establishment.

Samaritans were descendants of Jews in the northern Kingdom of Israel, who had stayed behind when some other Jews were being deported to Babylonia. They were accused of having intermarried with gentiles and of having corrupted their religion. Samaritans had their own story to tell, of the snobbery and discrimination to which they had been subjected by the returning Jews of Judaea, who inserted Scriptural passages (so Samaritans claimed) hostile to the northern kingdom. Excluded from worship in the Temple in Jerusalem, they performed their national rituals on Mount Gerizim in Samaria, which they regarded as the original sacred place for the Children of Israel. Jews and Samaritans were forbidden even to associate with each other, a prohibition illustrated by the story in John's gospel of Jesus and the Samaritan woman at the well. [John 4:4–42]

Before looking directly at the parable, we must pay still closer attention to the context. Jesus had openly challenged the claims of the Jewish tradition, and a traditional scholar has tried to trap him by asking, in essence, what are those principles that He is making the basis of this new teaching that has been working wonders? Christ's answer is to cite two unconnected pieces of the Torah, which He–but not the supposed expert–understands. In the subsequent exchange–the expert's question and the parable as answer–what is at stake, primarily, is the moral adequacy of the Jewish tradition.

The *nomikos* wants to put Jesus to the test–the verb *ekpeirazein* reminds us of the tests to which Satan subjected Him. This requires a bit of explanation. The verb–and its simpler uncompounded form (*peirazein*)–are typically translated by the English "tempt," but the meaning of that word has changed so much since the early 17th century (when the Authorized Version was commissioned) that it is quite misleading. To "tempt," in this and other passages including the *Lord's Prayer,* is not to entice or trap but to put something or someone to the test in order to find out what he (or it) is. A closer English word might be "assay," as in, "The chemist assayed the ore to determine whether it was gold or iron pyrite."

Since He is dealing with an expert in the Torah, Jesus naturally gives him the Scriptural response from Leviticus about loving one's neighbor. [Lev 19:18] As it is set up, then, the parable of the Good Samaritan is designed to expose the hollowness of an official Judaism that was more concerned with outward observance of the law, and it may also be relevant that Jesus [John 8:48] was accused of being a Samaritan, perhaps because he preached the inner meaning of the Law while not always observing every external rule.

This contrast between the Old and New Testaments is strongly emphasized in the traditional readings for the twelfth Sunday after Pentecost where the story of the Good Samaritan is paired with St. Paul's explanation [II Cor. 3] that the letter of the Old Law is a condemnation to death, while the spirit of the New gives life. A similar contrast is implied in the readings for the 13th Sunday that pairs the Samaritan leper who, alone of ten afflicted men healed by Jesus, returns to give thanks. "Your faith", responds Jesus, "has made you whole"—a phrase that can be also be translated as "Your faith has saved you." In both stories, faith in Jesus and a willingness to follow the spirit–and not the letter–of the law brings salvation.

The story of the Good Samaritan is so familiar to all of us that we rarely pause to puzzle over the details. That is why it is so easy for Christian Marxists to play it as their trump card. Although, neither in this parable nor anywhere else in the New Testament, is there any reference to government intervention in the economy, much less to state socialism, socialists like John C. Cort (Cort, 2020, p. 38) have no trouble in invoking it in support of their ideology. Indeed, Cort quotes triumphantly from a like-minded socialist ethicist: "Spontaneous, simple love, following the dictates of its own concern for persons in need, grows into concern for the formal structure of society" (Mott, 2011, p. 58), a passage entirely devoted to social change without a hint of understanding of "biblical ethics."

For socialists, Christian or not, the Samaritan and the robbery victim are universal everymen, which means that the entire planet is made of neighbors to whom we owe the same responsibilities. If this had been the intention of the parable, it has been rather botched in the telling, because in that case we should have expected both the priest and the Levite, in contrast to the Samaritan, to be the victim's neighbors in the conventional sense that they lived nearby. We have come to expect lies and nonsense from socialists, but many Christians these days are inclined to being sentimental do-gooders, and they are frequently lured into the tents of wickedness by Marxists who have borrowed and misapplied Scriptural phrases and examples.

The expert's question is a more complex question and a sharper challenge to Jesus than it might seem, because the Scriptures have two quite different words for "neighbor." This distinction is made in the Hebrew and Septuagint Greek texts of the Old Testament, and in the Greek text of the New Testament and in the Latin Vulgate. Unfortunately, it has not been preserved in any English version with which I am familiar. Let us look a little closer.

The ordinary English word "neighbor" is used, primarily, to refer to someone who lives next door or nearby. There are passages in the New Testament in which the word for "neighbor" (*geiton*) is used in the ordinary Greek sense of people who live nearby and can be expected to help in an emergency or take part in a celebration as in the parable of the woman who lost a coin. When she finds it, she calls her friends and neighbors together to rejoice with her.

This is not, however, the word used either in the New Testament nor in the Septuagint Greek text of Leviticus [19:18] that Jesus is citing. In those and many other passages, the expression is *ho plesion* (Latin *proximus*), which mean, roughly, the one nearby or in colloquial English, "the next man"–as in, "I like a pedantic Greek exposition of Scripture as much as the next man." While these words might be used in reference to a literal neighbor, their meaning is generally more inclusive and, in Scriptural translations, more precise. The phrase *ho plesion* is used consistently in the Septuagint Greek version of the OT to translate a Hebrew word *rea* meaning, roughly, someone to whom one is morally attached, as in friend, husband, or (perhaps most commonly) fellow-Jew. It does not refer to people who just happen to reside in the vicinity.

The distinction is clear in Exodus, where Jewish women, on the eve of the great departure, are instructed to "borrow" valuable items from their Egyptian next-door neighbors in order to despoil them. While such conduct is far from unknown even today–everyone, probably, has bad neighbor stories to tell–it is not the ordinary behavior expected of a neighbor, and it would be absolutely forbidden to those who are "neighbors" in the moral sense. The expert in the Torah, then, thinks the neighbors he is supposed to love are made up exclusively of kinsmen, friends, and fellow-Jews: no Gentiles or Samaritans–or perhaps in an extreme case even Galileans–need apply.

Indeed, Jewish commentators on the Torah have consistently maintained that the Law, including the Ten

Commandments, applies differently or not at all when a Jew is dealing with a Gentile. This was one of the reasons ancient writers regarded Jews–and therefore Christians–as misanthropic–because they allegedly had a double-standard that conflicted with the moral understanding of all the Greek philosophical schools.

On the first and most obvious level, then, the parable is aimed at refuting the Jewish moral double standard and prejudice against non-Jews, an argument anticipated in prophetic books such as Jonah and Job. The parable does not, however, instruct us to be indifferent to human differences. The man helped by the Samaritan is not a criminal or an invading enemy. He is only an ordinary respectable person requiring assistance. He is not Everyman around the globe but an unfortunate fellow human being whom our common humanity requires us to help when we see him in misfortune.

The Jewish and thus the Christian notion of *neighbor* (in its moral, non-geographical sense) is not a universal term nor does it refer to someone who accidentally lives nearby: It is rather more precise and even restrictive. It is a moral bond, like brotherhood and friendship, and it does not extend to people trying to harm us or our children or to hypothetical strangers who may live a thousand miles away. If we live next door to an anti-Christian abortionist, he is not our *neighbor* in the Christian sense, while if someone living a Christian life lives across town, he (even if his views are heretical or he belongs to a Christian sect we happen to loathe), he has certain moral claims on our time, resources, and attention.

THE JUSTICE OF FRIENDSHIP

Friendship is not itself a moral principle, much less an abstract or universal proposition, but, if the family is the seedbed of the commonwealth, then friendship is the seedbed of morality, and if we can once grasp the significance of friendship, we shall have an enriched understanding of the moral complexity of human experience.

We have, then, a stark contrast between the modern way of analyzing moral duties and the older way of looking at moral relations. On the one side stand the abstract and universal principles of right and wrong that each society advances as true, while on the other are arrayed the primary bonds of attachment that claim our loyalty. Since Descartes (for more remote sources we may even go back to the ancient Stoics), Western man has tended to maximize the importance of abstract concepts of right(s), while ignoring or denigrating or condemning sub-rational loyalties. To some extent, this unrealistic attitude has been the product of utopian philosophers from Plato and the Stoics to Immanuel Kant and John Rawls. By the 18th century at least, moral and political philosophy were dominated by abstractions that made the common sense of everyday life as irrelevant as *The Gospel Learned at My Mother's Knee*, the title (in translation) of a fine book of everyday morality by my late friend, the philosopher Pier Luigi Zampetti. These abstractions have alienated ordinary men and women not only from the traditions of their ancestors but from the reality of human nature.

This is not to say that moral philosophy does not require principles and universal abstractions, but that such principles must be induced from the historical experience of the human species and not imposed from on high by the semi-divine legislators known as moral philosophers. Friendship is, as I have been trying to show, a rather messy moral category that includes a variety of relationships that are not necessarily reducible to neat formulations and explicit rules, but on a fundamental level it is, like hunger and sexual desire, a part of human reality. Friendship is also, however, a necessary pre-condition for moral life, and in overlooking it–you may search the indices of academic books on ethics and not even find the word *friend*–the philosophers have dreadfully misled their students and their readers, and, through those of them who became teachers and writers, virtually everyone who has gone to school.

At its highest level, friendship is, after all, a non-erotic form of love that seeks the good of the friend even more than the good of the self. In this aspect, friendship resembles that form of love which St. Paul termed *agape* and which was translated into Latin as *caritas*. St. Thomas asked if friendship were charity, and answered the obvious objections to this equation by pointing out that friendship is a mutual feeling that requires communication.

> "Accordingly, since there is communication between man and God, inasmuch as He communicates happiness to us, some kind of friendship must needs be based on this same communication of which it is written, 'God is faithful: By whom you are called unto the fellowship of his Son.' The love which is based on this communication is charity: wherefore it is evident that charity is the friendship of man for God."[Sum. Th. II ii. q. 23]

Gregory the Great ends his *Life of Saint Benedict* with a miracle wrought by his sister Scholastica, who wept when he insisted on leaving her to return to the monastery. Suddenly a great storm came up that delayed his departure. When Benedict complained, his sister told him the Lord had granted her request, and the two spent the night in edifying conversation. Gregory concludes his anecdote by praising the "miracle that, by the power of almighty God, a woman's prayers had wrought."

Is it not a thing to be marveled at, that a woman, who for a long time had not seen her brother, might do more in that instance than he could? She realized, according to the saying of St. John, "God is charity" [1 John 4:8]. Therefore, as is right, she who loved more, did more.

Christ was not reluctant to call his disciples his friends nor to describe his voluntary submission to torture and death as the action of a friend: *Greater love hath no man than this, that a man lay down his life for his friends.* [John 15:13]

Friendship, which may exist at the lowly level of fishing buddies and brothers who have grown apart but continue to do favors for each other, may rise, as we mature, to a self-sacrificing love that brings us closer and closer to God. Greater even than faith and hope, this concrete and pragmatic love of the other–and not any abstract conception of duty, rights, or equality–lies at the heart of the two Great Commandments enjoined by Jesus Christ.

REFERENCES

Belfiore, E. S. (2000). *Murder Among Friends: Violation of Philia in Greek Tragedy.* Oxford University Press on Demand.

Blundell, M. W. (1991). *Helping Friends and Harming Enemies: a Study in Sophocles and Greek Ethics*. Cambridge University Press.

Brunt, P. A. (1988). *The Fall of The Roman Republic*. Clarendon Press Oxford.

Cort, J. C. (2020). *Christian Socialism: An Informal History, With an New Introduction by Gary Dorrien*. Orbis Books.

De Montaigne, M. (1958). *The Complete Essays of Montaigne* (D. Frame, Trans.). Stanford University Press.

Dover, K. J. (1994). *Greek Popular Morality in the Time of Plato and Aristotle*. Hackett Publishing.

Earp, F. R. (1929). *The Way of the Greeks by FR Earp*. Oxford University Press.

Konstan, D. (1996). Greek Friendship. *American Journal of Philology*, 117(1), 71–94.

———— (2006). *The Emotions of the Ancient Greeks: Studies in Aristotle and Classical Literature*. University of Toronto Press.

Lewis, C. S. (1991). *The Four Loves*. Houghton Mifflin Harcourt.

Mott, S. (2011). *Biblical Ethics and Social Change*. Oxford University Press.

Price, A. W. (1989). *Love and Friendship in Plato and Aristotle*. Clarendon Press.

Taylor, L. R. (1949). *Party Politics in the Age of Caesar.* (No. 22). University of California Press.

KINSHIP: KINFOLKS
OR SUBJECTS

And the brother shall deliver up
the brother to death, and the father
the child: and the children shall
rise up against their parents, and
cause them to be put to death.

— Matthew 10:21

I N THE TENTH CHAPTER OF SAINT MATTHEW'S GOSPEL, Jesus
is instructing the twelve apostles on their mission. He
predicts they will be rejected by some of their hearers,
who will hand them over to the courts and scourge them in
the synagogues. They should not fear these persecutions,
even though they will be accompanied by the terrors of a
dissolving society, but they are to remember that He did not
come to bring peace to the world but to set brother against
brother.

The predictions are alarming. In the context of His entire
teaching, which insists on respect for the Commandments,
He cannot be interpreted to mean that strife among family
members is a good thing. It is worth recalling that His followers, before they adopted the term Christian, had called
each other not only friends but brothers. Among Christians,
the law, while it has not been replaced, is fulfilled in the
love of people who regard themselves as friends and brothers. In this sense the literal blood-ties that bind brothers

together are the model for the more metaphorical ties of Christian love. No prophecy could, then, be more terrible than conflict between brothers. This strife and division, far from being a desirable state of things for spiritualized beings, will come as just retribution for mankind's stubborn rejection of His demands for justice and charity. For over two millennia, these demands have divided Christians, not only from their enemies in other traditions, but also among themselves, since Christians are not immune to the changes in fashion that go by the name of progress.

In modern times, there are many controversies that divide Christians from the leftists, liberals, and "conservatives," whose thinking is everywhere defined and circumscribed by the categories of the revolutionary tradition. While the children of the revolution believe firmly in a human progress that insures that every day and in every way things will be getting better and better, Christians have been promised a day of judgment that will come in response to a horrifying social breakdown in which brothers betray each other to the authorities, parents kill their children, and the children rebel against parents and compass their death. St. Paul, echoing the Master, says that in the last times "men shall be lovers of their own selves, covetous, boasters, proud, blasphemers, disobedient to parents, unthankful, unholy, *without natural affection.*" [2 Tim 3]

In our own day, when brothers and sisters live thousands of miles apart and face neither punishment nor shame for neglecting each other, when mothers are lauded for killing their unborn children, and euthanasia is either celebrated enthusiastically as a virtue or accepted with gentle regret as a necessity, the prediction sounds less like the last days than a description, albeit graphically expressed, of contemporary experience. No one blinks an eye when the son and brother of a crooked financier testify against him, and, no one scorns the children of celebrities when they publish attacks on their parents. In fact, these ghost-written libels are so popular that they make the disloyal children rich and their mercenary publishers richer. "It's nothing personal, it's just business."

The contempt for family and kinfolks is so pervasive we are not likely to be outraged when a red-diaper baby turned neoconservative boosts his career by publishing a book in which he denounces his communist father, or when public officials urge school children to inform on drug-abusing parents, or the media condemn misguided parents who bribe universities to admit their children. Bribery–like communism and drug abuse is worthy of condemnation–but what normal human being cannot sympathize with parents–even if they are Hollywood celebrities–who want to help their children?

The criminals in these cases are the university administrators, not only those who accept bribes but all those who have prostituted the honorable profession of scholarship and teaching to the exigencies of career development. Jail time for the crime of parental affection could only be demanded by men and women whose natural instincts have been suppressed by a culture of ideological indoctrination that turns healthy human animals into robots.

THE BONDS OF KINSHIP

Strife among relatives and kinfolks is taken for granted in postmodernity. In Jesus' own time, however, and in most ages previous and subsequent to the Incarnation, there was no worse crime than parricide and no sin more serious than disrespect for parents and failure in the duty owned to kindred. Jesus' depiction of the last days has much in common with the prediction of Hesiod, a Greek poet who lived some seven centuries earlier. In *Works and Days* [170 ff.] Hesiod imagines a future age when children will be born with grey hair, fathers and children will quarrel, and brothers will not love each other or respect their parents. In portraying the ultimate inhumanity of broken loyalties, such stories of the end times, whether revealed wisdom, as in the Christian case, or merely insightful fiction, as in the case of Hesiod, give us an insight into what earlier generations thought normal human life was supposed to be like. Every negative commandment, after all, entails a positive opposite.

Failure to show proper respect to one's relatives was an abomination for Romans as well as for Greeks and Jews, and Cicero advised orators to make use of this horror both to aggravate a murder charge [*De Inventione* I. 103] and to blacken the character of a defendant who has failed to fulfill "his obligations to country, parents, or other people joined by blood." [II.66]

Over thirteen hundred years later, the Christian Dante is close in spirit to the Greeks, who thought of kinship as the defining form of friendship. In Italian, kinship is often expressed by a phrase such as *i miei* ("my folks"), which can include both family members and friends. In *Purgatorio* [VIII 120] one of his characters (Currado Malaspina) says with pride: "Ai miei portai l'amor"–I bore love to my folks. By contrast the evil and malicious *barrator* (a bribe-taking public servant) from Navarre boasts [*Inferno* XXII 110] that he is so full of spite that he can cause harm *ai miei* ("to my own people"), presumably those closest to him. Thus political and legal corruption eats at the very core of morality and society.

The relationships of parents and children and between siblings, while the most immediate and demanding of blood ties, are not the only degrees of kinship that impose obligations. There have been many societies–and not all of them "primitive" or non-European–in which second or third cousins enjoy the right to inherit property or find themselves subject to penalties for crimes committed by fairly distant relatives.

Strong ties of kinship have been a human norm down into the 20th century, and when we try to ignore this reality, we cut ourselves off from our history and our literature. It is difficult to read Shakespeare with understanding if we fail to understand the horror with which audiences reacted to the murder of King Hamlet by his brother Claudius or to the young princes murdered in the tower at the order of their uncle, Richard III, or to the mistreatment inflicted on King Lear by his disloyal daughters. In Shakespeare's England, as in Hesiod's Greece or the Israel depicted in the Old Testament or in Roman Judaea in the time of Christ, it was understood that the ties of kinship were the foundation of all human society. Jesus could, therefore, take it for granted that, when he referred to his disciples as his "brethren," they would correctly interpret brotherhood as a relationship entailing profound responsibilities.

The alternative–a society in which kinship did not matter–was only conceivable to a few philosophers who imagined they might build their utopias on some other basis than the brute facts of human nature. Even Saint Augustine, for all his severity toward Greco-Roman society, has to concede some virtues to a pre-Christian civilization that fostered moral decency. Although the men in the Terrestrial City, in their pursuit of the good things in life, engage in violent conflict at every level, "non autem recte dicitur ea bona non esse quæ concupiscit hæc civitas, quando est et ipsa in suo human genere melior," [*C.D.* 15.4] that is, it is not right to say that those things this [terrestrial] city craves are not good, since the city is itself better in its human fashion than man in his natural state.

Augustine goes so far as to concede that even conflicts between cities may not be entirely bad if they result in a larger political community that brings peace to squabbling districts, especially if the more righteous cause prevails. He goes on to say that the commonwealth is an improvement upon the natural man, and an important part of this improvement lies in the realm of what is now sometimes referred to misleadingly as "family values"–an expression that implies that maternal affection and filial loyalty like commodities that can be traded in the market.

Kinship, which in its broadest sense includes sisters as well as cousins and aunts, entails an inventory of duties and prohibitions, and Augustine admits, albeit somewhat grudgingly, that some progress has been made by pagan civilization in the matter of incest. In the first generation of the human race, men had to marry their sisters, and this practice, permitted in the beginning only out of necessity, did not die out all at once. [*C.D.* 15.16] Ancient Romans, by contrast, were comparatively strict and, without outlawing marriage between first cousins, had strongly discouraged a custom that might weaken aversion to brother-sister incest. Since custom (*mos*) serves to control lust, traditional restrictions on incest must be honored. Augustine adds the sociological insight that incestuous marriages do nothing to encourage the integration of society that is brought about by uniting two families in a marriage: This advantage is lost when the couple has only one father-in-law.

On the other hand, as he suggests quite shrewdly, it would have been dangerous to run to the extreme of exogamy (out-marriage): The fathers of old, he argues, had a religious concern lest kinship (*propinquitas*) itself, little by little loosening its ties in the course of generations, might fall apart and cease to exist. For this reason early Romans had prescribed marriages between families but within the clan (*genus*). In Augustine's vision, incest rules, complemented by solidarity among kinfolks, was the basis for a stable social order.

Even Augustine, then, was willing to take instruction from the Roman order. He might have been encouraged by a sentence from St. Paul: "For when the Gentiles, which have not the law do the things contained in the law, these, having not the law, are a law unto themselves." [Romans 2:14] Taken out of context, the phrase "a law unto themselves" is often misapplied to moral anarchy; however, Paul's point is the opposite: Even though pagans had not studied the moral law found in the Pentateuch, they were capable of following moral principle, "which show the works of the law written in their hearts." [2:15]

Paul's insight is not always grasped by self-satisfied Christians, who routinely use "pagan," as a term of abuse for egregious violators of the moral law. Philanderers and adulterers are called pagans, and so are drunkards, gamblers, and wasters "who do not feel the moral beauty" of getting up with the birds to spend eight hours at a soul-destroying job. St. Paul, though he was ever ready to cast the first stone at the foolish pagans who drank and fornicated their way to Hell, knew that some of them, at least, did their best to be decent spouses and dutiful parents. They had the moral law engraved upon their hearts, because, as he told the Athenians on the Areopagus, He "hath made of one blood all nations of men for to dwell on all the face of the earth."

Unfortunately, too many Christians in every age of history are fond of exaggerating the vices of non-believers as a contrast to their own (all too often exaggerated, even illusory) virtues.

Religious propaganda, if not pressed too far, has its uses in stimulating perseverance in Christian moral discipline, but it can also encourage the self-righteous hypocrisy that blinds a believer both to his own vices and to the virtues of other sects and other religions. Some Fundamentalists ridicule Catholics who, they say, are free to sin on Friday night in the knowledge that their sins will be forgiven once they go to confession on Saturday and receive communion on Sunday. Many serious Catholics return the favor by assuming that all Protestants are moral anarchists, whose religions were created by the uncontrolled libidos of Henry VIII and the "renegade monk" Martin Luther, who condoned bigamy. In casting aspersions on Luther, Catholics conveniently forget the checkered histories of French monarchs, whose sexual peccadillos also sometimes went unchastised, and the Renaissance Popes whose gross immoralities had outraged Luther.

Christian complaints about the decline of the family in post-Christian countries are usually limited to the weakening of the nuclear family or, at the most, to the disappearance of grandparents from the domestic scene. That is partly because Christians, as much as non-Christians, suffer from the strains of modernization that have eroded family functions and reduced awareness of kin to the immediate family plus, in some instances, grandparents.

It is a commonly accepted truism, associated with the sociologist Talcott Parsons among others, that industrialism is compatible only with the nuclear family. Cousins, aunts, and uncles have become more or less ornamental figures in the modern family scene. By contrast, Greeks and Romans and Jews, whatever other sins and follies they might have committed, were rather more prone to over- rather than to undervalue the ties of blood.

CHRISTIAN KINSHIP

Some Christians might respond to the arguments I have been making by citing a predictable collection of proof-texts chosen to show Jesus' hostility to family and kinship. In a typical example, one of his disciples asks: "'Lord, permit me first to bury my father.' But Jesus said unto him, 'Follow me; and let the dead bury the dead.'" [Mat 8:21-22, cf. Luke 9:59-60.]

The most alarming statement occurs in all the synoptic Gospels:

> "If any come to me, and hate not his father, and mother, and wife, and children, and brethren, and sisters, yea and his own life also, he cannot be my disciple."[Luke 14:26]

These declarations, taken by themselves, are startling, but, if Jesus' point lay in rejecting the bonds of family and kinship, he would not have needed to add, "yea, and his own life also," which rather makes it clear that He is asking us not to neglect our families but to make a radical choice between the most important things of this world, no matter dearly we love them, and the heavenly kingdom. A Christian's highest priority cannot be his own life, with all its affections and duties, but his loyalty and obedience to God. If he is willing to lose his life, he must also be willing to lose his family.

However, short of martyrdom, he must fulfill every jot and tittle of the law, which prescribed "Honour thy father and thy mother."

The Law that Christ came to fulfill was rooted in the duties of kinship. In the Old Testament, the system of descent is patrilineal. A mother's family is thus not kin to her child. There appears, secondarily, to be some preference for endogamy, that is, for marriage within the tribe or kindred. This practice is reflected in the commandment concerning the daughters of Zelophehad [Num 36:6]: "Let them marry whom they think best; only, they shall marry within the family of the tribe of their father."

That this practice was seen as desirable by the Hebrews can be seen in Judges 14:3, where Samson's parents lament the fact that their son wants to marry a Philistine woman: "Is there not a woman among the daughters of your kinsmen, or among all our people, that you must go to take a wife from the uncircumcised Philistines?" Ideally, Samson's spouse would be a woman from his kinsmen (i.e. his patrilineage). If he did not want to marry one of them, his parents would have preferred any Israelite woman, rather than for their son to marry a foreigner.

Another text that may be taken as confirming the Hebrew preference for endogamous marriage is Judges 12:9, which specifically mentions that Ibzan gave his children away in marriage "outside," presumably to another tribe of Israel, though a union with foreigners would not be impossible. This passage occurs in the section of Judges that details the rapid moral decline of the Israelites after entering Canaan. There would seem to be no reason for this detail to be mentioned here unless the author was trying to use it to illustrate moral decline.

By the time of the Book of Tobit (roughly 200 B.C.) was being written, Jews had suffered displacement (exile in Assyria and Babylonia) and a return to Israel, but kinship was still a determining factor in marriage and social responsibility. Among the instructions Tobit gives to his son are [12]: "Be on your guard, son, against every form of immorality, and, above all, marry a woman of the lineage of our forefathers. Do not marry a stranger who is not of your father's tribe...Therefore, my son, love your kinsmen."

If we knew more about Jewish kinship and social life during the Roman period, we might have a better idea of what structures of family and kinship were taken for granted in the age of the Apostles. We do know that Paul is able to cite his own tribal affiliation, and that Jesus, who grew up in Nazareth, probably picked eleven out of 12 disciples from his own small region of Galilee of a bit more than 1000 square miles or the size of two midwestern counties.

Christianity, so far from repudiating the demands of kinship, used the language and values of kinship as the metaphor for the Church. Jesus' followers treated each other as kinfolk. Until the mission at Antioch developed under the divided leadership of Peter and Paul, they had no other names for each other but "brother" and "friend." Paul, in instructing Christians to be especially careful to do good to other Christians, refers to them as "members of the household of the faith." [Gal. 6:10]. This is no mere metaphor, and the Greek word *oikeios*, while it means pertaining to or belonging to the household, also connotes kinship and friendship. It is a more intense word than the Latin domesticus or any English phrase used to translate it. When something (or someone) is *oikeios* to you, it or he is part of you. Among Stoic philosophers, there was an explanation of moral development called *oikeiosis*, the process by which first parents, then friends and neighbors, fellow-citizens, and eventually all mankind become your own. The Church, then, functions as a broadly extended network of kinship in which the members discharge the duties of love and friendship to each other.

There is, unfortunately, a strain of thought in Christianity that tends to discount the significance of kinship. Misinterpreting Christ's dramatic appeal to let the dead bury the dead [Luke 9:60, Mat 8:22] or the admonition to would-be disciples to put love of kindred second to love of God, indeed, to hate their fathers and mothers, brothers and sisters, wives and children [Luke 14:26], some Christians have concluded that, in accepting Christ as their savior, they are exempt–or at least somewhat detached–from the ordinary rules requiring respect for parents, affection between spouses, and care of children. Nothing could be farther from the truth. Indeed, no one is more subject to foolish temptations than those who, believing they have reached a higher spiritual plane than their fellows, can join with the Pharisee who thanked God he was not like other men.

Ordinary pagans, who scarcely had a higher morality than the everyday duties owed to family, kinfolk, neighbors, and fellow-citizens, were less subject to such a high-minded temptation. Lofty idealism was left to philosophers who, from Socrates on, preached higher moralities, but in all ages of the world the preaching of philosophers generally falls on deaf ears. The most impractical idealisms, once they entered the world of human experience, had to accommodate themselves to reality.

The philosopher Epicurus was a hedonist who taught his disciples to be indifferent to human suffering, but he was, nonetheless, tender-hearted towards his friends. His heart reasoned better than his mind. The early Stoics did preach a doctrine of universal obligation and world-citizenship that diminished the moral significance of blood ties, but in Roman hands this philosophy was reshaped (by, for example, Musonius Rufus, Seneca, and Marcus Aurelius) to account for the specific obligations that arise from one's station in life.

Extravagant idealism, if it is going to escape the trap of hypocrisy and false piety, must come to grips with human nature. In his *Meditations*, the Stoic Emperor Marcus Aurelius resolved the conflict between his everyday duties and Stoic cosmopolitanism by thinking of himself as a dual personality. As a philosopher, his devotion was to a moral ideal, but as a son and father, as a Roman and as an emperor, he was bound to fulfill specific obligations. While the philosopher must always bear in mind that "all that partakes of reason is akin and that to care for everyone is according to man's nature", he should also act as a good Roman in every circumstance. He will tell himself that while one thing comes from God, another from chance, and still another

> ".... comes from a member of the same tribe, a kinsman, and a fellow (one with whom life is shared), even when such a fellow is ignorant of that which accords with his nature. But *I* am not [ignorant], and therefore I treat him kindly and justly in accordance with the natural law of fellowship."[III.11]

Even under the highly cosmopolitan Roman Empire, then, the power of kinship and fellowship was strong enough to hold its own against a powerful philosophy that regarded all men, whatever their blood or nation, as brothers.

THE NECESSITY OF KINSHIP

Human brotherhood is a noble ideal, preached–albeit in different ways–by Stoics, Christians, and post-Christian leftists some of whom include orangutans, dolphins, pet cats, and mountains in their moral universe. I am not joking about mountains. Once, at a conference of "environmentalist philosophers," I heard a paper in which the presenter said human beings had no right to interfere in the "intentionality" of a mountainside by carving images of American presidents into the surface.

Kinship, unlike our theoretical oneness with the entire universe, is a gritty and sweaty reality that can be dispensed with only by sages and saints and ignored, even by them, only at great peril. Universalism is a moral and intellectual luxury, like *foie gras* with a Taitinger Comtes de Champagne. Kinship is the everyday roast beef food and Chilean cabernet no one wants to (I should say "can") do without. To starve yourself and your children in the pursuit of luxury is worse than foolish: It is as perverse as sex without procreation.

Kinship and its duties are not a noble ideal to aim for but an essential part of humanity's survival kit. In the modern or postmodern world, both law and mass culture have made steady inroads into the solidarity of families and kindreds; nonetheless, family reunions, Christmas letters, genealogical data bases and social networking sites are used to remind distant cousins of their connections. When I receive a message or telephone call from a long lost relative, I am surprised by the delight I take in reconnecting myself with some I hardly knew or have never met. In modern societies, where mobility can dissolve the most intimate bonds, our connectedness beyond our more immediate relatives is difficult to maintain, but even in more traditional societies, obligations toward more distant kin are only felt strongly when they are strengthened by familiarity. "Kinship certainly gives rise to special rights and duties, but when unsupported by local proximity it loses much of its social force." (Westermarck, 1908, p. 202)

The loosening of natural ties that has led to the modern sense of alienation, aggravated in postmodernity, can be felt by people untouched by either Christian doctrine or respect for the past. A deracinated and much-divorced entertainer wondered, "Doesn't anybody stay in one place any more?" In my own limited experience, connections can be maintained more easily among people who all have experience of a living ancestor, but when the grandparents are gone, the bonds are weakened, especially if family members are scattered across the continent. In earlier centuries, separated relatives tried to maintain their ties through correspondence, but letters fail, eventually, and social networking is a cruel delusion.

The extent to which different degrees of kinship are acknowledged or translated into obligations varies widely from one society to the next. Some of the relevant factors–whether causal or merely correlative–are the strength of political entities beyond family and kin, *e.g.*, as in the modern state with its rules on inheritance and incest; however, an important element that strengthens kinship bonds beyond siblings is geographical proximity.

We only rarely reflect on what we may be missing in our isolation. Ignoring the reality of kinship does not lessen its force or significance any more than ignoring the law of gravity will enable us to fly. The consequences of kin-ignorance may take longer to be felt than the consequences of gravity-ignorance, but they are equally disastrous.

Athens: A Commonwealth of Blood

In modern Europe and North America, where kinship ties are weak and families scattered across a continent like so many handfuls of breadcrumbs flung out to the birds, it is hard to form a mental picture of how the obligations of kinship can hold a community together. It is easier to appreciate the importance of kinship by looking at pre-modern societies, such as the cities of Medieval Tuscany or the wandering children of Israel. Tuscany, it might be objected by skeptics, was recovering from the Dark Age of Christian superstition, and the fanatical tribes of Israel existed before the arts of reason had begun to liberate mankind from the shackles of superstition.

Then perhaps we should turn to a society that cannot be condemned for excessive religiosity or primitivism. A convenient place to begin our inquiry is classical Athens, a city routinely held up as a model of enlightened detachment from the superstitions of blood and religion. Athens was "the birthplace of democracy," where the lights of progress and philanthropy were first kindled. This sentiment has been expressed in the sublime words of a poet (Shelley): "Let there be light! Said Liberty, And like sunrise from the sea, Athens arose!" and the hackneyed phrases of a president's (Obama's) speechwriter:

We're indebted to Greece for the most precious of gifts – the truth, the understanding that as individuals of free will, we have the right and the capacity to govern ourselves. (Applause.) For it was here, 25 centuries ago, in the rocky hills of this city, that a new idea emerged. Demokratia. (Applause.) Kratos–the power, the right to rule–comes from demos–the people. The notion that we are citizens–not servants, but stewards of our society. The concept of citizenship–that we have both rights and responsibilities. The belief in equality before the law – not just for a few, but for the many; not just for the majority, but also the minority. These are all concepts that grew out of this rocky soil.

If one were to believe literary interpreters and popular historians, Æschylus' *Oresteia* is "all about" the triumph of democracy over blood ties, Sophocles' *Antigone* is a celebration of feminist individualism, and Thucydides' history displays skepticism on the matters of religion and kinship. In fact, Athenian writers–Æschylus, Sophocles, and Thucydides in particular–have left us a rich legacy of literary, philosophical, and legal evidence for the enduring attractive power of family and kin, community and religion.

Athens, in the era before the Persian Wars, was a kin-based society, and while the ties of blood were subjected to stress and raveling in the decades following the Greek victory, family and kindred remain at center stage in Athenian social and political life, and the tension between the claims of the city and the claims of blood is a prominent theme in Attic tragedy, from Æschylus' *Seven Against Thebes*, which pitted brother against brother in a war to determine the very survival of the city, to Sophocles' *Antigone,* in which a young woman, in defiance of her uncle the ruler, has to carry out the obligations of kinship that are normally discharged only by men, to Euripides' *Orestes,* in which Orestes, after killing his mother, who had murdered his father, is threatened by her father, betrayed by his uncle, and supported by his sister.

Both in tragedy and in Greek religion, the human social world is mirrored at a higher level by the divine. Greek pagans worshipped a bewildering multiplicity of gods whose relations were determined by their position within the divine family and kindred. Zeus and Hera were siblings and spouses, and, with their brothers Poseidon and Hades, they ruled the human universe in company with their children (whose genealogies were sometimes contrived). In his so-called "Ode to Zeus" in the *Agamemnon,* Æschylus (following Hesiod) goes so far as to explain the universe in terms of the violent succession of divine dynasties, from Uranus to Cronus to Zeus.

If there could be wars in the Greek heaven, families, too, had their conflicts, and while it was considered bad form for an Athenian to take his relatives to court, disputed legacies and personal disagreements incited family members to attack each other. The arena for these legal combats was the Agora. Crimes and disputes involving religion were handled in the *basileios stoa,* where a troublesome philosopher (let us imagine in 399 B.C.) has gone for some business involving a suit that has been lodged against him. (The *Stoa Basileios,* the King's basilica, was the place where the *archon basileus,* who inherited some of the religious powers of the Athenian kings (including jurisdiction over homicide), conducted business.)

The philosopher has been accused not only of teaching atheism but of making religious innovations (the charges may seem contradictory). Worst of all, he is to be put on trial for corrupting the young, a charge that touches on the integrity of the family and on the authority of parents. The philosopher meets a young acquaintance, who asks what business takes him to the court, and, when, Socrates (to give the philosopher his name) ironically praises his accuser as a man who knows enough about politics to start at the right end–with the education of the children–Euthyphro (for that is the young friend's name) misses the joke and declares that in accusing Socrates, the politician Meletus is destroying the city "from the hearth," a proverbial expression that suggests Socrates' accuser is attacking the very core of civil life.

Young Euthyphro's court business turns out to be even more curious than the prosecution that will cost Socrates his life; he is prosecuting his own father for homicide. Since homicide prosecutions at Athens had to be instigated by private individuals, generally by the victim's relatives, Socrates tries to find out what connection there was between Euthyphro and the victim. The young man responds by mocking the philosopher, insisting that the gods do not make such distinctions. The pious young man, who is all for a strict interpretation of the law, is no respecter of persons. He is, like most modern ethical philosophers, a universalist who believes that, when we are making moral decisions, such distinctions as kinship, ethnicity, and nationality are irrelevant.

As it happens, there are circumstances that mitigate the father's guilt. A servant, it seems, had killed a slave, and Euthyphro's father had tied up and neglected the guilty party until he could receive official instructions. In the meantime, the murderer died. The case really comes down to an accidental homicide that resulted from an attempt to comply with Athenian law, and a son, of all people, should not be prosecuting his father. None of these considerations–motive, legality, or filial piety–carries any

weight with a young man convinced of his own righteousness. While the exact circumstances of Euthyphro's case are
not entirely clear, (Kidd, 1990, pp. 213-21) he was accusing
his own father of the homicide (probably accidental) of one
slave who had killed another.

The rest of the conversation turns on the question of piety,
and it is hard to miss the connection between Socrates'
accuser and Euthyphro. Both of them assume that they
know what is right and best for the city, and both are in
fact destroying the city "from the hearth": Meletus, in the
metaphorical sense that in prosecuting an honest moral
philosopher, he is undermining justice, which is the foundation of civil life, while young Euthyphro is literally attacking
his own household in the person of his father.

KINSHIP — THE SOCIAL CONTEXT:

Euthyphro's mistake, from the conventional Greek point
of view, was not that he overvalued piety toward the gods
but that he failed in his duty to love and respect his father. Ancient Greeks were hardly unique in putting a high
value on filial piety, familial solidarity, and the duties of
kinship. These are moral tendencies so common, both in
primitive societies and advanced civilizations, that they
can be regarded as universal human traits. Of course, every
traditional society has its own peculiar customs and laws,
which make generalizations difficult; nonetheless, ancient
Greeks, Romans, and Jews, as well as Medieval Italian and
North European societies, converge upon a norm that can
be detected under the surface of the details.

Convergent norms are not iron laws, and it is a mistake to
draw broad generalizations from what might be eccentric

examples. Sir Robert Filmer's patriarchal theory of human society is a good example of taking a basically true position to almost absurd lengths by looking only at a few extreme examples. Filmer, a 17th century royalist writer whom John Locke targeted in his first *Treatise of Government*, based the absolute authority of kings on the father's right to rule his family. Filmer's theory was certainly closer to human reality than his opponent's speculations about an imagined social contract, but in universalizing the Roman family and using it as the base for absolute monarchy, he laid himself open to ridicule.

In making his broad generalizations about patriarchal authority, Filmer was overly impressed by Roman law and the stories of Old Testament patriarchs, but he was not entirely wrong to emphasize paternal authority as a necessary constituent of human society. No other Mediterranean society may have accorded the lifelong power of life and death a Roman father exercised (mostly in theory) over his children; nonetheless, they all required affectionate respect from children, whose affection and respect were often expressed by the terms of addressed they used toward their parents, just as the parents' view of the children was indicated by the names they gave the

Names are often a clue. Americans are prone to name their children after celebrities or to pick fashionable names out of a book; Athenians tended to name the first son after his paternal grandfather; and even modern Jews often name children after a dead ancestor as a means of keeping a memory alive.

The Romans, and this is typically Roman, were a bit more systematic. In the later Roman Republic, a conventional name, for a member of the élite, such as Gaius Julius Cæsar, included three elements, *prænomen*, *nomen*, and *cognomen*, which precisely located a man's identity within a lineage group. The *nomen* identified him as a member of a broadly extended kindred (the Julii), while the *cognomen* placed him in a narrower descent group (the Julii Cæsares). The *prænomen* (Gaius) was selected by his parents from a rather short conventional list that was narrowed still further by family tradition.

One key to the social dissolution of North America in the 21st century can be found in the very lack of familial and social cohesion suggested by children named Justin or Dylan, Brittany or Morgan, and by the prevalence of names drawn from entertainment celebrities. Still more alarming is the decision to give children names that are not specific to one or the other gender, as if being male and female were a matter of preference like ice cream flavors or the width of a necktie. The Roman system, by contrast, is a good indicator of the social cohesion that derives from family solidarity.

The highest Roman virtue was *pietas*, the reverent loyalty we owe to our parents and our gods. Vergil's *pius Æneas*, who escaped from Troy with his household gods, leading his son by the hand and carrying his aged father Anchises on his shoulder, was the exemplary Roman. Even after his father Anchises' death, Vergil's Æneas sought his counsel by undertaking the perilous journey to the Underworld, where he is granted a vision of the souls who will distinguish themselves in future Roman history. Æneas' descent into Hell to see his descendants—who are also the ancestors of the Romans of Vergil's time—is a brilliant play on the Roman reverence for dead ancestors.

This reverence assumed concrete form in Roman rituals. In the second week of February, Romans celebrated the festival of the *Parentalia*, which culminated in a procession of the living family members who carried food to the tombs of their ancestors. Indeed, throughout the year, families marched through the streets, on great public occasions, carrying the masks of their departed predecessors. "In the midst of life we are in death," proclaims the Anglican burial service, but this important fact was perhaps appreciated even more acutely in traditional pagan societies.

From Household to Kinfolk

In everyday English usage, kinship is a broad term that covers everyone related by common descent, whether siblings or second cousins. Anthropologists, however, prefer to separate the relations between members of a nuclear family from kinship, which is used to describe the broader connections among members of a descent group or lineage. The traditional family's realm of authority, sometimes known as the familial domain, is the household, (Fortes, 2013) which was seen (and to some extent still is) as inner-directed and semi-autonomous, a familial island in a sea of, if not strangers then at least outsiders.

The image of an island is somewhat misleading, if we think of chunks of dry land widely separated from each other. Ancient Greek and Jewish families were not isolated fragments but constituent parts of archipelagoes of kindred and clan. Single households were not directly integrated into the broader society, much less into the commonwealth that coordinated their activities; instead, they acted through the mediation of the lineage–that is a group believed to be descended from a common ancestor, while lineages themselves were integrated into still broader groups, such as clans or tribes.

In Athens, a citizen might describe himself as the son of his father and a member of a particular deme and belonging to one of the Attic tribes. These demes (the word means "people" and could also refer to a village or neighborhood) and tribes (*phylai*) were *somewhat* artificial political constructions that replaced the loosely connected villages and neighborhoods and the traditional Ionian tribes of the archaic age. However, the demes, though arbitrarily established by Cleisthenes before the Persian Wars, tended nonetheless to be clusters of family groups.

There were also lineages or clans known as *gene* (singular *genos*), which also played an important role in Athenian social life. For example, disputes over citizenship and thus inheritance were not settled exclusively among individuals or households but involved either the *genos* or *phratry*. The unity of households and extended families was necessary for the protection of the members, and, likewise, the unity of the clan was necessary to advance the interests of the familial households. When the authority of these broader lineage-groups is eroded, nuclear families turn inevitably to the power of government to support their rights or resolve disputes.

The broadest generalization one can make about kin and family relations is that they include a universal pattern of deference: Children defer to parents, youth to age, women to men. This reality lies behind Aristotle's observation that friendships (which includes kinship) between fathers and sons are unequal. [Eth Nic VIII.7, 1158b16] In a traditional society, kin relationships are typically between unequals (husbands and wives, parents and children, seniors and juniors), though they were none the less binding. Close relatives were supposed to assist each other in a variety of ways, and the more severe the crisis, *e.g.*, loss of parents, the greater the burden on the kin, whose duty it was to assist and support their relatives.

Kinship is largely a natural relationship by blood and sexual pairing, but it is also construed socially in different ways by different peoples. In the extreme case, the social construction may even confuse or obscure the natural connection between sex and children, though one has to be careful in reading earlier anthropological accounts that claimed that this or that group of Australian aborigines did not know how babies are made. If an anthropologist today were to visit an American suburb and ask carefully crafted questions, he might dutifully record that the inhabitants of Schaumburg, Illinois, thought men and women had the same physical and attributes, that one could easily switch from one gender to the next, that homosexual unions were as happy and stable as Christian marriages. If the same anthropologist were to visit a local tavern later that night, the jokers around the bar would quickly disabuse him of his illusions.

The vast possibilities of kin relations are reflected in the variety of terms used by different languages to describe different relationships. Many European languages, *for example*, ancient (and modern) Greek and modern Serbian, distinguish between uncle as mother's brother and as father's brother and, in the case of Serbian, between the husband of father's sister and the husband of mother's sister. While English has lost such fine distinctions, we once had the word "eme" (Germanic *Oheim*) for a mother's brother or brother-in-law, and we still have the clumsy term "orthocousin" to distinguish the children of same-sex siblings from mere cross-cousins.

It is possible, of course, to devise a comprehensive and precise set of terms to cover all possible relationships, and, to clarify these relations, anthropologists have devised several useful terms. If you have an agnate relative, the two of you share descent from a common male ancestor. This social structure can also be termed "patrilineal." If you are cognates, you may be related through either a male or female ancestor, while affines, by contrast, are relatives by marriage.

Societies where social position and property are inherited through the female line are described as matrilineal. As for the terms patriarchal and matriarchal, they are imprecise and misleading. If by "patriarchal," we mean that a society is politically, socially, and economically dominated by males, then all known human societies are patriarchal, and there is no such thing as matriarchy. So long as we are aware of the realities, we can apply "matriarchal" to societies in which women overtly play a larger role than is common, but it is important to bear in mind that there is no necessary correspondence between ideologies of gender and the reality of human life. It used to be said that in France, where women had few if any legal rights, they reigned supreme, while in England, where legal rights were guaranteed by law, women exercised far less influence. An even clearer example is presented by classical Athens, a city in which a strong patriarchy was declared by law and custom, but it was Athenian men who created some of the strongest tragic heroines—Clytæmestra, Antigone, Medea, and Phædra—and where Aristophanes (in *Lysistrata*, *Thesmophoriazusæ*, and *Ecclesizusæ*)—could imagine a rebellion of wives against their husbands.

Abstract terminology can, however, obscure the social and cultural realities of kinship that are more effectively (if not always precisely) expressed in a natural language. I know a Serbian couple in which the husband is from Vojvodina (northern Serbia between Belgrade and Hungary) and the wife from Nis (in Southeastern Serbia near the Bulgarian border). She is quite careful in using the precise terms to distinguish maternal from paternal relatives, while he is negligent and, according to his wife, cannot always remember the proper terms. Some of the differences may be due to temperament or gender, but they may also reflect a differing valuation of kin relationships in the more traditional southeast from the more westernized north.

A similar problem crops up when we speak too broadly, as I did above, about the ancient Greek distinction between paternal and maternal relations. In Homer and in archaic poetry, it is true, such distinctions are made, and they are recorded by later grammarians. (Miller, 1953) In Attic Greek (spoken in classical Athens), however, there is no distinction between maternal and paternal uncles, and there is only one term (κηδεστς) used to refer to "one's sister's husband, one's daughter's husband, and the father or brother of one's wife. The term is even applied to one's stepfather and to the husband of one's wife's sister." (Thompson, 1971) One might speculate—though I have no wish to do so at this point—that this simplified terminology has something to do with the Attic legal system that put emphasis on bilateral descent and on the significance of male affines.

Conventionally, anthropologists and historians have categorized descent systems as patrilineal, when property and/or status are inherited from or through the father's line, matrilineal, when it is through the mother's, or some form of *cognatic* system in which both sides are taken into consideration. Human realities, as we shall see when we take up marriage, can be more complicated.

Kinship is rooted in genetic reality. Genetically, I inherit 50% of my makeup from each parent, but they are not necessarily my closest relatives, since I am potentially anywhere from 50% to 100% related to siblings. I share only 25% with grandparents, aunts and uncles, and 12.5% with first cousins, and so on. It would be possible, then, to construct a kinship system based on these percentages, but such a system, if applied to any real society, would not take account of other preferences which might privilege vertical descent over other relations, male over female (or vice versa).

Kinship is primarily a social structure, if anything *the* social structure. It is also, however, a moral structure that dictates forms of behavior. Summing up a survey of several African societies, Meyer Fortes emphatically stated the basic premise of his widely influential research: "Kinship is binding; it creates inescapable moral claims and obligations." (Fortes, 2013, pp. 239-42) The closest analogy he can find is with the Christian notion of charity. In this sense then, kinship is the means by which human beings learn to treat each other fairly, kindly, and generously, and it shares moral territory with friendship, brotherhood, and citizenship.

The familial law of love, translated into the domain of kinfolks, becomes what Meyer Fortes has termed the "axiom of amity," a moral imperative for members of the kindred to help each other. Universalized in the early Church, it becomes the that virtue of charity which St. Paul regarded as supreme and indispensable. If virtues are not the mere abstractions to which they have been reduced by the liberal tradition, then they are forged in childhood by the experiences of kith and kin. It remains to be seen whether we can learn to treat our fellow citizens–much less all men–as brothers if we do not know how to treat our literal brothers and cousins.

THE FAMILY COMMONWEALTH

The idea of the family as a little commonwealth upon which the health and safety of the greater commonwealth depends is very old. Aristotle treated the familial household as the genesis of the political community, while Cicero (echoing earlier philosophers) described the family as the *seminarium*, that is, the seed-bed of the commonwealth. This way of thinking and talking about the family, taken over by the Christian Church, featured prominently in the English Common Law tradition in which the framers of the American Constitution were educated. Few of the leading American rebels–the obvious exceptions being Franklin and Paine–had any idea of attacking the family, either in the narrow or extended sense, but in retrospect we shall be able to see that a secession from the authority of the Crown and the Parliament gave an opportunity to social revolutionaries who wished to liberate the individual from the familial ties that bind.

Neither Socrates nor his student Plato (who wrote the *Euthyphro*) are the first people one would think of as defenders of family values. Socrates neglected his own wife and children in order to improve the minds of his fellow-citizens, and Plato proposed a model republic in which marriage and parenthood (as the Greeks understood those institutions) were virtually eliminated from the ruling class. Plato's *Republic*, however, was speculation; when the time came for a practical decision on who would run the Academy after his demise, the choice was not Plato's most brilliant student, Aristotle, but his nephew Speusippos.

Socrates, whatever his shortcomings were as husband and father, seems genuinely disturbed by Euthyphro's disloyalty to his father, more shocked, perhaps, than many of us today might be, since we are frequently told that it is our duty to inform on friends or parents who take drugs, possess illegal weapons, or harbor subversive political views. In the modern era we do not feel as tightly bound to our immediate family, and we might be tempted to side with Euthyphro, who could justify his suit by pointing to a large number of legal cases in the United States and Europe. There are, for example, children who have sued their parents for divorce or have testified to abuse or neglect. In one celebrated Cold War case, a twelve year-old son of immigrants from the Ukraine refused to return home with his parents and gained the support of the US State Department. The story was repeated in 2000, when the father of Elian Gonzalez tried to reclaim his son, who had been virtually kidnapped by his late ex-wife's relatives. Since the Cold War was over, law and common sense prevailed, and Juan Gonzalez was able to take his son home to Cuba, but other fathers (and husbands) have not got off so lightly. In both cases American conservatives, demonstrating a fatal mixture of political cynicism and moral obtuseness, sided with government against the actual families.

Wives have accused their husbands of "marital rape," which would have struck many people, until recent years, as a contradiction in terms, and some have been compelled to testify against husbands accused of child abuse. Judges have even imprisoned pregnant women in order to protect their unborn children from the effects of the mother's drug-taking, although the same judges would uphold the mother's right to abort the child.

An ordinary Athenian would be astonished, not only by these cases themselves, but also by the social and political system that could give rise to them. An Athenian (or Roman or Jewish) family was not one of our own powerless and feeble nuclear families but as a semi-sovereign community. Economically, the family and extended kin were autonomous: there was no social security–it was up to children to take care of aged parents just as it was a strict obligation of fathers and guardians to provide dowries for girls. Any breach would result in loss of social status. Although there were laws against incest and, at times, against marriage with non-citizens, the household (*oikos*) "enjoyed a stable position as the basic social unit of classical Athens throughout the Classical period..." The citizens who passed regulations were themselves members of families, often heads of families, and "most of the time they evidently preferred that the *oikos* should be left to manage its own affairs." (Roy, 1999) There were no state schools, much less school attendance laws, no truant officers, welfare case workers, child protection advocates. Within its own sphere, kinship reigned supreme.

The classical Greek *polis* give us clear examples of a civilized and urban people that preserved more than a few traces of a social organization based on kinship. These *poleis* (or city-states) were regions, usually small, with an urban capital. Beneath the upper level of the polis, with its political institutions, there was "a network of subdivisions of the citizen body..some territorial, others based on personal relationships," which were in origin kin-relations whose ties of blood had gradually become fictionalized, as in the Scottish clans. (Hanson, 2006, p. 114)

Among some less-developed peoples, kinship must do duty for political organization, but there is no one single pattern that can be made an archetype. In Medieval and modern Europe (as well as in the United States), the overall significance of the extended family may be overstated or understated, depending on the point of view of the interpreter and the subject he has chosen to study.

The terms of the debate were set by the exceptionalist arguments laid out with clarity by Bernard Bailyn, who emphasized the growing individualism stimulated by New World experiences. Other historians have (correctly) emphasized on the continuity of British family patterns in the New World, (Greven, 1972) and pointed to persistence of family pressures even in the absence of traditional patriarchal structures. (Snydacker, 1982, pp. 42-43)

Cross-cultural generalizations are difficult, and within the United States, different customs were practiced in different regions. Even in the study of one state, such as South Carolina, different conclusions can be drawn from studying upcountry rural communities and a commercial center like Charleston. (Crowley, 1986) Upcountry farmers tended to mention extended kin in their wills (as beneficiaries or executors), whereas in Charleston, a commercial city marked by high mortality, social mobility, and contractual relations, non-kin are mentioned at least, as much if not more, so than kin.

Generally speaking, rural, traditional, and homogeneous societies tend to be more kin-based than those that are urban, cosmopolitan, and ethically mixed, but this bland generalization is an overstatement.

In 14th-century Ghent, a commercial center in what is now Belgium, "most persons felt kinship with a far greater number of individuals and nuclear families than do their modern counterparts." (Nicholas, 1985, p. 117) So long as a nuclear family was intact, there was little opportunity or necessity for intervention, but if, for example, a father died, the extended kin stepped in to assist the family. In such a society care of the elderly is the responsibility of their children, or, failing them, the broader kin-group, and, if a girl's father is dead, then her brothers. In giving up the constraints exercised by clan and extended kin, nuclear families also sacrifice the security such broader connections afford.

Advocates of state-controlled social services say inevitably that governments have merely responded to the failure of families and kindreds to regulate their own affairs. Sometimes, the failures are ascribed to crises such as industrialization; others, it is human nature itself that is at fault. A Machiavellian or a student of Public Choice Theory may be forgiven a little skepticism: Why is it that in every crisis it is government agencies and agents that increase their income and power? At the beginning of the 20th Century, the radical Georges Sorel posed a similar question, asking why it was that every revolution waged in the name of human rights ended by consolidating the power of the State?

Suppose, for a moment, that Euthyphro came asking for our advice. What should we say to him? Social workers and judges would no doubt give the predictable answer that justified their own powers, but someone with no personal stake in the game might wonder if it can be right to prosecute your own father, even if you are acting according to the highest and noblest of motives. Most Athenians would have been shocked by such a prosecution, which, although it was not illegal at Athens (as it would be in Rome), offended their deep sense of family autonomy. Athenians were not even supposed to go take their distant kinsmen to court, and when they did (in cases of disputed inheritance) they often felt the need to justify their action.

What lessons can we take from this rereading of Athenian social life? Leftists, progressives, and liberals who are committed to the Revolutionary tradition will simply sigh and conclude that while the Athenians may have built a beautiful city and written great works of literature, they were only a first attempt, albeit an interesting one, at liberating mankind from the shackles of blood and fear. Such people may prefer the art of Picasso and Pollock, the music of Schoenberg and Cage, and the plays of David Mamet, August Wilson, and Neil Simon. Peace to them and their house, and may they never have their eyes opened, never realize what they have done.

Many people living in this new millennium experience a conflict between their minds, which have accepted all the usual precepts of liberty, equality, and fraternity, and their hearts which continue to pump the blood of our ancestors and feel the tidal pull of kinship much as their senses feel the tug of beauty when they first see the cathedral in Pisa or Sienna. Educated liberals and conservatives, however, may find cold comfort in the realization that the art and literature they were brought up to admire—everything from the Parthenon and Euripides to Vergil and the Pantheon, Dante and the cathedrals of Tuscany, Shakespeare, Milton, and Christopher Wren—were created by retrograde societies that revered the ties of blood and feared divine wrath. Turning uneasily to our own society, whose art and literature (if they have any taste or discrimination) they must deplore, they might begin to wonder if the political ideology on which they have been nurtured really corresponds to human reality.

If once they have experienced this wonder, it may quickly turn into a feeling of bewilderment that will demand further investigation. If the ties of blood have bound human beings in families, kindreds, and communities in such places as Greece and Rome, Israel and Medieval Europe, what is the nature of those ties and how have they been realized in human institutions and societies? Was it entirely wise for Western legal systems to have devastated kinship and reduced our sense of family to one or two generations? They may even begin to ask whether, in liberating ourselves from all the ties of blood and affection, we have constructed a new Eden or fallen into a posthuman darkness that is not the savagery of wild animals but the depraved bestiality of zoo animals.

REFERENCES

Crowley, J. E. (1986). The Importance of Kinship: Testamentary Evidence from South Carolina. *The Journal of Interdisciplinary History*, 16(4), 559–577.

Fortes, M. (2013). *Kinship and the Social Order.: The Legacy of Lewis Henry Morgan*. Routledge.

Greven, P. J. (1972). *Four Generations: Population, Land, and Family in Colonial Andover, Massachusetts*. (Vol. 134). Cornell University Press.

Hanson, M. (2006). *Polis: An Introduction to the Ancient Greek City-State*. Oxford University Press.

Kidd, I. (1990). The Case of Homicide in Plato's Euthyphro. *Owls to Athens. Essays on Classical Subjects Presented to Sir Kenneth Dover, Oxford*, 213–21.

Miller, M. (1953). Greek Kinship Terminology. *The Journal of Hellenic Studies*, 73, 46–52.

Nicholas, D. (1985). *The Domestic Life of a Medieval City: Women, Children, and the Family in Fourteenth-Century Ghent*. University of Nebraska Press.

Roy, J. (1999). Polis and Oikos in Classical Athens 1. *Greece & Rome*, 46(1), 1–18.

Snydacker, D. (1982). Kinship and Community in Rural Pennsylvania, 1749-1820. *The Journal of Interdisciplinary History*, 13(1), 41–61.

Thompson, W. E. (1971). Attic Kinship Terminology. *The Journal of Hellenic Studies*, 91, 110–113.

Westermarck, E. (1908). *The Origin and Development of the Moral Ideas*. (Vol. 2). Macmillan.

Kinship: Embracing and Refraining

Those privileged to be present at a family
festival of the Forsytes have seen that
charming and instructive sight–an upper
middleclass family in full plumage.

So John Galsworthy begins his "saga" of the Forsyte
clan, adding that a psychologically astute observer
would have

"gleaned from a gathering of this family—no branch
of which had a liking for the other, between no three
members of whom existed anything worthy of the
name of sympathy—evidence of that mysterious concrete tenacity which renders a family so formidable
a unit of society, so clear a reproduction of society in
miniature. He has been admitted to a vision of the
dim roads of social progress, has understood something of patriarchal life, of the swarmings of savage
hordes."

Galsworthy was writing of the late 19th century, when bour-
geois families were not yet isolated households that grudgingly acknowledged bonds extending no further than from
grandparents to grandchildren; they were in fact ramified
kin-groups of considerable complexity. Almost servile in
their obedience to the conventions of society, Galsworthy's
fictional Forsytes appreciated the advantages of the stable

217

home. "To break up a home is at the best a dangerous experiment, and selfish into the bargain." Young Jolyon Forsyte, who had broken up a home, reflects,

> "The core of it all," he thought, "is property, but there are many people who would not like it put that way. To them it is 'the sanctity of the marriage tie'; but the sanctity of the marriage tie is dependent on the sanctity of the family, and the sanctity of the family is dependent on the sanctity of property. And yet, I imagine all these people are followers of One who never owned anything. It is curious!"

Galsworthy wrote in an age when the extended family, rooted in property and inheritance, was beginning to crumble under the onslaught of, first classical liberal, then Marxist-socialist legislation. Despite the cynicism of his tone, he was not unaware of the value of the old stability:

> "Is there any institution—religious, moral, philanthropic, or cultural—that is not ballasted by ties of interest and property? Can there be any attitude more naive than that of the skeptical dreamer who imagines human life could, even in a monastery, do without its selfish foundations? Certainly, the One who lived without property or marriage, did not think so. A naive Jesus would have told his host at the wedding of Cana to drink plain water and would have sent bride and bridegroom packing, to reflect in solitude on higher things than marrying and begetting heirs."

In speculating on his imaginary Jesus, Galsworthy might have been reflecting on some Gnostic "gospel," which portrayed Him as a fanatical ascetic. In the canonical Gospels, the Master, while holding out the promise of abundant life, was not immune to the ordinary sentiments of the humanity He had in common with his kinsmen and disciples. He subjected himself to his parents, showed no reluctance to express his affection for the family of Lazarus, and selected most of his disciples from the region in which he had grown up. His disciples did not learn to call each other "friends" and "brothers," because their teacher despised friendship and kinship.

DIGRESSION: THE FAMILY FIRM

Galsworthy's Forsytes were an extended family, that is to say, a complex network of kinfolks, tracing their descent from an 18th century farmer named Jolyon Forsyte–their interests have intersected and interconnected in such a way as to view them as a family business.

There are many well-established business dynasties, such as the Rothschilds, the Rockefellers, and the Kennedys, but by far the most successful and famous of them all are the descendants of Albert of Saxe-Coburg and his wife Victoria, in other words, the British royal family whose surname today–if we properly take the name of the senior male progenitor at his birth–is Battenburg. The implications were best summed up by Prince Philip, as he is known, who once wrote a letter informing his daughter-in-law that by her indiscretions she had "let down the firm."

Any corporation not based on a family suffers from nepotism and conflicting loyalties, but a family firm–*the* family firm in particular–has a great obligation to maintain solidarity and keep up a good face. The estimated net worth of the Battenburg/Mountbatten-Windsor family approaches

90 billion dollars. As their pervasive presence in British and American newspapers attests, the family brand is worth a great deal, so much, indeed, that it has survived the shenanigans of Albert Edward, otherwise known as Edward VII or Eddy, the brief reign and disastrous marriage of Albert Edward's grandson Edward VIII, the sexual escapades of Queen Elizabeth's randy son Andrew and vulgar wife, her sister's and daughter's divorces, to say nothing of the failed marriage of her spoiled son and heir, Charles, and his even more spoiled wife. As if this were not enough scandal to bring down any monarchy including the papacy, they had to face the hijinks of Prince William's brother and his Hollywood wife.

As the marriage of Prince Charles and Princess Diana was falling apart, there was talk of either dissolving the monarchy or passing over Charles in favor of his son William, but "time that puts all things to sleep" quiets gossip and calms temperaments. Charles has grown into an obedient son, who with his son William, provide shelter for the family during the trials created by a B-list actress who snared the celebrity she so eagerly pursued. Prince Philip, an admirable bastion of the proprieties that do not depend on moral virtue, *is said* to have informed Prince Harry that of course one steps out with actresses, but one does not not marry them.

As the family closes ranks and adjusts its tactics, it is hard not to hear echoes of lines, from other branches of the same profession, that "the show must go on." I can almost hear the Queen applying the language of the movie *Forty-Second Street*, as she urges on the ingenue daughter-in-law who has to step in to fill the void created by the defection of Meghan Markle:

"Now, Middleton, you listen to me and you listen hard. 200 people, 200 jobs, $200,000 dollars [multiply all the numbers by a thousand], five weeks of grind and blood and sweat depend upon you. It's the lives of all these people who've worked with you. You've got to go on, and you have to give and give and give. They've got to like you, they've got to. Do you understand? You can't fall down, you can't, because your future's in it, my future and everything all of us have is staked on you. All right now, I'm through. But you keep your feet on the ground, and your head on those shoulders of yours and go out. And Middelton, you're going out a youngster, but you've *got* to come back a star."

"Marrying and begetting heirs" is as much a major concern of families and kindreds as is the preservation of property, and, while the acquisition of heirs and property is an important right within any conceivable society, these rights cannot be exercised or maintained, if the possessor does not accept the burdens that go with them. Generally speaking, then, it can be said that kinship confers both benefits and obligations. Of the debts owed to kinfolks–particularly the debts of blood–more will be said in the next volume. It is the benefits that occupy our attention here. The primary formal benefit derived from kin relations is the capacity to inherit property and social (and civic) status. Since the perpetuation of identity and the transmission of property are essential features of marriage and kinship, they are circumscribed by rules, determining not only who may inherit what from whom, but, even more basically, who can legitimately marry whom in order to produce legitimate heirs.

I N C E S T

The question of who may marry whom is raised in one of the most famous scenes of English literature: The dialogue is between Prince Hamlet and his Uncle Claudius, who has married the widow of Hamlet's father.

> *Claudius*: But now, my cousin Hamlet, and my son.–
> *Hamlet*: A Little more than kin, and less than kind.

Hamlet's response to his uncle/step-father has puzzled some readers and critics for centuries. Does he refer to himself, as seems natural in the dramatic context, or to Claudius? Our answer depends in part on what we think the words mean. "A little more than kin" is easy enough, since Claudius has married his brother's wife, Hamlet's mother Gertrude, but how "less than kind"? Etymologically "kind" refers to the nature we have by birth or descent from our ancestors, but even in Shakespeare's day it could be used as an adjective with the meaning "gentle" or "charitable." Some readers have taken Hamlet's sarcasm as a reference to Claudius' lack of kindness in murdering his brother and taking his wife, but others–and surely they are right–have thought of the unnaturalness of Claudius' incestuous union with Gertrude and his kinship with the young man who is both nephew and stepson. (Even the sentence structure seems to demand that "kind" be a noun parallel to "kith.") If this interpretation is correct, then it makes little difference whether Hamlet is referring to himself or to his uncle/father. It is exactly by being more than kin that they are in an unnatural relationship with each other.

Kinship systems have many functions, and one of the most important is the power to declare who may marry whom. In the ancient and Medieval Church, marriage with a deceased brother's wife was forbidden–hence Hamlet's condemnation a few lines later of his mother's

> wicked speed, to post
> with such dexterity to incestuous sheets.

The prohibition goes back to the Old Testament. While a brother was obliged to beget children by a dead brother's wife, if her husband had died without heirs, such a marriage was otherwise forbidden. John the Baptist was killed for criticizing Herod Antipas' marriage to his brother's wife Herodias. [Luke 3:19-20]

Speaking in broad terms, one can say that most societies have prohibited marriage between persons who are related vertically in close degree: Parents and grandparents may not marry their children or children's children nor brothers their sisters, though the Athenians permitted marriage between siblings with different mothers.

For reasons that have most to do with inheritance and the preservation of family property, Greeks had an inclination for marriage between cousins and between uncles and aunts with nieces and nephews. In the later Roman republic and under the empire, Roman law forbade marriage both between an ascendant and a descendant, and between siblings. A man could not marry his sister's daughter, granddaughter, or great granddaughter. Too much is made of the Emperor Claudius' marriage to his niece Agrippina. (Treggiari, 1991, pp. 37-39) He was emperor, after all, and his example, though imitated by a few sycophants, did not alter Roman attitudes. In earlier times marriage between first and even second cousins was prohibited at Rome, though later on these became acceptable. (Shaw & Saller, 1984) Romans also generally applied their rules to relations by adoption and by marriage. A man could not, for example, marry either his stepmother or stepsister.

There are some obvious advantages to avoiding close inbreeding: Some genetically transmitted defects are carried on recessive genes that are more likely to remain unexpressed until they are matched with the same gene; inbreeding also eliminates the beneficial genetic variation that results from outbreeding, though it is also argued that excessive outbreeding can result in physiological difficulties.

In theory, a successful mating strategy would take the middle road: a preference for mates that were similar to one's relatives but sufficiently different to avoid dysgenic effects and encourage variety. It has been argued that the most effective means of eliminating undesirable genetic traits would be to encourage inbreeding that would hasten the death and non-reproduction of individuals bearing those traits,(Bateson, 2005, pp. 33-35) but this is a strategy that few men and women would knowingly adopt. To what degree incest-taboos are a stockbreeder's response to genetic problems or a socially constructive mechanism for building stable families is a matter of dispute I shall leave to the dueling advocates of biological and environmental determinism, but the development and enforcement of these taboos may well be, as Westermarck argued, a means of suppressing behavior that has been acknowledged as abnormal.

The Roman kinship system was rational as well as comprehensive. If I may not marry my brother's daughter, I may also not marry, were my wife to be deceased, my brother-in-law's daughter. A reformer would doubtless find these minute regulations overly fussy; however, legal tinkering with such a system might seriously damage the familial and social fabric. In an early 20th century novel, Nancy Mitford's *Love in a Cold Climate*, Lord and Lady Montdore have a daughter who wants to marry her aunt's widowed husband who was also, to make matters worse, Lady Montdore's lover. The news scandalizes an old-fashioned friend, Lady Alconleigh, who has only just learned that such a marriage is now legal in Britain:

> "Would you believe that anything so disgustingly dreadful could be allowed?...What a law. Whenever was it passed? Why it's the end of all family life."

Lady Alconleigh's consternation is understandable, since marriage to an uncle-in-law was legalized only in 1931, roughly the dramatic date of the novel.

Early Christian rules combined Jewish and Roman traditions. The resultant system of the Middle Ages was unbearably strict, forbidding, potentially, marriage between a man and woman related up to seven degrees of consanguinity.(Sheehan, 1997, pp. 119-125) If applied severely, the rule would have prohibited marriage between sixth cousins. Fortunately, common sense and the Church's dispensing power worked to ameliorate the harshness, but disputes over marital regulation played an important part in the Protestant revolt and even afterwards continued to divide Anglicans from Calvinists.

Incest avoidance rules play an important part in defining family and kinship. They were not created by governments or even by the Medieval church, which elaborated them beyond a reasonable degree. They developed, instead, through countless interactions between and among families and kin-groups seeking to perpetuate their identities and their properties. As irrational as these rules may seem–for example, the Roman inclusion of adoptive relationships–they make part of larger social structures that can be tampered with only at risk of causing difficulties that are not always easy to foresee. When prohibitions on second-cousin marriages became inconvenient in the Roman world, the prohibition was not eliminated by an imperial fiat: It simply faded away gradually. Modern governments, however, by a stroke of the pen, can legalize any marital union. Indeed, the incest taboo appears to be the next barrier to be broken by the revolution against marriage and the family. Marriages between uncles and nieces are becoming legal, and the Ethics Council that advises the German government has recommended a relaxation of incest rules for siblings.

These moves have not gone unchallenged or uncriticized, but the principal object of the opponents of liberalization seems to be to protect children from predatory older relatives. What they appear not to recognize is the fundamental threat to family and kinship. In traditional societies, close kin and family relations are virtually defined by the prohibition of marriage, and, as is the case with any complex eco-system, tampering with one aspect of a system can have far-reaching consequences. While each man's death may not diminish us, our understanding and valuation of marriage and family may well be diminished by a revolutionary abolition of traditional rules.

Of course rules on incest vary: Marriages between cousins or uncle and niece, while frequently taboo, are in some societies legal and acceptable, but if such rules are changed arbitrarily, these changes entail–or ratify–deeper changes in the social structure. No sane society could permit siblings to marry with each other or parents with children, because such unions in principle violate the very nature of the family. If governments legalize such unions, then those governments have redefined family much as they have, in legitimating same-sex unions, redefined both marriage and family. If I may marry my sister in New Jersey, it is because the ruling class of New Jersey has decided that family members are mere individuals, no different from anyone else.

DEATH IS NOT THE END

Modern men and women tend to look at relatives outside the immediate family in largely in economic terms. From whom can we expect a legacy? Who might hit us up for a loan? How expensive a gift do we have to provide when a nephew graduates or a niece gets married? Jews, Greeks, and Romans, while they were perhaps even more keenly interested in such material advantages and disadvantages, were also interested in the continuity of the bloodline and in the carrying out of ritual obligations,

Although we moderns look at questions of inheritance largely in economic terms, Jews, Greeks, and Romans were also interested in the continuity of the bloodline and in the carrying out of ritual obligations, particularly to the dead testator and his ancestors. The eldest son in a Jewish family, in return for his larger share in the wealth, had to carry out funereal duties for his father and take his place in the religious tradition.

In Athens, where citizenship had to be proved by the phratry, the vital fact of citizenship was bound up with dead ascendants. Places of burial were not "memorial gardens" to be visited only occasionally: The place of burial bound the living to their ascendancy:

"In Athens, when the archons-to be are examined for their eligibility, they have to prove their full citizenship not only by naming their parents and grandparents but also by stating 'where they have their Zeus Herkeios and their Apollo Patroos and their family graves.'"(Burkert, 1985, pp. 255-256)

The survival and success of the *oikos*–the "house" as a metaphor for the family as a property-holding corporation that lived on from generation to generation–was a major concern for Athenians. In adopting an heir, a man was insuring the continuity of his *oikos*, but it was essential to both the birth and the adoptive families that the adopted son forfeit all claim to the property of the family into which he had been born.

The family's continuity insured the maintenance of the sacrifices and rituals owed to dead ancestors. Among the most important of these duties was the burial of a deceased kinsman. The heir had the primary responsibility to see that the rites were carried out properly without any involvement of the dead man's enemies. Families had their own places of burial, and part of an Athenian's proof of citizenship was his ability to identify where his family buried.(Lacey, 1968, pp. 147-150) The city's interest in these rituals was not limited to questions of citizenship. In a political community like Athens, the rituals of the family were mingled with community festivals, such as the Apatouria, at which the phratries paid honor to their dead, and the Anthesteria, during which the ghosts of dead ancestors were revered and dismissed for another year. The Romans, if anything, were even more reverent toward their dead ancestors.

At a funeral during the Roman Republic, there were grave formalities to be observed: The procession was led by musicians, followed by sons with veiled heads and bareheaded daughters. Men wore the masks of their ancestors and put on the garments that typified the high offices held by those ancestors. According to Plutarch and Polybius, an effigy of the dead man wearing his own mask was carried on a funeral bed.(Turcan, 2001, p. 27)

For Romans (and other traditional peoples), the dead have not entirely gone away. They may, in the manner of Greek heroes, bless their descendants and people in the neighborhood, or, if they are offended, they may prove troublesome. Once a year at the *Parentalia* (nine days in February), Roman families honored their ancestors, whose shades (*Manes*) were brought offerings, and exorcised any malevolent intentions that might have been provoked. Ovid tells the traditional tale (which he does not believe) that when on one occasion the rites had not been observed, ghosts left their tombs and threatened Rome. [*Fasti* II 533 ff.] In May they celebrated the *Lemuria*, whose rites were generally aimed at exorcizing evil spirits. Traditional Catholics preserve this understanding of the awesome dead by celebrating All Saints and All Souls.

There are countless Christian rituals and customs honoring dead ancestors. In many families, the names given to children pay tribute to grandparents or more distant ancestors whose memory is preserved by a living descendant. The Orthodox Serbs have a unique custom, the *Slava,* an annual ceremonial meal that honors the family's patron saint, which is the patron of the father's ancestors, and commemorates the day on which a remote pagan ancestor was christened.

We have nothing quite like the Greek and Roman attachment to places of burial in the American experience;

nonetheless, tending graves used to be taken seriously by family members. In the South, this obligation was felt very strongly. The importance of place and the family burial ground is a commonplace in the list of North/South distinctions. "What do you do for a living?" the Northerner inevitably asks, while the Southerner just as inevitably responds (or used to respond) with his question, "Where are you from?" or sometimes, if he is speaking to another Southerner, "Where do your people bury?" Andrew Lytle, who frequently made this distinction in conversation, celebrated familial piety in his family memoir, *A Wake for the Living,* whose very title is evocative. In the world in which Lytle grew up, the connection to kinfolk was a vital necessity, but in the world in which he grew old, the bonds had weakened:

> "If you don't know who you are or where you come from, you will find yourself at a disadvantage. The ordered slums of suburbia are made for the confusion of the spirit. Those who live in units called homes or estates–both words do violence to the language–don't know who they are. For the profound stress between that union that is the flesh and the spirit, they have been forced to exchange the appetites."

Mr. Andrew (as he was known to friends and disciples) had lived long into postmodernity. The last time I saw him was the occasion of his 90th birthday. After the ceremony, he invited Mel and Marie Bradford–with me as an appendage–to the Log Cabin for quiet conversation. He was tired, after so much rigmarole, but his mind was still lively, though it dwelt much on the past I could not help thinking that he was, perhaps, fortunate in not living any longer. He would have been far more at home in the Roman Republic than in Schaumburg, Illinois.

At an American funeral in the 21st century, relatives and friends arrive at the funeral parlor or church, dressed in every style and color, and, when they are not consoling the widow and children, they speak casually of sports and entertainment. I frequently hear people even older than I am say things like, "I am so glad we don't have to wear black any more–dark colors are so depressing, don't you think? Aunt Joan would not have wanted us to feel sad..." Nonetheless, we still take sufficient interest in the dear departed, when there is money or property to be inherited.

Men and women who have little regard for past ancestors will probably not waste too much energy thinking about future descendants. It is all too common for Americans, when they retire, to go in search of eternal youth in Florida or Arizona. moving far away from the friends of their youth, their children and grandchildren. If they are rich enough, they can afford to visit and receive visits, occasionally, from their descendants, but if they are of limited means, visits may be limited to once or twice a year. I wonder what postmoderns think of the comic French film *Les Visiteurs* in which a Medieval French knight (Jean Reno) is transported to the 1990's. Seeing his descendant, some 20 to 30 generations later, he sighs, "Ma descendence!" My posterity–it sounds odd in English, because we cannot imagine anyone caring about distant posterity, much less envisioning our whole posterity summed up in a single person. In the beginning of his descent on modern France, the knight is simply a fool who is terrified of traffic and does not understand the use of soap. By the end of the film, even a dull-witted modern should begin to sympathize with his bizarre attachment to a remote descendant.

S T A T E L E S S   C O M M U N I T I E S

If our Medieval knight had fallen into the hands of a team of academic philosophers, they would have poked and prodded him to find out what makes him tick. One might ask him, "Do you have similar feelings of obligation to your ancestors?" And, when he answered in the affirmative, they might have pushed further, and asked, "But what about other people's ancestors and descendants?" At this point the would be puzzled, recalling that most of his closest friends and neighbors, who were cousins to one degree or another, would share some ancestors and descendants with him. Exasperated, one of the professors might ask, "All right, then, what about a Saxon, a Chinese, a Hun?"

As the conversation broke down into incoherence, a professor of politics would inquire about Norman law. "Does the law or the state require such duties, and if so, shouldn't they be universal?" Sensing his bewilderment, the political philosopher reassures him: "Forget my colleague's question about Huns and Chinese and stick only to your own country. Didn't France or Normandy have oppressed minorities–Celtic Bretons, for example, or serfs? Shouldn't the state require you to apply some of your sense of obligation to victims of discrimination?"

Before the Norman begins to draw his sword, he might well ask what this thing called "the state" is, that it would presume to interfere in matters of familial devotion and feudal loyalty. In resolving our knight's dilemma, solving young Euthyphro's problem, or treating any one of the myriad social and moral problems that afflict any human society, our first task today (unless we are anarchists) would be to find out the laws that would justify the intervention of the state in the lives of individuals.

When we turn from a fictional knight to historical societies such as ancient Athens, our modern assumptions get in the way, because there was no good word for "the state," either in classical Greek or Medieval Latin or French. Though political theorists insist on translating the Greek word *polis* (city) as state, that is as an institution (at least as we understand it) which really took shape only at the end of the Middle Ages and during the early Renaissance. While the *polis* was primarily a place inhabited by interconnected kindreds, the state is an omnipotent institution–Hobbes called it "a mortal god"–that is distinct from the peoples it governs. To use an analogy, an ancient commonwealth–whether democratic, aristocratic, or autocratic–was something like a community softball team, where ties of blood and neighborhood made themselves felt even by those who were the sponsors and managers of the team. The modern state, by contrast, is something like a professional major league team that buys and sells players who can, by standing up to the management, negotiate not only their salaries but also their sale or trade to another team. It is the difference between a communal and a competitive relationship, the difference between friendship and strife.

While we today often think of the individual as being either the victim or beneficiary of the state, this way of thinking has limited relevance for the political communities that created our civilization: ancient Greeks, Romans, and Jews, Medieval Italy, France, England, and even the early American republic.

A Greek *polis,* such as Athens, was neither a corporation (as in Medieval Tuscan towns) nor a merely legal institution: It was first and foremost a community of people living in a specific place that was no random collection of land and buildings, but a particular place hallowed by gods and by the bones of dead ancestors. As a functioning community, it was not a collection of individuals, each pursuing his own preferences and opportunities, but something more like an extended family or set of interconnected families and clans. Athens, like other Greek cities was a community of households, kindreds, and other corporate groups that shaped the moral, social, religious, legal, and political lives of the people. The most important social reality was that of kinship.

Many anthropologists make a sharp distinction between the family or household, which tends toward autonomy, and the ties of kinship by which families are integrated into society. On one level, this distinction is useful, but if pushed too far it obscures the reality that each family is an outpost of (typically) one kindred united with another by marriage. The household family, then, is the basic element of the kindred just as the kindred is the basis of society or the commonwealth.

While conservative advocates of social causes like to talk about "family values," most of their policies–tougher divorce laws, stricter legal definitions of marriage, and subsidies to children from poorer families–have the effect of further subordinating the family to the state. There was a time, not so long ago, when people involved in political discussions had a basic knowledge of European culture, ancient and modern, and their historical vision was not limited to the conditions and events of their own lifetime.

The household of the 1950s and 1960s, already dependent on state-provided education, retirement benefits, and regulation, is hardly an ideal model for family independence. Even in modern Greece, the family is far more powerful than it has been in the United States for over 100 years.

Before drawing up plans to strengthen the family, conservative social reformers should divert their attention from the past two centuries, when the family has been in decline, and look instead to the formative periods of our history, when the organic bonds of kinship were stronger than the mechanical apparatus of government.

The most basic organic unit of human society, as Aristotle points out in the *Politics*, is the household. He used the word household rather than family, because neither the Greeks nor the Romans really had a good word corresponding precisely to our own concept of the family–by which we typically mean a nuclear household made up of a man and wife plus their offspring. For us, grandparents, poor relations, servants are, for the most part, viewed as temporary add-ons rather than part of the basic definition. The Greek household (like the Roman) possessed greater complexity than can be accounted for in the modern theory of the nuclear family.

Generally speaking, ancient cultures looked at what we call the family from two perspectives, the one spatial and economic, the other temporal or genetic. In a spatial sense, the family was defined by co-residence in an economically and socially autonomous household that might include more than parents and children. Since Greek has two closely related words that can be translated, depending on the context, as house, household, or family, to speak of "the family in ancient Greece" can be misleading.

Though Athenians like other Greeks had no good word for the family in our restricted sense, they made do with some rather more precise alternatives. The physical house itself was usually known as an *oikia*, while the more metaphorical meanings of house as a domestic arrangement or as a group defined by descent from a common ancestor were covered by the related–and more basic–word *oikos*. The distinction is not always as clear as historians would like, but it is *oikos* that is used when referring to "the line of descent from father to son through successive generations." More generally, the line of descent from both mother and father was known as an *anchisteia* (from *anchistos*, "nearest"), a term that indicates a capacity for inheritance or for assuming a familial obligation, *e.g.*, the duty to prosecute the killer of a relative.

Athenian law, it has been said by an authority on the subject, is a law regulating individuals, not families, since family relations are not covered by law. (MacDowell, 1999, p. 15) This statement, while true enough in one sense, is susceptible to misconstruction, because most of what went on within families is not mentioned by law precisely because the family was sovereign within its own sphere. What is more, it is by membership in a household that an Athenian was part of the larger social and political frameworks that made him subject to the law. A man without citizen-ancestors (at least on one side) could not typically be a citizen. Unless he had a citizen who protected him, the outsider possessed few legal rights, including the legal right to have his murderer punished.

Try not to think of an Athenian household as one our own powerless nuclear families but as a semi-sovereign community. Economically, the family and extended kin were autonomous. Since there was no social security, it was up to children to take care of aged parents just as it was a strict obligation of fathers and guardians to provide dowries for girls. Any breach would result in loss of social status. No police could enter; there were no schools, much less school attendance laws, no truant officers, welfare case workers, child protection advocates. Within its own sphere, kinship reigned supreme.

Ancient commonwealths were all different in their social arrangements, but there were many common themes. A Greek household was made up of the related people living under one roof, though it did not theoretically, in contrast with Rome, include the slaves. Another important difference between classical Athens and Rome is that the Athenian father did not possess a life-time *patria potestas* (paternal authority) that included a power of life and death over his adult children, though he was supposed to command their respect.

At Athens a new household was formed by a married couple. The important fact of life that sealed the marriage was that the bride moved in with the groom, either to his family's house or to a new one. The marriage had to be registered with the husband's phratry, a broader kin-group that was a cross between a clan and a religious fraternity. The purpose of marriage was, at it has always been, the production of children, and a wife had the right to have children. When the Athenian tyrant Peistratus married the daughter of his ally Megacles, the head of the powerful Alcmæonid clan, he refused to have normal sexual relations, for fear of begetting an heir whose maternal connections might encourage trouble and favor the Alcmæonid heir. The refusal to engage in procreative relations was a deadly insult and broke his political alliance with Megacles and his family. As in the story of Onan, the offense was not the unnatural sexual act but the attempt to avoid procreation.

When children came to a Greek household, they too had to be presented to the phratry brothers (*phrateres*) who, if the child's citizenship or right to inherit were challenged, might later be called upon to testify to the facts. The phratry, then, was a formal intermediary, integrating the members of a family into the commonwealth.

In ancient Greece as in Medieval and Renaissance Italy, a familial or kin relationship (that is, an *anchisteia*) can be roughly defined in both positive and negative terms. On the negative side, as a man's relative, I can also be made, whether in early Athens or late Medieval Florence, to share his criminal guilt. When (in the later 7th century) an Alcmæonid (also named Megacles) killed a group of Athenian conspirators who had taken refuge in a temple, it was not only he who was exiled but the entire clan of the Alcmæonidæ. However, on the positive side of the balance sheet, I am an *anchistes*–a blood-relative and potential heir–to someone else if I have a legal capacity to inherit property from him. In such a society, with rights and duties dictated by the structures of kinship, any man who mistreated his father, no matter how noble the cause, could be considered monstrous.

Conclusions

The ancient societies to which we owe the greatest debts expressed the significance of kinship by imposing strict rules on marriage and inheritance and reinforced them through a multiplicity of funereal and sacrificial rites. In the course of the past several centuries, the rules have been bent, weakened, and abolished and the rites decayed to the point that men and women now see themselves–and are strongly encouraged to see themselves–as individualists looking out for their own interests.

Even before national governments began in earnest to reduce familial households to dependency upon the state, they had come to regard clans and kindreds as a threat to their own growing power. One family by itself can hardly stand up against a king, but Scottish clans did just that, as did the kin-based factions that supported the Yorkist or Lancastrian claimants on the English throne during the Wars of the Roses, which were a sort of blood feud writ large. Violence between kindreds and clans, it is true, disrupt the peace and order of a society, but there can be no real peace, no order, no liberty in a society whose political class has eliminated all obstacles to its own absolute power. That is the great success of the modern state, whether it goes by the name of fascist dictatorship, People's Democracy, or the Constitutional Republic of the United States.

References

Bateson, P. (2005). Inbreeding Avoidance and Incest Taboos. In A. P. Wolff & W. H. Durham (Eds.), *Inbreeding, Incest, and the Incest Taboo: the State of Knowledge at the Turn of the Century*. Stanford University Press.

Burkert, W. (1985). *Greek Religion*. Harvard University Press.

Lacey, W. K. (1968). *The Family in Classical Greece*. Cornell University Press.

MacDowell, D. M. (1999). *Athenian Homicide Law in the Age of the Orators*. Manchester University Press.

Shaw, B. D. & Saller, R. P. (1984). Close-kin Marriage in Roman society?. *Man*, 432–444.

Sheehan, M. M. (1997). *Marriage, Family, and Law in Medieval Europe: Collected Studies*. University of Toronto Press.

Treggiari, S. (1991). *Roman Marriage: Iusti Coniuges From the Time of Cicero to the Time of Ulpian*. Oxford University Press.

Turcan, R. (2001). *The Gods of Ancient Rome: Religion in Everyday Life from Archaic to Imperial Times*. Taylor & Francis.

KINSHIP:
INHERITING THE PAST

A good man leaveth an inheritance to his
children's children: and the wealth of
the sinner is laid up for the just.

— Proverbs 13:22

A STABLE SOCIAL ORDER RESTS ON MANY FOUNDATIONS,
not the least of which is the secure possession
and orderly transmission of property from one
generation to another. Anyone with even a slight familiarity
with history must be aware that, whether he lives 30 or a
hundred years, he is floating on the thinnest surface of a
sea too deep to be plumbed. A Christian or Muslim, in
moments of faith, looks forward to eternity, but, in making
plans for next year, he may be assaulted by the knowledge
of his impotence and futility. Man is not the only creature
to face old age and death, but he is the only one cursed
with the knowledge of his mortality. "The body dies, the
body's beauty lives" is poetry, but the prose version would
read, the person dies, but he lives on in his children and
kinsmen.

Life is brief, but a kindred may go on for centuries. Our natural immortality begins in marriage, which, in uniting two
sexes and kindreds, is the foundation of the family, and if,
as people once believed, the basic function of marriage is to
create heirs to whom property and status is passed down,

then systems of kinship extend the range of the marital functions. This characterization applies to Anglo-American traditions on marriage, family, and kinship, but also to the ancient and Medieval societies from which we derive our basic understanding of how to be human. This understanding of kinship and inheritance was once universal and is still, as Wendell Berry says, the characteristic of

> "a man who knows that the world is not given by his fathers, but borrowed from his children; who has undertaken to cherish it and do it no damage, not because he is duty- bound, but because he loves the world and loves his children..."(Berry, 2006, p. 39)

Ancient Jews

Given the brevity of life and the hopes we put in our descendants, it is not surprising that the records left by earlier civilizations should display so much interest in the passing down of property. The legal systems of ancient Greeks, Romans, Indians and Chinese laid down precise rules on who could inherit some part of an estate. The Scriptures of the Old Testament also have a great deal to say about inheritance. To bequeath a good legacy to children, grandchildren, and (presumably) beyond, is a mark of virtue and divine favor, while the loss of an estate to another bloodline is a punishment for injustice. The Jewish social order rested on principles of succession and inheritance, and the rights of heirs were not dependent on the whims of a testator: In general, property was transmitted from generation to generation according to principles that were spelled out in detail by law and tradition.

Since the preservation of the family's identity and property depended upon resolute men, a man's property went to his sons, the first-born receiving a share double that of each of his brothers. In other words, if a father had four sons, his property was divided into five parts, two of which went to the eldest son, and one to each of the others. This favored status was treated as a gift from God and not as a mere human privilege, and a less favored older son, such as Esau or Reuben, might only on the rarest occasions be passed over in favor of a younger favorite. This rather limited primogeniture was not a one-sided affair but entailed corresponding duties. The first-born, who enjoyed greater power and respect than did his brothers, had the burdens of assuming a sacerdotal duties, maintaining the dignity of the family, and, probably, taking care of his mother and sisters. The fact that an eldest son had the right to decline both the double inheritance and the duties that went along with it tells us plainly that this blessing came at a price.

If a father failed to produce any sons, Moses granted a dispensation that permitted daughters to inherit [Num 21], though it was later stipulated that such heiresses must marry within the tribe to prevent the property from passing to strangers. [Num 36]. This law is a parallel to a more stringent Athenian provision that such an heiress must marry the closest male relative on her father's side.

Since the Jews were polygynous, problems might arise if a father was tempted to prefer the son of a younger wife, but he was, nonetheless, generally constrained [Deut 21:15-17] to award the double share to the son of his less favored older wife. Hard and fast rules of this type tend to discourage family disputes by removing inheritances from the whim of a capricious proprietor. In such traditional societies, the current possessor is looked upon not as a self-made individualist but as only one link in a long chain going back generations.

Inheritance was so precious to ancient Jews that it was a metaphor for the blessings they had received from the God who had granted them the Holy Land.

> "Be strong and of a good courage: for unto this people shalt thou divide for an inheritance the land, which I sware unto their fathers to give them. [Josh 1]"

Christians applied the same metaphor to the Kingdom of Heaven. In the first chapter of Colossians, Paul tells us to give:

> "thanks unto the Father, which hath made us meet to be partakers of the inheritance of the saints in light."

CONVERGENCES AND DISTINCTIONS

Inheritance customs stipulated by the Old Testament have parallels in the older societies of ancient Mesopotamia. In the early days, it would seem that land was inherited and held jointly by members of the family, and, as common property became more difficult under more urban circumstances, the sons of a property-holder (and sons of a dead brother) inherited jointly. Dowries were established either by the girl's father before his death or, if he died without making provision, by her brothers (Postgate, 2017, pp. 96-97).

Israelites and Babylonians were hardly unique in paying both high regard and careful attention to inheritance. Parallels are to be found among Sumerians and Persians, Greeks, and Romans, as well as among the Germanic tribes that destroyed the Roman Empire in the West.

Ancient Egypt provides some of the earliest surviving documentary evidence of inheritance laws; however, since Egyptian civilization spanned a period of over three millennia, generalizations are dangerous. In general, the eldest son was the principal heir, though he was supposed to support his siblings. At some point, women gained (if they had ever lacked it) the right to inherit equally with male heirs, and enjoyed the right to bequeath property (Blerk, 2019). While succession rules were probably strict in the earlier periods, a famous document of about 1000 B.C. the will of Naunakhte in the Ashmolean museum, a mother disinherits ungrateful children.

The laws and customs that regulate inheritance can teach the observer two important lessons: First, their universality—despite the great diversity—is strong evidence for the overriding importance of kinship in human societies; and, second, the diversity of the specific arrangements themselves provide insight into the nature of the societies and their hierarchy of value. In patriarchal Israel, the preservation of the patrilineal family was encouraged by restricting the heirs to male offspring, and the duties to the dead father were carried out by the eldest son, who consequently received a larger share. In Egypt, where social roles were more a function of status than sex, daughters inherited along with sons, though Egyptians, in connecting succession with obligations to the dead, showed the same concern for the afterlife that they did in other aspects of their social life.

Property and inheritance seem to have been frequently communal in the early stages of society. Although the earliest histories of societies are usually shrouded in darkness, property in ancient Mesopotamian cities was held and transmitted in common. Parallels can be found in the South Slavic *zadrugas*, patrilineal clans whose members resided on property they jointly owned, and vestiges of such a system can be seen in Athenian law, where, in the absence of a legitimate son, a dead man's male agnates (descendants of a common male ancestor) assume the rights and duties of heirs. At the other end of the spectrum is postmodern America, where in many states a father is free to disinherit his children or leave at least a large part of his estate to whomever or whatever he likes.

THE CALCULUS OF BLOOD

Complex and far-reaching rules on marriage presuppose the recognition of kinship beyond the level of the immediate family and the current generation. How far beyond can vary greatly, and the breadth or narrowness of kin-recognition is a defining element in any social system. Some suburban Californians can barely maintain contact with their siblings, while in parts of the American South, much time is still spent calculating possible kinship with new acquaintances.

One of the marks of a traditional aristocracy is an awareness of family history and an acknowledgment of kinship. In *Gone With the Wind*, Margaret Mitchell depicts the complex interrelationships of the Wilkes clan:

> "Half of Atlanta was kin to or claimed kin with Melanie and India. The ramifications of cousins, dou-

ble cousins, cousins-in-law and kissing cousins were so intricate and involved that no one but a born Georgian could ever unravel them.... They had always been a clannish tribe, presenting an unbroken phalanx of overlapping shields to the world in time of stress, no matter what their private opinions of the conduct of individual kinsmen might be."

The categories of friends, neighbors, and relations are not watertight compartments. Even first cousins may not become close if they do not have the opportunity for frequent encounters. Property, whether shared or inherited, can always strengthen such ties, and in Andalusia first cousins frequently married in order to keep property intact. A similar tactic was adopted in colonial South Carolina, though such unions were frowned upon in contemporary England. (Glover, 200, pp. 9-10) It is observed in *Gone With the Wind* that even in the mid-19th century, "Wilkeses and Hamiltons always marry their own cousins." Whatever her limitations were as a novelist, Margaret Mitchell was a careful observer of the society into which she had been born. It was part of her own inheritance.

Rules of descent and inheritance, which are the bones of human social orders, offer insights into the social priorities of a people. In establishing and enforcing rules on inheritance, a society not only protects the family but defines it in relation to the social and legal system. Property and inheritance laws, even more perhaps than incest prohibitions, are a clear indication of how societies structure their priorities. In many modern countries, a citizen may write a will leaving much or all of his wealth to person or persons outside the family; in more traditional societies, by contrast, custom and law regulate and may even dictate succession. In 16th century England and British North America, for example, estates often passed from father to eldest son by the traditional custom of primogeniture, just as in most European monarchies, a king was succeeded by his eldest son.

Primogeniture was by no means a universal rule or even a dominant tendency in inheritance laws: In many societies all the sons–or sons and daughters–might inherit equal shares. But even in societies where estates were normally passed to the eldest son, some provisions were generally made for the heir's younger brothers, who might inherit incomes or goods, and sisters, who would be provided with dowries.

To survey the variety of privileges accorded (or denied) to first-born sons would require a tedious and distracting diversion from an argument intended only to establish the enduring ethical significance of inheritance rules in general. For this present purpose, the details of any particular system do not matter, but the point lies rather in the universality of such systems in human societies.

ATHENIAN KITH AND KIN

In early Athens, there was no such thing as a will, since a man's entire estate (*kleros*) passed by strict rules to his male heirs: to his sons, if he had any still living, or, if the sons had died leaving legitimate male offspring, to his grandsons, or even more distant descendants. For his daughters he was expected to provide a dowry, which constituted their inheritance. Sons automatically inherited equal shares of the estate, unless they had been adopted into another family. If there were no sons or issue thereof, the daughters or their children inherited, but daughters were legally required to marry a close kinsman of their father, if he wished to exercise his right in order to preserve the estate. Failing any living descendants, a man's collateral relatives on his father's side became the heirs. The preference went to males up to the degree of children of first cousins. The object was to preserve the ongoing line of descent by keeping property within the network of kinfolk.

Athenian law eventually did leave room for maneuvering. A man without children might adopt a son, who would automatically inherit the entire estate or, if sons were born subsequent to the adoption, an equal share with the natural sons. A childless adult male could also make a will, devising the property to a specific set of relatives or friends. By the fourth century, even a man with sons might leave a portion of his property to others, though the nearest male relatives of the deceased could sue to have the will overturned.

Members of a Greek household generally handled their own affairs without going to law with each other. These household family groups were part of a broader clan or network of kinfolks, the *genos* (descent group), whose senior members could resolve inter-familial disputes and help to preserve common customs. The more important descent groups usually played a dominant role both in their neighborhood and in the politics of Attica.

In pre-classical Athens, the *genos* was the arbiter of disputed inheritances, and the property-owner's desires counted for little. Solon is credited with introducing the will as a legal instrument to cover cases of *epikleroi* (daughters without brothers) or families with no offspring. Whoever the author and whatever the inspiration for them, the availability of wills have an advantage in discouraging (though hardly preventing) family feuds over inheritance.

Athenian courts must have been clogged with cases of disputed succession, and virtually the entire surviving corpus of Isæus' speeches (early fourth century B.C.) is devoted to disputed legacies. A particularly rich example is the case of Cleonymus' heirs preserved in the speeches of Isæus [1]. Cleonymus had died without children, having made a will, many years before his death, giving his property to a set of friends who were also distant relatives. His sister's sons, however, made a stink, and when the heirs agreed to share with them, the nephews felt emboldened to sue for everything.

The nephews based their case on two allegations. Their first claim was that Cleonymus had only disinherited them because he was quarreling with their guardian, whom he did not wish to control his property or have responsibility for his funeral. When that guardian died, the boys moved in with Cleonymus, who helped to settle their debts and provide for their education–a fact the boys cited as evidence of their uncle's affection. In their second claim, they declared that on his deathbed Cleonymus had called for a magistrate's clerk to bring his will, presumably intending to change it, but his designated heirs would not allow the clerk to enter the house.

The nephews' case would not stand scrutiny for a moment in an American or English court, but the boys were counting on the jurors to sympathize with them. Their real case did not rest on their somewhat dubious claims about what might have happened but on the fact of blood, and their argument reveals an Athenian predilection for kinship over individual preferences, even when those preferences were set forth in an unambiguous legal document. In general, it can be said, Athenian juries were more skeptical of documents, which could always be forged, and more attentive to the probabilities of human character. In their calculations, the propinquities of blood might matter more than a piece of paper, however meticulously drawn up.

"It is only right that you should, as in fact you do, give your verdicts on the basis of the truth of the matter and on the grounds of blood-relationship (*genos*) rather than siding with those who contest the case on the basis of a will. For you all know what the relationship of the *genos* is; that cannot be falsified, but many people have falsified wills, some by making complete forgeries, in other cases wills are made by people not in their right mind."

The nephews are obviously suggesting that any uncle who would disinherit his beloved nephews would have been out of his head, thus the will–which he allegedly drew up in a fit of anger–is false on one of two counts: either because he intended to change it, but his badly chosen heirs prevented him, or because he did it in anger against the guardian but not with any rancor toward his next-of-kin. To gain the sympathy of the jurymen, the nephews declare, at the beginning, that it grieves them to go to law against their kinsmen, and that they would feel as bad in damaging the interests of kinsmen as they would in being unjustly deprived of their property by such people.

In every legal action, our view of the case at issue is colored by the point of view of the speaker. In the dispute over Cleonymus' will, we can read only the arguments of his blood-kin, with whom we naturally tend to sympathize. We hear something of the other side of such cases in a speech, "Ægeneticus", written perhaps a little earlier by the Athenian orator Isocrates. Here a sickly man named Thrasylochus has died, leaving his estate to the boyhood friend who had taken care of him during his illness. The friend has also been instructed to marry the dead man's sister. The friend is thereupon sued by the testator's illegitimate half-sister, a woman who had shown hostility to both him and his brother. In his defense the designated heir argues not only that he is the best friend of the deceased but that their families had been previously and are now again connected by marriage. The laws have made such a will legitimate, and thus both law and friendship favor the cause of the heir.

Although, like all Greeks, Athenians were busybodies who liked meddling in their neighbors' business, the political and legal system of the *polis* had so few coercive mechanisms at its disposal that troublesome citizens took each other to court rather than invoke the power of the non-existent policemen, social workers, and bureaucrats, who exercise authority over American families. Cleonymus' nephews expected to persuade their fellow-citizens on the moral grounds of kinship, ignoring the plain facts of a written will.

ROMAN PIETY

Athenians were by no means an unusual people in viewing kinship through the lens of inheritance. The Romans were, if anything, even more narrowly focussed on what are sometimes termed "succession strategies." In the early days of the Roman republic, inheritance laws were as strict in their own way as Athenian laws had been, though there were important differences. If a man died intestate, his property passed automatically in order, first to his children and (in certain cases) wife, next to his nearest male relatives, and then to kinsmen who shared the family name. By the end of the Republic, however, a father was obligated only to bequeath a fourth of his estate to his sons; nonetheless, the evidence (drawn from wills, literary sources, and legal codes) paints a picture of a society in which property was expected to go to the natural heirs (Saller, 1997, p. 163). The mere fact that fathers could alienate most of their property did not mean that they actually did so.

The revolution by which Christianity was made first a licit, then a favored, then the virtually exclusive religion of the Roman Empire, did not subvert, much less overthrow the pre-Christian social conventions that dictated respect for parents, affection for family members, and loyalty to kindred. Family and kinship remained vital forces in maintaining the Roman social order, and the gradual infusion of Christian morality into legislation did little or nothing to loosen the ties of blood. The rules on incest were, in fact, more sharply drawn, and the evidence of wills suggests that, of those Roman citizens, Christian or pagan, who possessed enough property to make wills a practical necessity, most continued to favor close relatives (Champlin, 1991, pp. ff.).

AFTER THE FALL: THE FEUDAL ORDER

Gothic and Burgundian Germans, by the time they came to write down their legal codes, had long been subject to Roman influences, but the Lombards, before their king Alboin led them into Italy (about 570), were among the Germanic peoples who had fallen least under the influence of Roman civilization, and the *Edict of King Rothair* (643), though written in Latin, reflects traditional Lombard custom with little or no Roman influence. Under its provisions, a man's property, upon his death, was partible, that is, it was divided among his male offspring. Legitimate sons had the right to the lion's share in their father's estate, but natural sons inherited a smaller portion.

Sons could not be disinherited except on such serious grounds as plotting against the life of their father or other family members, striking the father, or sleeping with a step-mother. Inherited property was not held in common by the heirs, but the accumulated property of past generations could not be easily alienated. Preservation of the estate intact was a concern for many Germanic peoples, including the Anglo-Saxons (Stenton, 2001, pp. 317-318), and such rules could only be tolerated in a society that put a high value on the continuity of family and kindred.

Feudal England

English law, which is ancestral to the laws of the American and Canadian commonwealths, follows a similar path of development as the other Germanized provinces of Rome. With the collapse of Roman authority and the failure of Romano-Celtic principalities to defend themselves against Germanic aggression, England fell under the control of illiterate pagan Angles, Saxons, Jutes, and Danes, only to be subdued ultimately by the Norman French and their allies.

Reflecting the complex history of the island, English laws and customs governing inheritance were as complicated, if less thorough-going, than the Roman, and they did not give way entirely to social revolution until the 20th century. In America, unfortunately, that revolution broke out before the ink had dried on the Treaty of Paris that acknowledged the reality of American independence, and the most funda-mental traditions of marriage, household autonomy, and inheritance were parched and withered under the hot light of irrationally applied reason. To understand the American revolution against kinship, we have to know something of, first, the tradition that the revolutionaries were rebelling against and, second, the theories of individual property rights that they invoked to justify their proposals.

Throughout Medieval Europe, the building up of estates–and the preservation of the power that accompanies property–became a major objective of families. In England, where the traditions of feudal law dictated the nature of possession and inheritance, primogeniture became a primary value for the upper classes, originally because the estate had to be possessed by a single person capable of discharging his obligations, largely military, to his liege, and later because the prestige of the family took precedence over the particular interests of daughters and younger sons.

In Celtic and Anglo-Saxon England, inheritance rules were fairly loose, and fathers could and did divide their property among their children. The Norman Conquest changed the situation and first sons came to be privileged, not because the invading Normans had a long tradition of primogeniture: In much of Normandy, they did not. It was largely the circumstances of the Conquest itself and William's policy that caused the feudal revolution in England (Douglas, 1964, pp. 266 ff.). As king, whose barons were necessary to his rule over an alien people, William had an urgent need to keep his barons dependent upon himself. This was easier in England than elsewhere, since the vast majority of land titles changed hands in the years following the Conquest. Nonetheless, on the continent at almost the same time, longstanding feudal traditions were being stiffened and organized by the Emperor Frederick Barbarossa.

To oversimplify a complicated legal evolution, the Normans in France and in England–for some time following the conquest–distinguished between property held on military tenure and property held on civil terms. In the latter case, the property-holder had the right to bequeath the property according to his desire, but, if he held it on military terms, it had to pass down to his eldest son, who also inherited the obligation to provide military service to the liege lord from whom the property was received. The necessity for such a connection between property and military service–the essence of feudalism–was most obvious in the case of noble and royal titles, though it took some time for it to have the force of law. William the Conqueror, apparently, was able to distinguish between his inherited title and property as Duke of Normandy, which he had to pass on to his eldest son Robert, and conquered England, which he was free to leave to his second son William Rufus.

While primogeniture may have been increasingly the norm for inheriting estates by the time of William's great-grandson, Henry II, the principle was ignored when the barons preferred the claim of Henry's youngest son John to the claim of his deceased older brother Geoffrey's son, Arthur of Brittany. (John, was of course, the unpopular ruler who sparked the barons' revolt that led to the drafting of *Magna Carta*.) Under Norman succession rules, John was the appropriate choice, while under Angevin rules–Henry II, the father of Richard and John, was son and heir to Geoffrey "le bel" Plantagent of Anjou–Arthur was the heir. The point became moot, when the unfortunate Arthur fell into John's hands and disappeared from history, but the issue was still significant enough to claim Shakespeare's attention in his play *King John*.

Several of Shakespeare's greatest plays turn on the disinheritance of the proper heir. The series of revolutions and wars that made up the Wars of the Roses were sparked by the unlawful succession of Henry of Lancaster, who defeated and murdered his cousin Richard II and usurped the throne of Richard's presumptive heir, Edmund Mortimer. In *Macbeth*, the unscrupulous hero not only kills King Duncan but usurps the place of Duncan's son and heir, Malcolm, who at the end of the play succeeds to the throne. In *King Lear*, the elderly king capriciously demands his daughters to display sycophantic affection, and when his one loyal daughter respectfully declines to flatter the old fool, he disinherits her with disastrous consequences to himself and his realm.

Lear ignored the admonition of Ecclesiasticus [33:19-23]: "To son or wife, to brother or friend, do not give power over yourself, as long as you live; and do not give your property to another, lest you change your mind and must ask for it. At the time when you end the days of your life, in the hours of death, distribute your inheritance." Lear wished to live in ease and comfort, but he had failed to bring up two of his daughters to know their responsibilities to the man from whom they inherited wealth and power.

THE DECLINE OF FEUDAL INHERITANCE

Feudalism was never a static system but a constant ebb and flow of power among contesting parties: Kings and Emperors naturally strove to assert their rights by emphasizing the contingency of lands granted on condition of service, while their barons did all they could to insure the automatic transmission of this property to their heirs. When the central authority was strong, rulers might declare that an inheritance depended on fulfillment of duties and even on the will of the sovereign. Their barons, while doing their best to make their properties automatically pass to their heirs, insisted on their own authority over lands granted to their own men, whether lords or knights.

In English law, as it developed, primogeniture, basically, could work two ways. If a man died intestate, his estate–down to a fairly trivial level of household articles–went in its entirety to his eldest son. However, a well-to-do man could also make a will, in which he either restricted or strengthened the rights of his first-born son by a process known as entailment (Cecil & Baron Rockley, 1895).

In the early days, a tenant could sell property in his own lifetime, thus depriving his heir of part of the estate and his lord of his feudal dues, though this loophole was eventually eliminated by the *Statute of Uses* passed in the reign of Henry VIII. The duties of military service, which had become an anachronism by the 17th century, were swept away, a process of erosion that eventually made automatic primogeniture a legal nullity. Nonetheless, primogeniture lived on as a device that could be used by property-holders to preserve their estates by entail or fee tail (*foedum talliatum*). A fee, fief, or *foedum* is the right to the use of a property, and a foedum talliatum–a "cut fee"–restricts that right by stipulating that the property be passed on to the owner's "heirs of his body." Such a stipulation frequently (though not always) included a provision for primogeniture.

The *custom* of primogeniture in wills, in other words, continued in strength even as the *legal obligation* was falling into abeyance. The purpose of entailed primogeniture was the perpetuation of the family's property, wealth, and social position, and it was the obligation to pass on this precious inheritance undivided and even improved according to an orderly rule of succession (Jamoussi, 1999, pp. 9-14).

While it was possible to convey an estate by means of a "tail general," which included female descendants, the "tail male", restricting succession to males, was more common. More than one English novel, *e.g. Pride and Prejudice,* turns on the exclusion of daughters from the succession. However, the category of the disinherited included not only daughters but younger sons. From the ancient Greek or modern American points of view, such exclusions–whatever the objective–seem patently unfair. They did, nonetheless, drive many an enterprising younger son into useful careers in the military, in the Church, or in commerce.

Loving fathers, whatever the law or family interest may dictate, do not generally wish to leave their daughters or younger sons destitute, and a variety of legal instruments, such as fee simple possession (a non-feudal form of property right) and gifts in marriage to a person and his/her heirs, were devised to enable a father to transfer a heritable estate to daughters and younger sons. Love will, as the saying goes, find a way even among the rich and great. Less fortunate families tend to be less interested in preserving estates they do not have than in helping the children of all their children. In the fourteenth-century, peasants, when primogeniture laws were in full force among the gentry, did not have to worry about discharging feudal obligations, and they made strict provisions for the rights of widows and younger children.

The more ruthless aspects of primogeniture and entail were gradually curbed by recourse to such principles as gavelkind, a complex Anglo-Saxon legal tradition that enabled a man to leave his lands to whomever he liked and, where there was no will, portioned out the property equally among his sons. In British law, gavelkind survived in cases of intestate succession, that is, where the deceased had made no will and, where an estate was supposed to descend intact, it became possible for a daughter, if she were the only child, to inherit. In cases of intestacy in colonial America, however, surviving wives frequently enjoyed a life-interest in the estate, and children inherited equal shares.

This brief survey of the evolution of property rights, over-simplified as it is, should be sufficient to establish a simple point. The residuum of Medieval laws that were codified in Britain and America at the time of the Revolution were far from Draconian. In general, as societies change, people find moderate measures by which they can "work around" the obstacles presented by laws and traditions that have out-lived, at least in some aspects, their usefulness. More rad-ical measures, inevitably presented as necessary reforms, often have unanticipated consequences. The legal rebellion against primogeniture and entailment, although it was jus-tified on the grounds of fairness and the redress of wrongs, was also part of a broader intellectual and social revolu-tion whose primary object was the liberation of individuals and the weakening or even abolition of such obstacles to individual freedom as monarchy, established churches, and social classes.

Rationalizing Kinship Out of Property

The philosophical reinvention of property and property rights was a fruit of the same intellectual tradition that has reinvented marriage, the family, and all the political institutions of Europe and the Americas. This darkening of the human mind has inevitably been termed the Enlightenment. It is far from my intention to present a critique, much less a history of Enlightenment thought, but since we are nearly all, liberals and conservatives, Christians and atheists, children of the Enlightenment movements that have turned society upside down and reinvented all our social and religious institutions, some few words about the impact of this revolution on kinship and inheritance are in order.

To get an idea of how society was viewed before the Enlightenment, we can turn to that great reactionary, William Shakespeare. In *Troilus and Cressida*, a dramatic sidelight on the tale of Troy, the Greeks were being hard pressed by the Trojans. When Agamemnon, the leader of the expedition, polls his lieutenants, asking why they and the men are so downcast, Ulysses explains that their failure is the result of insubordination and the collapse of the social and political hierarchy that is a reflection of the natural order. The orders and degrees of human societies, argues Ulysses, reflect the order of the universe:

> The heavens themselves, the planets and this centre
> Observe degree, priority and place,
> Insisture [fixedness], course, proportion, season, form,
> Office and custom, in all line of order....

Failure to preserve the hierarchy of rank and birth results in chaos both in the material world and in human society:

Take but degree away, untune that string,
And, hark, what discord follows! Each thing meets
In mere oppugnancy: the bounded waters
Should lift their bosoms higher than the shores
And make a sop of all this solid globe:
Strength should be lord of imbecility,
And the rude son should strike his father dead:
Force should be right; or rather, right and wrong,
Between whose endless jar justice resides,
Should lose their names, and so should justice too.
Then every thing includes itself in power,
Power into will, will into appetite;
And appetite, an universal wolf,
So doubly seconded with will and power,
Must make perforce an universal prey,
And last eat up himself.

The order in the heavens was proof for Shakespeare, as it
had been for Saint Paul, that the social order was an expression of natural law:

How could communities,
Degrees in schools and brotherhoods in cities,
Peaceful commerce from dividable shores,
The primogenitive and due of birth,
Prerogative of age, crowns, sceptres, laurels,
But by degree, stand in authentic place?

The privileges of the first-born were, along with the rights
of rank and age, kinship and kingship, rooted in natural
and divine law.

In *King Lear* [I.ii] the villainous bastard complains about
the unfairness of it all and contrasts the freedom of nature
with the servitude of law:

Thou, nature, art my goddess; to thy law
My services are bound. Wherefore should I
Stand in the plague of custom, and permit
The curiosity of nations to deprive me,
For that I am some twelve or fourteen moon-shines
Lag of a brother? Why bastard? wherefore base?
When my dimensions are as well compact,
My mind as generous, and my shape as true,
As honest madam's issue?

OPENING SHOTS

Shakespeare seems to be putting into the bastard's mouth
the opinion of Montaigne, who in his "Apology for Raymond Sebond," had offered a list of "popular and wild
opinions, and of savage manners and beliefs" beginning
with drunkenness, religious relics, and human sacrifice and
ending with fortune-telling. Sandwiched in between is the
bestowing titles to be inherited by a firstborn son.

It took some time for Europe to follow where Montaigne had led, but two generations after Shakespeare's
death (in 1616) John Locke, as part of his refutation of the
patriarchal theory of government, made a systematic attack on primogeniture. In his *First Treatise on Government*,
Locke's primary objective was to discredit the argument
that the king's authority was derived, on the principle of
primogeniture, from Adam's authority over his children.
Anticipating his theory of the state of nature and the social contract in the *Second Treatise*, Locke asks his readers
to believe that all of Adam's children would have inherited
equal shares. Though that is not consistent with what we
know of Jewish inheritance laws. He concludes from this

false premise that a father/proprietor is obligated to bestow his goods and property on his children equally [104-105].

Since the principle of primogeniture was the basis of most European monarchies, Locke was naturally eager to oppose it, but he went further, arguing that a possessor might do anything he liked with his property, including destroy it. Paradoxically, he also insisted that children have a "right" to inherit an equal share of their father's property, though it is an empty right if the father has, before his death, burned his house, sold the land, and squandered the money on women and gambling. Absurd or not, Locke's elevation of the acquisitive individual to a moral plateau above family and tradition was to echo throughout the liberal tradition, drowning out the ancient arguments of blood. English and American Conservatives who take their stand on classical liberal grounds are apparently unaware that they are supporting the first phase of the revolution they imagine they are opposing.

Locke's argument is so confused that it can be taken as evidence either of his ignorance or duplicity. If the "laws of God" include the Old Testament, he is entirely wrong, and his conversion of parental duties to children's rights is a sleight of hand that could not hoodwink anyone who had read Saint Thomas or Aristotle.

A characteristic of Enlightenment social and political theory is the tendency to turn away from the existing base of historical evidence, which at that time consisted of European legal traditions, the histories of Greece and Rome, and the Scriptures, and move in the direction of abstract arguments about an imagined state of nature. This can be observed, for example, by comparing Richard Hooker's *Laws of Ecclesiastical Polity*, with their rich historical detail, and Locke's two treatises, whose arguments derive from speculations about imaginary men living in a fictional "state of nature."

It is not that Enlightenment writers were ignorant of the classics–that is far from the case–or did not appreciate Greek and Latin literature, but when Voltaire or Rousseau write about the human condition, it is as opponents of the Church and as defenders of the new speculative approach to society. When "evidence" is brought forth, it is often extracted from travelers' tales of exotic and savage nations. Montaigne celebrated South American cannibals, and many an 18th century anti-Catholic intellectual subjected his own society to a withering critique from fictive Turkish, Chinese, or Persian visitors. The best of these fairy tales is probably Montesquieu's early work, his *Lettres Persanes,* in which the author, a propertied French nobleman, uses a two-edged satirical sword to dissect both French and Persian pretensions.

In his most important work, *L'Esprit des Lois,* Montesquieu was more cautious and dealt seriously with the question of inheritance. The work constitutes a lengthy and erudite argument to sustain his basic principle that there is no one system of laws for all nations, since every nation adopts laws congenial to its character and historical experience. He devotes a considerable space to laws regarding succession to property and title. He wisely, perhaps inevitably chose to concentrate on Roman law, which is probably the richest legal tradition in matters of property and succession.

Montesquieu begins at the beginning of the Roman commonwealth, with the founder and first king Romulus, whose laws insured the orderly transmission of property within a bloodline. The necessity of keeping estates in the hands of families, he argues, led to laws forbidding children to inherit their mother's estate. Feudal law on property and succession would have interested him less, because Roman Law was far more strict in limiting the cases by which possession and succession could be infringed by government. He appears to have well understood the danger to property rights posed by abstract theories of natural right and explicitly declares, in his title to chapter 15 of book XXVI "That things that depend on the principles of civil law ought not be determined by principles of political law."

Montesquieu's prudent respect for particular traditions and the ambitions of propertied families was not shared by many of his warmest admirers. Antoine Destutt de Tracy, though a professed admirer of Montesquieu, was a representative thinker of the French Enlightenment. His strong advocacy of deductive reasoning is on display in his Commentary on Montesquieu's *Spirit of the Laws* (1808), and it is put to devastating use in his discussion of inheritance. He begins with an axiomatic assumption that a republic has an interest in preventing the emergence of great wealth. The solution is to abolish primogeniture and other privileges and to require an equal distribution among children. This would mean the end to inherited monarchy and nobility. [Book XI]

After all, he argues in a pure Enlightenment style, no one in his right mind would make the position of coachman, cook or lawyer hereditary, and yet "in obeying a monarch who derives power this way, nothing preposterous presents itself to the great mass of mankind; it is those only that think, who are confounded at human inconsistency."

Jefferson's Self Evident Folly

Such an attitude inspired the Enlightened Thomas Jefferson–though it would certainly have run counter to his own projects as an aristocrat who took great care to nurture the careers and fortunes of his extended family in Virginia. Jefferson had read Destutt de Tracy, particularly his *Treatise on Political Economy*, with enthusiasm and proposed a comment of his own for insertion into the translation, though for one reason or another it was apparently not published. [Letter to Joseph Milligan, May 1816] Apprehensive that politicians might conclude, on reading the work, that government should take wealth from more industrious families and share it with the indolent, he observed that a more fair result could be obtained by imposing partible inheritance: "If the overgrown wealth of an individual be deemed dangerous to the state, the best corrective is the law of equal inheritance to all in equal degree: and the better as this enforces a law of nature, while extra-taxation violates one."

Jefferson actively promoted Destutt de Tracy's commentary, but it was not the original source of Jefferson's opposition to primogeniture. Like most men of his background and education, he had read with approval Locke's two *Treatises*, and he had the example of Massachusetts, which had already abolished the legal practice, to guide him.

Jefferson's argument, summarized in the sentence "the earth belongs to the living, not to the dead," was aimed at liberating property from the constraints imposed by ancestors, and it enabled a current holder to treat both ancestors and descendants with contempt.

Jefferson, although he was no enemy of family tradition or inherited rank, makes his position explicit in a letter to James Madison [September 6, 1789]:

> "I set out on this ground which I suppose to be self-evident: 'That the earth belongs in usufruct to the living;' that the dead have neither powers nor rights over it...We seem not to have perceived that by the law of nature, one generation is to another as one independent nation to another."

That phrase "self-evident" is almost always a clear sign that a writer is stating a principle he has accepted as revealed wisdom but is unable to justify, much less prove. The Age of Enlightenment was dominated by self-proclaimed skeptics who doubted revelation and wisdom and then went on to take their stand on unexamined first principles.

Jefferson believed that the current generation had the right and freedom to dispose of their property and to alter their constitution. In a famous letter to Thomas Earle [September 24, 1823], Jefferson affirmed his belief that the land belongs to the living, and went on to explain, first, that most civil countries empower the testator to make any arrangement he likes, and, while the laws of our ancestors should not be lightly overturned, "but this does not lessen the right of that majority to repeal whenever a change of circumstances or of will calls for it."

Jefferson led the successful campaign to end both entail and primogeniture in Virginia, and Alexis de Tocqueville, the French aristocrat who came to the infant United States to see if democracy could possibly work, grasped Jefferson's point: The elimination of large estates was conducive to democratic equality in America. The snake in the pretty grass of Jefferson's social revolution is the tendency to detach a current possessor from the entangling network of family ties. This effect would not have pleased Jefferson, a man solidly enmeshed in a complex network of kinship that connected him to nearly every family of note in Virginia.

Even in modern America law, where inheritances are for the most part determined by the passing mood of the testator, the property of a man dying intestate is awarded, in most states, to next-of-kin according to a fixed order and formula that varies from state to state. In Wisconsin, for example, the formula goes in the order of the surviving spouse, the children, grandchildren, great-grandchildren etc, then parents, siblings, and, nieces and nephews, and so on. In some states, a surviving spouse splits the estate with surviving descendants. Far from making a family more dependent on government, such a law reinforces the traditional relationship between blood and property. Laws of intestate succession can fairly be said to represent a legal consensus that acknowledges the propriety of traditional patterns of inheritance.

When the bulk of an estate consists of lands and property inherited from previous generations, it is easier to see the current possessor as only one link in a long chain, but in modern societies a father's wealth depends very largely on his own efforts. Should he not be able to dispose of the fruits of his labor as he sees fit?

These days even an arch-reactionary is tempted to say *yes*, but this line of reasoning ignores two facts of life: The first and perhaps less significant fact is that most prosperous people are indebted to parents and perhaps grandparents for their lives, education, and the moral outlook that made success possible. My parents were not wealthy people, but they worked hard, provided a decent home, encouraged disciplined habits and serious reading, and sent me off to college. They also left me a modest legacy that came in very handy to an impoverished young writer. I cannot repay them for all this, but I can discharge some of my obligation by passing what little wealth that governments have left me onto their grandchildren.

There is also the biological fact, perhaps of greater significance, that I am genetically the sum of my parent's contribution to my being, just as my children are the sum of the genetic contribution made by my wife and me. Liberals–both classical liberals and the leftists who claim to be liberals–who persist in believing that there is an unbridgeable chasm between the realm of biological facts and moral values will not accept this argument, but the minds of such people are impervious to reality.

Wealthy Americans like J. Howard Marshall appear to feel no shame in partially disinheriting their children or in leaving a large part of their estates to women a third their age (the case of Anna Nicole Smith). In earlier times, such an act was viewed as despotic and a sign of a mental and social disorder. In Greek legend and literature the most famous dissension between parent and child involved Orestes, son of Agamemnon and Clytemnestra. After Clytemnestra and her lover murdered her husband Agamemnon, they drove the dispossessed Orestes into exile. He could only reclaim his estate and position as king by murdering the guilty pair, an act that drove him mad. The disinheriting of Orestes is only one vile act in a multi-generational sequence of crimes, but it is a sign that something is rotten in the state of Mycenæ (or Argos), just as there was something rotten in the state of Denmark, when young Hamlet is not permitted to succeed to his father's throne.

Moral Skeleton

Kinship is not, then, merely a matter of warming sentiments or shared experiences, but the bones of our moral order that sustain the flesh and organs of private property and inheritance, marriage and the family. As a necessary part of human nature, it is rooted in our biological being. Descendants from a common ancestor share common genes. While social structures may sometimes obscure one or another aspect of genetic reality, we may not safely assume that pre-modern or primitive peoples did not understand the basic principle of biological descent. The very complexity of their kinship terminology and their carefully constructed rules on inheritance betray a keen appreciation of sociobiological reality, even in societies in which the mechanics of procreation may not be well understood.

Kinship and genetic descent are obviously related but not necessarily identical. I may not get on well with some of my closest relatives, especially those with whom I may be competing for an inheritance. In a patrilineal society I might, for example, develop a strong bond with a maternal uncle or my sister's son. Germanic literature offers many examples of these bonds, such as Beowulf's concern for his cousin.

As the sister's son of the late King Hygelac, Beowulf is offered his uncle's throne, though he is reluctant to displace Hygelac's son. However, when the son is killed, Beowulf succeeds to the kingship. In the Anglo-Saxon poem "The Battle of Maldon," Byrhnoth's sister's son is one of the first to die fighting to avenge the death of his uncle (Seebohm, 1902, pp. 68-72). Among the patrilineal Anglo-Saxons, the inheritance and succession rights from father to son are predictably observed, but even in wills, some property often passed, by the informal system of the avunculate (that is "uncleship"), to a sister's son (Whitelock, 2011).

Though some efforts have been made to connect the Anglo-Saxon avunculate with an earlier matrilineal or totemic system, such ingenious explanations are not necessary: Kinship structures are flexible and adaptable, and without more precise information about early German social life, speculation is fruitless (Glosecki, 1999). Kinship is an organizing principle of most societies, but it would be wrong to reduce all social obligations and affections to descent patterns: There are other forms of friendship, though brotherhood and kinship very often serve as metaphors for institutionalized affections not based on blood or marriage.

THE REVOLUTION: DISENTANGLING THE INDIVIDUAL

The decay of kinship ties is not one of those natural developments that must occur in any organic societies. As Montesquieu recognized, there is no one ideal form of government or system of law, and there is, one might add, no ideal structure of kinship and inheritance that will fill the needs of each and every society. The law must always be adapted to changing circumstances, and the rule of primogeniture had lost most of its feudal significance in England before the end of the 17th century, and it never had any in America. Nonetheless, Thomas Jefferson worked relentlessly to undo whatever vestiges of the custom remained. Jefferson's animosity to primogeniture and entail can only be understood in the context of an intellectual revolution that had been brewing since at least the late 14th century. Those who would oppose the later phases of the revolution–Marxism, feminism, genetic engineering, animal rights, and transgenderism, would do well to consider how long they can with consistency and good conscience continue to uphold the earlier phases of modernity.

References

Berry, W. (2006). *The Unforeseen Wilderness: Kentucky's Red River Gorge.* Counterpoint Press.

Blerk N.J., v. (2019). The Basic Tenets of Intestate (Customary) Succession Law in Ancient Egypt. *Fundamina,* 25(1), 170–194.

Cecil, E. & Baron Rockley, E. C. (1895). *Primogeniture: a Short History of its Development in Various Countries and its Practical Effects.* J. Murray.

Champlin, E. (1991). *Final Judgments: Duty and Emotion in Roman Wills, 200 BC-AD 250.* University of California Press.

Douglas, D. C. (1964). *William the Conqueror: the Norman Impact upon England.* University of California Press.

Glosecki, S. O. (1999). Beowulf and the Wills: Traces of Totemism?. *Philological Quarterly,* 78(1-2), 15–47.

Jamoussi, Z. (1999). *Primogeniture and Entail in England: A Survey of Their History and Representation in Literature.* Centre de publication universitaire, 1999.

Postgate, N. (2017). *Early Mesopotamia: Society and Economy at the Dawn of History.* Taylor & Francis.

Saller, R. P. (1997). *Patriarchy, Property and Death in the Roman Family*. Cambridge University Press.

Seebohm, F. (1902). *Tribal Custom in Anglo-Saxon Law*. Longmans, Green & Company.

Stenton, F. M. (2001). *Anglo-Saxon England*. (Vol. 2). Oxford Paperbacks.

Whitelock, D. (2011). *Anglo-Saxon Wills*. Cambridge University Press.

From Kin to
Commonwealth

Home is the place where, when you have to go there,
They have to take you in.

— Robert Frost, The Death of the Hired Man

*E*VERY YEAR, AS THE GRASS AND LEAVES TURN BROWN and
the sun appears to die, large numbers of deracinated
individualists travel hundreds, even thousands of
miles to return, if not to their childhood homes, at least
to the places where their parents have chosen to spend
their declining years. During the panic of 2020, millions
defied the warnings of public officials and, putting on their
masks, filed into crowded airplanes to make a pilgrimage
of only a few days. Most of them were received joyfully
by parents and siblings who had missed them, and even
the black sheep among them could anticipate the appearance, if not the reality, of a heartfelt welcome. In times of
crisis, so the cliché runs, grown men think of their mothers.
To paraphrase another cliché, in the foxholes there are no
individualists.

More distant relations may also rely on ties of kinship as
the strands of a safety-net to be used in emergencies. The
Children of Israel, as they entered the Promised Land, were
organized on the lines of kindred and tribe, and in the first
and perhaps greatest work of Western literature (the *Iliad*),
a crisis impels the Achæan leadership to fall back on bonds

275

more primitive and less formal than the command structure of the army.

In the tenth year of the Trojan War, the war is going badly for Agamemnon. When a deceitful dream, promising victory, instructs him to attack, the commander decides to test the resolve of his troops by telling them that perhaps it is time pack up and go home. Instead of meeting with the massive protest he expected, his proposal triggers a rush to the ships that is stopped, just in time, by wiser heads. The outbreak of chaotic anarchy does not bode well for the future, and, once order has been restored, the aged Nestor tells the "lord of men" to muster the troops according to tribes (*phyla*) and clans (*phretres*). This will enable Agamemnon and the other leaders to judge who among the leaders is cowardly and which of the peoples is brave [II.362-65].

Nestor's advice, to return to a traditional order that is based not on the chain of command but on kinship, is a valuable reminder that, when an artificial hierarchy is weakened or threatened, human beings naturally learn to rely on more fundamental structures of family, kinship, and friendship.

Kinsmen and Clansmen

There is endless argument about the origin and significance of all Greek social institutions, from the *oikos* (household) to the *polis*, and debates over the intermediate groupings of tribes, clans, and brotherhoods may tell readers more about the outlook of the writers than they do about the social structures of ancient Greece. How we regard any kin-based association is almost inevitably determined by our more general view of human society and its development. The children of modernity, who put a high valuation on the twin sovereignties of the individual and the state, will tend to see intermediate social orders not as expressions of a universal human nature, but as historical phenomena that arise in particularly developmental stages or in response to troubled times and social dissolution, but the students of Aristotle and Thomas Aquinas, who are more likely to regard the commonwealth as an organism evolving out of marriage, family, and kinship, will regard clans and tribes as inevitable and necessary forms of social organization that flow from our common human nature.

Although the general title of this work, *Properties of Blood*, reflects an organic conception of social institutions, there is one aspect of the counter-argument, at least, that is worth serious attention. Historians, in trying to account for the persistence (or emergence) of clans and tribes, often argue that, while these broad associations of blood are only a social construction, societies in crisis often revert to such forms of institutionalized kinship. In Book II of the *Iliad*, Agamemnon, seeing his authority as commander dissolving, turns to more primitive and passionate elements of social order, the ties of blood.

There is no necessary contradiction in the assertion that clans and tribes are an outgrowth of human nature and the counter-assertion that they come to the fore during periods of political anarchy. Why should the social utility of an institution exclude a natural origin? Presumably, a Darwinist could argue that kindreds, age-grading, religious rituals, and a myriad of other customs and institutions have evolved to satisfy natural necessities and thus enhance the fitness of individuals who succeed in using them to their own benefit. The same might be said of marriage and the family, the violence of self-help and blood revenge, and the protection and comforts offered by small-scale intermediate institutions of kinship. The fact that marriage has been in decline for the past 50 or 100 or even 200 years does not constitute evidence that it is not a natural institution, and when, during the coming period of violent social upheaval, marriage reappears in full vigor, it would be absurd to say that our savage grandchildren will be reinventing marriage.

The tribes and phratries to which Nestor turns were a feature of Ionian Greek cities–including Athens and the East Mediterranean cities that gave birth to epic and elegiac poetry and to Greek philosophy. The Athenian phratry of later times was a religious brotherhood of male kinsmen who took part in common rituals. A man's phratry-brothers testified to his citizenship and to the legal descent of his heirs. To be *aphretor*–outside the circle of kinsmen–was to be an outlaw, someone who has no one and nothing, not even the law, to protect him. Many scholars have argued that the Ionian phratry and/or tribe, like the Scottish clan and Montenegrin *pleme,* were in their origins voluntary associations, created, more or less *ad hoc,* and only later reinterpreted as expressions of common descent. In any particular case, they *may* be right, but what we actually *know is that* Ionians and Athenians regarded them as both ancient and based (originally) on blood. As we shall see, adoptive and metaphorical kin-relations can exert as strong a pull as ties of blood.

Kinship in ancient societies bound men and women in networks of obligation that integrated them into the greater civil orders that claimed their allegiance: their city, a confederation of cities, a kingdom, or the entire Roman Empire. At festivals like the Athenian Apatouria and the Roman Lemuria, even the participation of the dead ancestors of the living was welcomed by the citizens of a commonwealth, which, by preserving its connection with previous generations, expected to survive for countless generations in the future.

In European monarchies, one could say, "The king is dead, long live the king." While the phrase appears to have been coined in early 15th century France, the sentiment is much older. In England, it was declared as early as at the death of King Henry III that the crown could never be vacant, because the successor–in this case Edward I–already existed. Modern democratic republics have a presumed immortality, because, despite the regular rotation of elected officials and ruling parties, the wheels of government roll on, greased by generation after generation of political mechanics. Thomas Hobbes's declaration that the state was a "mortal god" had it quite wrong. The state is no god, however divine its origins might be, but, while it exists, it is presumed to be *im*mortal, and the immortality of the Roman Empire or the British monarchy derives in no small measure from the continuity of the lower, more fundamental institutions of blood from which commonwealths derive their vigor and their authority.

The way we view a nation is inextricably linked with our conception of family and kindred. If cousins and great-grandparents mean little to us, we shall probably view the nation as nothing more than a set of laws and markets, "a land of opportunity," a place where (in the words of T.S. Eliot in "The Rock")

We all dwell together
To make money from each other...

And where mobility trumps every tie of family and home:

All dash to and fro in motor cars,
Familiar with the roads and settled nowhere.
Nor does the family even move about together,
But every son would have his motor cycle,
And daughters ride away on casual pillions.

But, where kinfolks and family members still count for something, a current generation of men and women may well wish to preserve what they have inherited from their ancestors for the benefit of their dependents. The political implications are obvious: The prosperity and comforts of the American people is the product of risks taken by earlier generations and the investments they made of themselves. The "American way of life," whatever meaning we choose to give that phrase, is therefore a precious legacy, one not to be shared with every foreigner who strays into our territory. Viewed from the perspective of angels or space aliens, such tenacious loyalty to kith and kin, hearth and land appear barbaric and bigoted, but looked at from the ground up, it is as natural and wholesome as the desire for food and procreation.

The Evolution of Society

It has been a commonplace among organic political theorists—Aristotle and Cicero, St. Thomas and Althusius, Sir Robert Filmer and French counter-revolutionaries—that the commonwealth is an outgrowth of the household or family. The proposed steps of this theoretical social evolution usually echo Aristotle's account that traces the coalescence of households into a village and villages into a city or commonwealth. Aristotle and St. Thomas, to name only two, could take for granted that their readers had some knowledge of household and village life and of the significance of kinship. Since modern writers are not fortunate enough to have readers embedded in powerful structures of family and kin, some little attention to how the process might work will not be wasted.

One phase in the transition from a married couple with children to the modern nation state is the development of broader kin groups of clan and tribe, in which artificial ties of kinship are eventually–and inevitably–recognized. We have already seen that in classical Athens, households were bound together by their ties, in decreasing order of closeness, to *genos* and *phratry*, deme and tribe. Each level of organization conferred certain benefits and required particular obligations. In the suit brought by the heirs of Cleonymus, the boys took their stand on the close relationship within the *genos,* whose ties should take precedence over the transient whims of an elderly testator.

To be functional, a clan or descent group need not be exclusively a formal network of actual blood ties. If we think of a highland clan, we shall recall that its ranks were filled out with poor relations and even fictionally adopted families. Clan Murray in Scotland was amplified, for example, by the adoption of Flemings, some of whom came to dominate the clan. Since *genos*, the Greek word for clan, is derived from a verb that means "to be born," the members of a Greek *genos* claimed to be descended from one common ancestor; they were bound together in a particular cult, which made the *genos* a kind of religious corporation; and they were also bound by ties of friendship and shame. (The English word clan, similarly, means "offspring" or "descendants."). A sense of shame was important because it instilled in a man the fear of doing ill or failing in his obligation to his family. In Athens it was considered bad form, though not illegal (as it was in Rome), to take one's kinsmen to court.

In Aristotle's analysis, households grow into extended families, villages uniting different linages, and cities, which may after generations still preserve some recognition of kinship. His highly schematic account of social evolution would not satisfy a sociologist today, but it remains useful as a structural outline. Greeks were as keenly interested as evolutionary theorists in the origins of species, customs, and institutions, and they were always seeking for the first man or god to have founded a city or developed an art or begotten a family or clan. It is as natural a way of thinking as it is to see the characteristics of parents in their children.

Aristotle's temporal account of social development can thus be viewed in more spatial terms, much as expressions of time are correlated with expressions of space. In English we can say, "I'll meet you at nine," much as we say, "I'll meet you at the bar." In Latin and Greek, the correlation is clearer. The ablative case in Latin, for example, can be used to show both the location and the time of an event. Similarly, the temporal hierarchy of the generations from great-grandfather to great-grand son is paralleled by the familial hierarchy of living members.

If we join Greeks, Jews, Romans, and older generations of Christians in honoring ancestors and predecessors, we shall probably be more predisposed to accept the wisdom of senior members of the family and the authority of those who bear responsibility. Contempt for ancestors, in other words, is accompanied by contempt for living men and women who are in positions that require (in traditional societies) respect from their community. Tradition is simply the notion of community extended over the generations–and *vice versa*. Chesterton, in one of his most frequently quoted aphorisms, summed up the weight of tradition with the phrase "the democracy of the dead."

The Greeks were not alone in emphasizing genealogies. Tribal Jewish kinship, it seems, was also expressed through genealogies (McNutt, 1999, pp. 76-78). The Pentateuch gives modern readers a powerful portrait of a society in transition from kindreds, ruled by patriarchal leaders–Abraham and Isaac and Jacob–to a loose confederation of tribal groups led by Moses to the Promised Land, where they are eventually pressed by circumstances into choosing a general king. The process is far from easy, and the frequent conflicts between tribe and tribe, Saul and David, the northern and southern kingdoms provide dramatic evidence of the difficulties the people encounter on their road to "statehood."

In a pre-literate or lightly literate society, genealogical facts can be maintained orally over several generations, though over the centuries the memory of some facts can be blurred and alien descent-groups can be grafted onto the family tree, though with intermarriage the distinction between real and fictional descent might be rendered meaningless.

People of my name in Scotland were clearly descended from Flemish immigrants, some of them weavers and others Flemish warriors who had flocked to William the Conqueror's standard. Some of them were grafted onto Clan Murray, into which they also married. The mere name "Fleming," then, is only rarely an indication of any genealogical connection, but this does not prevent me from resenting the depiction of a crooked lawyer named Fleming in an old movie, or from deploring Faulkner's creation of the redneck Fleming Snopes. On the other hand, when I met an African-American young lady named Fleming–with whom there could be only the remotest chance of kinship–we jokingly called each other cousin. Even more remote connections are possible, if only in jest. I once had lunch in Bruges with some leaders of the Vlaamsblok, a Flemish separatist party. When I arrived at the table, a young scholar in the party greeted me with, "Welcome home." Kinship is a natural way of interpreting the world, and we invoke it even when it is the accident of a name.

To maintain affiliation with a clan, the members must know their place in the genealogical scheme of things. Members of a wealthy family or political dynasty tend to preserve the memory of their distinguished ancestors, but, in our New World at least, poor people outside the rural South rarely have the leisure for genealogies. In graduate school I got to know a student in English. Since his first name was Forrest, I asked if he had been named after Nathan Bedford Forrest. He confessed he didn't know, and when I asked about his ancestry, he said he had grown up in Los Angeles and had no idea of where his parents had come from.

By contrast, Highland Scots and ancient Greeks of all classes tended to be proud of their lineage. Homer's aristocrats counted back two or three generations and, in the case of Homer's Diomedes, more than that. In Book Six of the *Iliad*, Diomedes is about to fight with a young Lycian named Glaucus. Diomedes is clearly the greater warrior, but Glaucus has fought so impressively that the Greek, wanting to make sure he is not, once again, about to fight with a god, asks who he is. Glaucus, with a wisdom beyond his years says it does not matter because *the generations of men* are like leaves blowing in the wind.

The Extended
Metaphor of Kinship

Glaucus' world-weary exhalation is sometimes mislead-ingly interpreted to refer only to the brevity of the lives of men, but the melancholy point is the brevity not of a single human life but of human memory of earlier genera-tions. Generations come and go, like the seasons, and the time comes when we are gone forever, like pagan gods who fade into inconsequence when none is left to worship them. Nonetheless, when Glaucus sketches out his family tree (go-ing back to the early hero Bellerophon), Diomedes rejoices to find a descendant of Bellerophon, who had been a *xenos* or guest-friend of his grandfather.

The word, *xenos*, means stranger or foreigner and is later also applied to a mercenary, but a *xenos* whom you have entertained in your house (or *vice versa*) is like an adopted friend or member of the family. You may not injure him or fight with him, and when you visit his town, or he vis-its yours, you are supposed to look out for each other's interests. This relationship is not automatically inherited over several generations, but since Diomedes and Glaucus acknowledge it, they will not attempt to kill each other in battle. They are now the equivalent of kinsmen. In a way, Diomedes' response to Glaucus complaint is an affirmation of continuity among men of good will.

In classical Greece, *xenia* was the mechanism by which mem-bers of different commonwealths could treat each other as friends and kinsmen. Like real kinsmen, *xenoi* were ex-pected to support each other by giving counsel, lending money, and, in times of crisis, taking care of each others' families, or even serving as stepfather to the children (Her-man, 2002, pp. 16-29). This remained a rhetorical commonplace at least down to the time of the Emperor Julian, who, in his "Panegyric on Eusebia," praised his patroness for honoring people whose ancestors had maintained *xenia* with her own. [116 C-D]

Friendships and alliances can develop independently of blood ties or lineage systems. If kinship is the model expression of social amity, then those who enjoy such amity begin to be regarded as something like kin. Though kinship may seem exclusive—an iron destiny dictated by blood—there are formal mechanisms in many societies by which outsiders can be adopted into the lineage. These range from transparent fictions—such as drinking out of the same cup and pledging *Bruderschaft*—where the burden is felt rather lightly—to ritualized adoptions that confer nearly all the rights and duties of kinship upon the adoptee. In Roman law, an adopted son was subject to the same rights, penalties, and incest prohibitions as a son by birth.

It is difficult if not impossible for the denizens of modern and postmodern societies to appreciate the significance kinship has had for most of the earth's societies. The great stumbling block is the liberal myth of individualism that dominates the entire spectrum of political debate and has so interwoven itself into our consciousness and dreams that we cannot read the tragedy of Antigone without making her an individual or even a proto-feminist martyr, when in fact her heroic action in burying her brother derives from the duty of kinship.

This danger is underscored by the anthropologist who has already been cited for his insights into the duties of neighbors in a Spanish village:

"A system of thought that takes the individual as its starting-point and assumes that he is motivated by self-interest, faces a difficulty in confronting the examples of behaviour that is not so motivated...the majority of the world's cultures do not share the individualism of the modern West and have no need to explain what appears to them evident: that the self is not the individual self alone, but includes, according to circumstances, those with whom the self is conceived as solidary, in the first place, his kin."(Pitt-Rivers, 1975, p. 90)

After this prefatory admonition, Julian Pitt-Rivers goes on to take up his subject, how kith become kin, that is, how we come to treat an outsider as a member of our kin group, imposing and accepting the bonds of altruism. There are, as can be expected, gradations of acceptance from casual friendship to ritualized forms of friendship ("This is your uncle Chris") to formal and ritualized brotherhood or adoption into the clan. A key role in formalizing these relationships is played by rituals, such as take place in Mediterranean societies when god-parents are named. In parts of Spain and Latin America a godparent or *compadre*, is not only treated as kin to the child and his family but also accepts certain responsibilities toward another *compadre* (Pitt-Rivers, 1961, pp. 107-08). A similar bond is expressed in Serbian by the word *kum,* which describes such relationships as godfather and something like the best man at a wedding. It is an enduring bond, not a transitory social convention.

The line distinguishing kin from kith, while real enough in biological terms, can, therefore, be blurred by oaths, rituals, and shared adventures. While it is probably too much to say that kin is always the model for kith or that the Greeks were right in using the same word, *philia*, for both sets of relations, it does seem probable that our ability to form stable friendships arises in part from our experience of kinship. Friendships come in different forms, for different motives, and with different levels of intensity. Comrades in arms or in work may drift apart as soon as the war is over or the job finished. Ritualized friendships, remade on the model of kinship, are more stable and anticipate the brotherhood of all faithful believers preached by the apostles.

KINDRED AND COMMONWEALTH

The ties of blood, even when limited and directed by legal and political institutions, did not disappear during the Roman Empire, when many of the primal responsibilities of kinfolks had been peacefully absorbed by municipalities and the imperial government. The political and legal claims of government, however, were shocked and shattered, as much as the walls of the cities themselves, by waves of invading barbarians: Goths and Vandals, Franks and Lombards, Angles and Saxons. By the sixth century, even in comparatively civilized cities such as Rome and Ravenna, there were few reliable alternatives to the bonds of kinship. The formal apparatus of feudalism, which made property and status contingent upon military service, did not develop evenly throughout Europe—and in Venice hardly at all. In much of France and Germany, the feudal order prevailed, but in some other places, notably in Rome, the Languedoc regions of France, and the maritime republics of Italy (*e.g.*, Pisa, Genoa, Venice), the power of blood and marriage ties contended successfully with the institutions of the Empire and the Church, both of which were challenged and coopted by aristocratic dynasties.

The demands made by human nature, while universal, are constantly being reconstrued to meet changing circumstances, and, as a society grows and comes to require more powerful and more universal legal and political authority, the significance of broader networks of kinship fades in the glare of more powerful authorities. In a virtually stateless community, such as archaic and classical Athens, kin associations were relied upon to discharge functions that would inevitably be taken over by more formal mechanisms of government, once they came into existence. These gradual transitions do not necessarily constitute a social revolution. The changing position of married women in 19th-century England and the United States, for example, demanded an increase in their legal capacity to own and bequeath property. The various "married women property acts" of 19th-century America were not inspired, much less carried out, by feminists eager to destroy marriage and the family; they were practical measures devised and executed by fathers, husbands, and brothers who were responding to practical necessities in order to protect the interests of the women in their families.

The ebb and flow of "kin power" (as we might term it) can be observed throughout human history. As political institutions develop, kin-groups must gradually surrender much of their power to protect and avenge their members to a formal legal system, though during times of chaos and unrest, the ancient demands of blood may reassert themselves. They have only completely surrendered to the forces of the modern state, though even in 21st century Europe and North America, grandparents continue to assert their rights, though most often in vain. Highly organized states generally put kin relations under the greatest stress. Sir Henry Sumner Maine, in discussing the house-communities of primitive Slavic settlements, concluded that these resilient and democratic associations of kindred had less to fear from the Islamic oppressors who made war on them than from the legal and political forces of advancing civilization (Maine, 1883, pp. 235-36).

The societies of ancient Greece, Rome, and Israel–among many others–had been incorporated into an empire that administered a large part of the civilized world by means of a uniform legal and political system, which, nonetheless, permitted a good deal of local variation and control. In Western Europe during the fifth century of the Christian era, the system was crumbling under the weight of heavy taxes and overwhelmed by barbarian invaders. The Christian millennium that followed the collapse of the Roman Empire in the West is often referred to as "The Dark Ages." Although the phrase is an overstatement, the European peoples who lived this period certainly experienced a steep decline in health and sanitation, lawfulness and civil order, literacy and rationality. The material and cultural decline, however, is not the main reason it was condemned by Renaissance intellectuals to whom any age must be dark, if it is informed by Christian teaching.

In the parallel dark ages experienced by Egypt, in the so-called "intermediate periods" between the First and Second and the Second and Third Kingdoms, and by the Greeks after the fall of the Mycenæan citadels in the Late Bronze Age, were also periods of robust creativity, when the collapse of bureaucratic infrastructure and the decline of international trade required Egyptians and Greeks to fall back on their own resources, within families and small communities, and to develop new institutions, technologies, and art forms. Medieval Europe experienced much the same sort of revival, as the descendants of both barbarians and Romans had to rely on networks of kinfolks and neighbors. The Archaic Greek revival can be seen in the rebuilding of cities, the energies expended on colonization, the development of Geometric art, and, above all, by the magnificence of the Homeric epics.

The fall of the Western Empire opened up a chasm that divided ancient civilization from our own time. This was the millennium we moderns dismiss as in Middle Ages, but it was during these creative centuries that Europeans rebuilt a civilization out of the ruins of the Empire. During this period, Roman law, though it survived to some degree in the canon law of the Church, was largely replaced by unwritten barbarian customs that hearkened back in spirit to the customs of Homeric Greece and the early Roman Republic. In medieval Europe the social and cultural revival is seen most brilliantly in the development of dynamic city states, Gothic cathedrals, and the elaborate machinery of feudalism.

In some Germanic successor states in Italy and Gaul, Romans preserved what they could of their own legal traditions, while the Franks, Burgundians, and Lombards developed legal codes out of their barbaric traditions. As time went on, the diverse traditions were inevitably intermingled, and, near the end of the period, medieval legal institutions were revivified by an infusion of Roman law. For this reason (among many others), nothing could be more confusing to study than medieval law, particularly laws on kinship and inheritance.

There is a ceaseless ebb and flow of authority between the power of kinship and the power of governments. The obligations of kinship begin to shrink and fade, as societies grow more complex and cosmopolitan, and alternate institutions, often dependent upon or at least related to the polity, take over the functions of family and kindred. However, in periods of social disintegration, such as the early Middle Ages, the bonds of kinship are strengthened. The Byzantine Emperor Leo VI "the Wise," in the 18th chapter of his *Tactica* describes the Frankish soldiery in graphic terms that might remind us of the *Iliad*. They are strong and ferocious but undisciplined, and their martial energies, which a Roman and Byzantine would regard as owed to the ruler and the people, are devoted to personal ends. One of the sources of their success is their organization by kin. As Gibbon renders the passage in *The Decline and Fall* (chapter 54): "Their ranks are formed by the firm connexions of consanguinity and friendship; and their martial deeds are prompted by the desire of saving or revenging their dearest companions" (Leo VI, 2010).

In most of Italy at that time, even village institutions had not yet come into force, and yet, as Chris Wickham observes of early medieval Italy:

> "The relative weakness of early medieval villages did not mean that peasants were socially isolated. Rather, they acted in informal groups of friends and neighbors, sought the help of patrons, and, above all, operated in webs of kinship." (Wickham, 2002, p. 140)

This retreat to the 'web of kinship,' although it manifests itself most clearly in the laws of blood revenge found in the legal codes of Germanic peoples, can be seen in all aspects of social organization. As is the case with so many periods of apparent dissolution–the Greek Dark Age, the primitive conditions of the American frontier–the ties of family and kinship were immeasurably strengthened.

THE REVOLUTION
AGAINST KINSHIP

The campaign to weaken and eliminate the ties of blood began as an intellectual movement whose leaders declared their intention of liberating men and women from the shackles of religion, monarchy, and aristocracy. At the very same time as Jefferson was attacking primogeniture in Virginia, some of his friends in France were taking direct action, not just against the French monarchy and the Catholic Church, but against the authority of husbands and fathers and the power exerted by extended families.

During the French Revolution, radical Jacobins, drunk on the abstractions of Locke and Rousseau, stigmatized all the social traditions they opposed—primogeniture, patriarchal marriage, the authority of extended families—as *feudalism*; they reinvented marriage as an agreement between consenting free individuals; and they limited the concept of the family to the nuclear household (Desan, 2004, pp. 174-76). The Revolutionaries, though anti-Christian to the depths of their souls, still clung to the Christian dream of brotherhood within the Kingdom of God, but they eliminated both gods and kings from their made-up universe. Where Christians had spoken of the obligations entailed by kinship and friendship in a world whose order was predicated on the Holy Trinity of Father, Son, and Holy Ghost, the Revolutionaries spoke of their duties to the fatherland and to mankind in a new world dominated by the unholy trinity of Liberty, Equality, and Fraternity.

In displacing kinship of blood, Revolutionaries have turned the benevolent reign of love into a brutal dictatorship in which the political class defines value, establishes norms, and enforces its will with a rigor that would arouse envy

in Hitler and Stalin. Ever since the revolutionary earth-
quake opened the chasm between social life pre-and-post
1789, utopian experiments and despotic regimes based on
utopian ideologies have waged war on the traditional institutions of everyday life until each of us has become an
outcast, an outlaw, and an alien:

> ...a stranger and afraid
> In a world I never made.

A Brief Excursus: Patriotism Versus Nationalism

The French Revolution, while the leaders agreed on what
they wanted to destroy, was not a simple phenomenon dominated by one political ideology, and Revolutionaries could
move back and forth between positions we should now
describe as nationalist and internationalist. Influenced by
Rousseau, the individualist who glorified the state, the leaders of Revolutionary France proclaimed their devotion to
the nation, though not the historic nation that acknowledged kings and the Church. In this spirit *The Declaration of
the Rights of Man* states that, "The principle of all sovereignty
resides essentially in the nation. No body nor individual
may exercise any authority which does not proceed directly
from the nation."

On the other hand, they also declared their support for
other revolutionary movements that would rise up to throw
off the chains of monarchy, feudalism, and Christianity. In
the *Proclamation of the Convention to the Nations*, December
1792, they declared: "We have conquered our liberty and we
shall maintain it. We offer to bring this inestimable blessing
to you, for it has always been rightly ours, and only by a

crime have our oppressors robbed us of it. We have driven out your tyrants. Show yourselves free men and we will protect you from their vengeance, their machinations, or their return." Stripped of duplicity, their appeal declared that the universal rights of men justify the French conquest of Europe.

In the 19th century, the revolutionary current would separate into nationalist and internationalist channels, the one leading to the formation of centralized nation-states in Europe and North America; the other inspiring Utopians and Marxists with their project of establishing economic justice in an international order. Each side has come to consider the other as its opposite and anathematizes the enemy as demonic. Globalists blame the nationalists for all the horrors of war, though Marxist internationalism has probably killed more people than the most aggressive nationalisms, and nationalists accuse globalists of lack of patriotism, though no movement has been more subversive of authentic national traditions than nationalism. As different as they may appear on the surface, both nationalism and internationalism are ideological movements that make war on all the little platoons in which the human character is formed and everyday life is lived.

The words nationalism and patriotism are often confused, and even when political theorists draw a contrast, the result is often a distinction without a difference or a bizarre twist of meaning that defies everyday usage. According to 19th century nationalists, the will of the nation, defined as an historic community of blood and tongue, had to find expression in a common and unified state. Hence, the Italian nationalist Mazzini spoke always of the twin principles of unity and nationality, and, in the name of these ideals,

Neapolitans and Sicilians were subjugated and robbed, exploited and murdered.

Italy presented a special case of a people that had not been unified since the fall of the Western Roman Empire and had been divided up into competing principalities, some of which were controlled by foreign dynasties, *e.g.*, the Bourbons of Naples, and foreign powers, particularly Austria. To liberate and unify Italians in a centralized state was the nationalist goal, one that naturally overrode all the local patriotisms of Sicilians, Venetians, Latins, and Tuscans—to say nothing of Catholics loyal to the Pope, whose estates were rudely stripped away by the French-speaking rulers of Piedmont. That process of unification culminated in the 1860's, when the more developed North conquered and subjugated the agrarian South. The parallel with the American *Risorgimento* did not escape the notice of Pope Pius IX, who regarded Jefferson Davis as a fellow-victim of nationalist aggression.

In almost every case nationalists have set their minds against the traditions of the historic nations they pretended to exalt. The French Revolutionaries, for example, destroyed churches, persecuted the clergy, and, not content with killing their king and queen, destroyed the ancient tombs of their earliest kings. Robespierre's France was the imaginary product of his scheming but uneducated mind, and the Jacobins reinvented French history as the struggle between the subjugated Celts and Frankish invaders who made up the aristocracy.

The pattern is repeated in nearly every national uprising. The Hungarians, to express their national freedom, had to repress the aspirations of Croats and Slovaks. Bismark, in unifying Germany around the core of Protestant Prussia, had to eliminate the challenge presented by Catholics in Bavaria, and the next logical step would be taken in the 20th century. Although the real Germany was divided between Catholics and Protestants, the Nazis' ideal German nation had to be unified, and Hitler was all the more ready to persecute his own family's Catholic Church, because it divided Germans and made some of them loyal to an international religion.

Nationalists always seem to have believed that they could only erect their fictional new nation on the ruins of the actual nation of their ancestors. Jacobin nationalists established the model. In attempting to build an abstract and artificially unified French nation, they made war on all other, more deeply rooted loyalties: They destroyed the Church, waged a war of genocide against Catholics in the Vendée, and did their best to obliterate the distinctive ways of life (*e.g.*, in Provènce and Brittany) that were responsible for the vitality of French culture. The predictable results, in France, Britain, and the United States (to name only three examples) is a for-profit mass culture in which the only "national identity" is the creation of commercial entertainment and state propaganda.

The instinctive loyalty to family and tribe has no name in English or in most European languages, though Edmund Burke intuited the concept when he referred to the "little platoons" that command our loyalties. Burke was fumbling to express a concept for which we have no word now, and if ever we did I have not found it in my Anglo-Saxon dictionary. The Latin *amor patriæ*, love of the fatherland, is the closest we can come, though the Serbian language does have such a word: *rodoljublje*, love of kith and kin, love of the stock (*rod*). The love of kith and kin is not based only on blood, but also on the language, culture, and traditions of the people from whom we are descended, in reality or in fiction, and while the process of loyalty begins with the family, it culminates in the commonwealth which fulfills, without superseding, lesser loyalties.

If the nationalist point-of-view narrows the human outlook, it also implies a willingness to divide the human race into the categories of "us" and "them," and to define "them" as an enemy to be eliminated or subjugated. This attitude, as George Orwell pointed out in his essay "Notes on Nationalism," stems from the habit of assuming that human beings can be classified like insects and that whole blocks of millions or tens of millions of people can be confidently labeled "good" or "bad." In identifying ourselves with a nation, he said, we place the state "beyond good and evil,...recognizing no other duty than that of advancing its interests" (Orwell, 1954).

Propaganda and ethnic bigotry are the hallmarks of developed nationalism. In the First World War, Thomas Hardy and A.E. Housman both deplored the hatred ginned up in the press against so kindred a nation as the Germans. As nationalism increased, such sentiments became scarce. While soldiers in the two world wars were sometimes willing to look upon each other as human beings, their governments, which enlisted distinguished writers in their propaganda campaigns, could only see enemies as cartoon villains. The Germans, who were portrayed as savage monsters by the allies, ridiculed the effeminacy of Britain and France and portrayed Jews and Slavs as subhuman. The United States, in denigrating the Japanese, resorted to the most sordid racial stereotyping. Such propagandistic stereotyping, on the part of the American government, goes back at least to the American Civil War, when government and newspapers alike depicted Southerners as cruel and inhuman slave-drivers. The propaganda was then used to justify the criminal actions of the Union government.

RESISTANCE AND COUNTER-REVOLUTION

It has taken centuries of violent outbursts and cautious "reform" to turn the abstract fantasies of the Jacobins into the nightmarish parody of reality in which most postmodern men and women live. In the course of more than two centuries, most resistance to the Revolution has come in the form of sullen resistance to the latest phase of destruction. The efforts of conservatives have been aimed principally at defending the most recent high-water mark of revolution. There have been exceptions, such as Edmund Burke, who composed his *Reflections on the Revolution in France* at an early stage of the Revolution. Declaring "the age of chivalry is dead," he went on to explore the political consequences of the Revolutionary project.

Burke saw the French and English nations as a rich legacy of many previous generations, an estate we have inherited, like our property, from our ancestors:

"By a constitutional policy, working after the pattern of nature, we receive, we hold, we transmit our government and our privileges in the same manner in which we enjoy and transmit our property and our lives. The institutions of policy, the goods of fortune, the gifts of providence are handed down to us, and from us, in the same course and order."

The analogy of constitutional order and property is not limited to forms of government; the ties of blood and faith are the cement of the political order.

> "In this choice of inheritance we have given to our frame of polity the image of a relation in blood, binding up the constitution of our country with our dearest domestic ties, adopting our fundamental laws into the bosom of our family affections, keeping inseparable and cherishing with the warmth of all their combined and mutually reflected charities our state, our hearths, our sepulchres, and our altars."

Burke sums up his argument with the famous aphorism that, "People will not look forward to posterity, who never look backward to their ancestors."

Burke was not the only thinking European to have responded with horror to the Revolution. Sir Walter Scott had also, at the very beginning, stared into the abyss and glimpsed the monsters it would cast up from its depths. Along with Goethe, Scott was the master-spirit of the Counter-Revolution, and the reading of one great Scott novel could do more to set back the clock than all the pamphlets, plans, and stratagems devised by conservative and reactionary politicians and theorists.

Scott was born in 1771, and at age of 19, in the same year when the Revolution was making a sharp left by nationalizing the Catholic Church and Edmund Burke was publishing his *Reflections*, the young law student wrote an essay on the feudal system, in which he tried to prove that feudalism was not, as Jacobins and English radicals claimed, the invention of German invaders who inculcated principles of royalist absolutism. To the contrary, Scott argued, feudalism "proceeds upon principles common to all nations when placed in a certain situation." In other words, there was nothing intrinsically innovative, much less oppressive, about a system based on kinship and loyalty, instead of on individual rights and legal contracts.

Walter Scott was once regarded as one of the greatest writers in the history of Britain and, indeed, of all Europe, and his literary works were to inspire a revival of interest in medieval institutions, including the habits and institutions of feudalism. Indeed, the power of his imagination to reconstitute traditions supposedly dead is the main reason he has been erased from the memory of modern men and women. In his first novel, *Waverley*, a young English officer, by visiting Scotland, goes back in time, first to the household of a Scottish Baron leading a life more typical of the Middle Ages or early Renaissance, and then into the Highlands, where he experiences tribal society, in all its power and danger.

In the *Heart of Midlothian*, one of his most popular works, a reader will find it easy to discern the outlines of the feudal mentality Scott was hoping to revive. The plot of the novel hangs on an historical incident: the story of a girl who would not lie in order to save her sister from hanging and walks to London to procure a pardon by appealing to the Duke of Argyle, a nobleman who looked out for the interests of his fellow-Scots.

Scott's depiction of the feudal residue ranges from the comical highland laird who does not allow the church bell to be rung until he is seen on the way to church to the reverence, fraught with political implication, shown to the Duke of Argyle by his own people. His heroine Jeanie Dean is the epitome of loyalty to kin, kith, and clan, and her simple assumption that the Duke will naturally be willing to take up the cause of a poor peasant girl expresses Scott's own conviction that feudal loyalties constitute a bargain with obligations on both sides. Her reasoning is clear: To the Duke, after all, since he represents Scotland to the king, all the Scots are his people, and as such they deserve his sympathy and assistance. Imagine, today, in a similar situation, some poor Wisconsin farm girl, who goes to a US senator in search of justice: Only a lobbyist or donor can get an appointment, unless there is a photo opportunity in the meeting. The feudal relation, by contrast, was personal and not based on wealth or influence or personal advantage.

The Duke understands perfectly, what his duties are, and, when Jeanie's cousin remarks that Scots are "clannish bodies," the Duke replies: "So much the better for us...and the worse who meddle with us." In the same novel Scott describes the kindness of a Scottish innkeeper living in England and comments on the willingness of Scots to help each other:

> "The eagerness with which the Scottish people meet, communicate, and to the extent of their power assist each other, although it is often objected to us as a prejudice and narrowness of sentiment, seems on the contrary to arise from a most justifiable and honorable feeling patriotism, combined with a conviction...that the habits and principles of the nation are a sort of guarantee for the character of the individual."[III.3]

When it is clear that the Duke of Argyle is willing to help the girl, Scott wonders if only a Scot can understand "how ardently, under all distinctions of rank and situation, they feel their mutual connexion with each other as natives of the same country...the high and low are more interested in each other's welfare; the feelings of kindred and relationship are more widely extended, and in a word, the bonds of patriotic affection...have more influence on men's feelings and actions" than in more advanced countries like England. [IV.1] Better perhaps than Edmund Burke, Scott understood the deep connection between "the bonds of patriotic affection" and "the feelings of kindred."

A man of Scott's medieval cast of mind was strongly attached to a social system in which each class knew its place, and every man recognized the duties incumbent upon his station. At the same time, he was repelled by snobbery and by any expression of contempt for the poor. Despite the persistence of sharp class distinctions, Scotland was a country marked by social solidarity, where kinsmen knew how to take care of each other. In a letter of 1817, Scott wrote:

> "In Scotland men of all ranks, but especially the middling and lower classes, are linked by ties which give them a strong interest in each other's success in life, and it is amazing the exertion which men will make to support and assist persons which you would suppose them connected by very remote ties of consanguinity...They have in the lower ranks a wholesome horror of seeing a relation on the Poor's role of the parish; it is a dishonor."

As Douglas Young pointed out in his book on *Edinburgh in the Age of Walter Scott*, the Scottish capital was not socially stratified by neighborhood–unlike London. Like ancient Rome, rich, middle-class, and blue-collar families lived on different floors of the same house, an arrangement that made for a far greater degree of social solidarity and diminished the temptation to class warfare (Young, 1965).

Scott was more than an instinctive Tory who happened to possess an extraordinary ability to fire the romantic imagination. He also had a shrewd legal brain and a practical understanding of politics. Late in life, when he was pressed by debts and lack of time, he wrote a *Life of Napoleon Bonaparte*, whose first volume is a succinct if not always entirely accurate account of the Revolution. The book was a popular success, though it was severely criticized by Whig reviewers, but it was not erroneous details that offended the critics but Scott's refusal to demonize the kindest man who had ever sat on the French throne and his insistence on connecting the principles of the Enlightenment with the horrors of the Revolution. Throughout his career, he was outspoken in opposition to the principles of the French Revolution and of the reforming Whigs in Britain who resembled the revisionist Marxists who have carried out Marxist revolution, both in Europe and in North America, by non-violent means.

In politics Scott was motivated largely by his patriotic affections both for Scotland and for the United Kingdom, and by a sincere desire for the common good. He was willing, in a good cause, to associate and even to work with the hated Whigs. His dislike for political antagonism led Scott to collaborate even with the Whiggish *Edinburgh Review*, and he was close for some years with its brilliant editor, Francis Jeffrey, but the *Review's* ill-tempered criticism of Scott, combined with the editors' increasingly open "liberalism," finally caused a rupture.

The difference between Scott and the Whigs was apparent in their different responses to the legal reform movement in Scotland. Of course there were irrationalities and inconsistencies in Scottish law, but Scott was very suspicious of reformist meddling and tampering. In his biography [chapter 15] Scott's son-in-law John Gibson Lockhart recounts an anecdote of 1806, when Scott met Francis Jeffrey on the street. Jeffrey engaged in his usual caustic banter over legal reform, but the usually amiable Scott was in no mood: "No, no–tis no laughing matter; little by little, whatever your wishes may be, you will destroy and undermine, until nothing of what makes Scotland Scotland shall remain." Scott then turned his face to the wall to hide his tears (Lockhart, 1838, p. 290).

Scott is one of those writers, along with Shakespeare, Dante, Sophocles and Vergil, who can cleanse the human spirit of some of its modern demons and banish the specters of the Enlightenment. That is why they are no longer taught or read, and, if they are taught, it is after their texts have been teased and tortured by postmodern critical methods into seeming to say the opposite of what the writers intended. One of the greatest triumphs of the perpetual revolution has been to alienate modern men and women from the insights of the classical and Christian traditions, which, in better times, formed the minds of the young and gave them a solid foundation for resistance.

THE REIGN OF LOVE: A CODA

Walter Scott viewed the Scottish commonwealth not as a formal assemblage of random persons bound only by contracts and laws, much less as a set of individuals whose only commonality lay in their dedication to a proposition. Scotland was not merely (or even) a state but a complex mesh of relationships of blood and love. His "feudal" vision of Scotland as a model society brings us back to the beginning of our inquiry into kinship.

Advocates of the modern "democratic" state make many different kinds of arguments in its defense: It provides equal justice to citizens of every type and degree, and to the extent it is able, also to non-citizens who enter its confines; it works to suppress forces of prejudice and repression that stunt individuality; and it gives scope to human individuals to follow their chosen paths to self-fulfillment. Visionary idealists might go so far as to claim that modern democracies, in the assistance they provide to children and minorities, the poor and disabled, the elderly and mentally infirm, are the fulfillment of the Christian dream of the Kingdom of Heaven. There are even self-described Christians who have cheerfully identified the Gospel's exhortations to brotherhood and charity with the the socialist policies of the welfare state.

The ethics of Christianity and socialism are, in fact, diametrically opposed. The roots of a Christian polity lie in kinship in its infinite variations, while the foundation of the modern state lie in the elimination of all the social ties that cannot be made as universal as a universal language or monetary system. A Christian commonwealth speaks different languages and acknowledges innumerable moral and social currencies, while the state speaks only Esperanto and accepts only its official Bitcoin as money.

The subordination of the Christian to the Marxian vision of society has been facilitated by the Christian tendency to read the Scriptures selectively, ignoring, so far as they can, the Old Testament's commendations of blood revenge and capital punishment, self-defense and war, and twisting the plain sense of the New Testament's teachings on justice, self-reliance, and the divine mission of the rulers. It is to remedy this peculiar disease that the next volume has been written. But even if we ignore the sword of vengeance entrusted to the rulers and all that goes with it, we have only our own blindness and perversity to blame if we convert the religion of Christ into the cult of modernity.

Christians stake their lives on the fatherhood of God and the brotherhood of Christians, while liberals and leftists dream of a world in which all men are brothers, regardless of blood or belief. Christians sing of the crucifixion, a concrete fact of human reality,

> O sacred head sore wounded
> Defiled and put to scorn.
> O kingly head surrounded
> With mocking crown of thorn.

Leftists rewrite the words as a pie-in-the sky dream of rootless brotherhood and sisterhood that gets more and more remote with every passing day in a world controlled by leftist anti-Christians:

> Because all men are brothers
> Wherever men may be,
> And women all are sisters
> Forever proud and free.

Human brotherhood, divorced from kinship and its rules and obligations, is not so much a dream as a nightmare that has claimed the lives of over a hundred million Russian, Chinese, and Cambodian victims, while in Western Europe and North America it is steadily eradicating the very foundations of human nature itself. Divorce and abortion on demand, the legalization of same sex unions, the growing acceptance of incest all point the path of mankind in the same direction toward the eradication of all the ties of blood that have drawn men and women into networks of respect and obligation. The liberation of the individual has already revealed itself as the enslavement of the human person.

REFERENCES

Desan, S. (2004). *The Family on Trial in Revolutionary France*. University of California Press.

Lockhart, J. G. (1838). *Memoirs of the Life of Sir Walter Scott, Bart*. (Vol. 2). Robert Cadwell, Edinburgh.

Maine, H. S. (1883). *Dissertations on Early Law and Custom*. J. Murray.

McNutt, P. M. (1999). *Reconstructing the Society of Ancient Israel*. Westminster John Knox Press.

Orwell, G. (1954). *Your England, and Other Essays*. Secker & Warburg.

Pitt-Rivers, J. (1961). *The People of the Sierra. London and Chicago*.

Pitt-Rivers, J. (1975). The Kith and the Kin. In J. Goody (Ed.), *The Character of Kinship*. (Vol. 17, pp. 89-106). Cambridge: Cambridge University Press.

Wickham, C. (2002). Rural Economy and Society. In C. La Rocca (Ed.), *Italy in the early middle ages: 476-1000*. (Vol. 6, pp. 118-138). Oxford University Press.

Young, D. (1965). *Edinburgh in the Age of Sir Walter Scott*. (No. 17). University of Oklahoma Press.

GENERAL BIBLIOGRAPHY

Adkins, A. W. (1960). *Merit and Responsibility: a Study in Greek Values*. Clarendon Press Oxford.

Bateson, P. (2005). Inbreeding Avoidance and Incest Taboos. In A. P. Wolff & W. H. Durham (Eds.), *Inbreeding, Incest, and the Incest Taboo: the State of Knowledge at the Turn of the Century*. Stanford University Press.

Belfiore, E. S. (2000). *Murder Among Friends: Violation of Philia in Greek Tragedy*. Oxford University Press on Demand.

Berry, W. (2006). *The Unforeseen Wilderness: Kentucky's Red River Gorge*. Counterpoint Press.

Bignone, E. (1916). *Empedocle: Studio Critico; Traduzione e Commento Delle Testimonianze e Dei Frammenti*. Fratelli Bocca.

Blerk N.J., v. (2019). The Basic Tenets of Intestate (Customary) Succession Law in Ancient Egypt. *Fundamina*, 25(1), 170–194.

Blundell, M. W. (1991). *Helping Friends and Harming Enemies: a Study in Sophocles and Greek Ethics*. Cambridge University Press.

Bremmer, J. (1987). *The Early Greek Concept of the Soul*. Princeton University Press.

Brunt, P. A. (1988). *The Fall of The Roman Republic*. Clarendon Press Oxford.

Burkert, W. (1985). *Greek Religion*. Harvard University Press.

Burnyeat, M. F. (1997). The Impiety of Socrates. *Ancient Philosophy*, 17(1), 1–12.

Cecil, E. & Baron Rockley, E. C. (1895). *Primogeniture: a Short History of its Development in Various Countries and its Practical Effects*. J. Murray.

Champlin, E. (1991). *Final Judgments: Duty and Emotion in Roman Wills, 200 BC-AD 250*. University of California Press.

Cort, J. C. (2020). *Christian Socialism: An Informal History, With an New Introduction by Gary Dorrien*. Orbis Books.

Crook, J. A. (1967). *Law and life of Rome*. Cornell University Press.

Crowley, J. E. (1986). The Importance of Kinship: Testamentary Evidence from South Carolina. *The Journal of Interdisciplinary History*, 16(4), 559–577.

De Montaigne, M. (1958). *The Complete Essays of Montaigne* (D. Frame, Trans.). Stanford University Press.

Desan, S. (2004). *The Family on Trial in Revolutionary France*. University of California Press.

Douglas, D. C. (1964). *William the Conqueror: the Norman Impact upon England*. University of California Press.

Dover, K. J. (1994). *Greek Popular Morality in the Time of Plato and Aristotle*. Hackett Publishing.

Dyck, A. R. & Cicero, M. T. (1996). *A Commentary on Cicero, De officiis*. University of Michigan Press.

Earp, F. R. (1929). *The Way of the Greeks by FR Earp*. Oxford University Press.

Fleming, T. (1985). Review of Jan Bremer's The Early Greek Concept of the Soul and David Claus' Toward the Soul. *The Classical Journal, 80*(2), 165-168.

———— (1988). *The Politics of Human Nature*. Transaction Publishers.

———— (2004). *The Morality of Everyday Life: Rediscovering an Ancient Alternative to the Liberal Tradition*. University of Missouri Press.

———— (2007). *Socialism*. Marshall Cavendish.

Fortes, M. (2013). *Kinship and the Social Order.: The Legacy of Lewis Henry Morgan*. Routledge.

Fränkel, H. (1975). *Early Greek Poetry and Philosophy*. Harcourt Brace Jovanovich.

Glosecki, S. O. (1999). Beowulf and the Wills: Traces of Totemism?. *Philological Quarterly, 78*(1-2), 15–47.

Glover, L. (2000). *All our Relations: Blood Ties and Emotional Bonds Among the Early South Carolina Gentry*. Johns Hopkins University Press.

Greven, P. J. (1972). *Four Generations: Population, Land, and Family in Colonial Andover, Massachusetts*. (Vol. 134). Cornell University Press.

Hanson, M. (2006). *Polis: An Introduction to the Ancient Greek City-State*. Oxford University Press.

Harrison, A. R. W. (1998). *The Law of Athens*. (Vol. 1). Hackett Publishing.

Harrison, E. (1960). Notes on Homeric Psychology. *Phoenix*, 14(2), 63–80.

Herman, G. (2002). *Ritualised Friendship and the Greek City*. Cambridge University Press.

Inwood, B. (1992). *The Poem of Empedocles*. University of Toronto Press.

Jamoussi, Z. (1999). *Primogeniture and Entail in England: A Survey of Their History and Representation in Literature*. Centre de publication universitaire, 1999.

Jones, W. (1807). *Speeches of Isaeus in Causes Concerning the Law of Succession to Property in Athens*. (Vol. 9). John Stockdale.

Kidd, I. (1990). The Case of Homicide in Plato's Euthyphro. *Owls to Athens. Essays on Classical Subjects Presented to Sir Kenneth Dover, Oxford*, 213–21.

Konstan, D. (1996). Greek Friendship. *American Journal of Philology*, 117(1), 71–94.

———— (2006). *The Emotions of the Ancient Greeks: Studies in Aristotle and Classical Literature*. University of Toronto Press.

Lacey, W. K. (1968). *The Family in Classical Greece*. Cornell University Press.

Leo VI (2010). *The Taktika of Leo VI*. (Vol. 49). Dumbarton Oaks Pub Service.

Lewis, C. S. (1991). *The Four Loves*. Houghton Mifflin Harcourt.

Lockhart, J. G. (1838). *Memoirs of the Life of Sir Walter Scott, Bart.* (Vol. 2). Robert Cadwell, Edinburgh.

MacDowell, D. M. (1999). *Athenian Homicide Law in the Age of the Orators*. Manchester University Press.

Maine, H. S. (1883). *Dissertations on Early Law and Custom*. J. Murray.

McDonnell, B. H. (2003). Is Incest Next?. *Cardozo Women's Law Journal*, 10, 337.

McNutt, P. M. (1999). *Reconstructing the Society of Ancient Israel*. Westminster John Knox Press.

Miller, M. (1953). Greek Kinship Terminology. *The Journal of Hellenic Studies*, 73, 46–52.

Mott, S. (2011). *Biblical Ethics and Social Change*. Oxford University Press.

Nicholas, D. (1985). *The Domestic Life of a Medieval City: Women, Children, and the Family in Fourteenth-Century Ghent*. University of Nebraska Press.

Orwell, G. (1954). *Your England, and Other Essays*. Secker & Warburg.

Pitt-Rivers, J. (1961). *The People of the Sierra*. London and Chicago.

Pitt-Rivers, J. (1975). The Kith and the Kin. In J. Goody (Ed.), *The Character of Kinship*. (Vol. 17, pp. 89-106). Cambridge: Cambridge University Press.

Postgate, N. (2017). *Early Mesopotamia: Society and Economy at the Dawn of History*. Taylor & Francis.

Price, A. W. (1989). *Love and Friendship in Plato and Aristotle*. Clarendon Press.

Roy, J. (1999). Polis and Oikos in Classical Athens 1. *Greece & Rome, 46*(1), 1–18.

Royce, J. (1904). *The World and the Individual*. (Vol. 2). Macmillan Company.

Saller, R. P. (1997). *Patriarchy, Property and Death in the Roman Family*. Cambridge University Press.

Schmitt, A. (1990). *Selbständigkeit und Abhängigkeit Menschlichen Handelns bei Homer*. (No. 5). Franz Steiner.

Schwabl, H. (1954). Zur Selbständigkeit des Menschen bei Homer. *Wiener Studien*, 67, 46–64.

Seebohm, F. (1902). *Tribal Custom in Anglo-Saxon Law.* Longmans, Green & Company.

Shaw, B. D. & Saller, R. P. (1984). Close-kin Marriage in Roman society?. *Man*, 432–444.

Sheehan, M. M. (1997). *Marriage, Family, and Law in Medieval Europe: Collected Studies.* University of Toronto Press.

Snell, B. (1953). *The Discovery of the Mind, trans. TG Rosenmeyer.* Author.

Snydacker, D. (1982). Kinship and Community in Rural Pennsylvania, 1749-1820. *The Journal of Interdisciplinary History*, 13(1), 41–61.

Sordi, M. (1994). *The Christians and the Roman Empire.* Taylor & Francis.

Stenton, F. M. (2001). *Anglo-Saxon England.* (Vol. 2). Oxford Paperbacks.

Taylor, L. R. (1949). *Party Politics in the Age of Caesar.* (No. 22). University of California Press.

Thompson, W. E. (1971). Attic Kinship Terminology. *The Journal of Hellenic Studies*, 91, 110–113.

Treggiari, S. (1991). *Roman Marriage: Iusti Coniuges From the Time of Cicero to the Time of Ulpian.* Oxford University Press.

Turcan, R. (2001). *The Gods of Ancient Rome: Religion in Everyday Life from Archaic to Imperial Times*. Taylor & Francis.

Westermarck, E. (1908). *The Origin and Development of the Moral Ideas*. (Vol. 2). Macmillan.

Whitelock, D. (2011). *Anglo-Saxon Wills*. Cambridge University Press.

Wickham, C. (2002). Rural Economy and Society. In C. La Rocca (Ed.), *Italy in the early middle ages: 476-1000*. (Vol. 6, pp. 118-138). Oxford University Press.

Young, D. (1965). *Edinburgh in the Age of Sir Walter Scott*. (No. 17). University of Oklahoma Press.

Zuntz, G., ... (1971). *Persephone: three essays on religion and thought in Magna Graecia*. Clarendon Press.

Ingram Content Group UK Ltd.
Milton Keynes UK
UKHW011945270323
419267UK00015B/420/J